The Other Price of
Hitler's War

Recent Titles in
Contributions in Military Studies

The Heights of Courage: A Tank Leader's War on the Golan
Avigdor Kahalani

The Tainted War: Culture and Identity in Vietnam War Narratives
Lloyd B. Lewis

Shaping a Maritime Empire: The Commercial and Diplomatic Role of the American
Navy, 1829–1861
John H. Schroeder

The American Occupation of Austria: Planning and Early Years
Donald R. Whitnah and Edgar L. Erickson

Crusade in Nuremberg: Military Occupation, 1945–1949
Boyd L. Dastrup

The Dogma of the Battle of Annihilation: The Theories of Clausewitz and Schlieffen
and Their Impact on the German Conduct of Two World Wars
Jehuda L. Wallach

Jailed for Peace: The History of American Draft Law Violators, 1658–1985
Stephen M. Kohn

Against All Enemies: Interpretations of American Military History from Colonial
Times to the Present
Kenneth J. Hagan and William R. Roberts

Citizen Sailors in a Changing Society: Policy Issues for Manning the United States
Naval Reserve
Louis A. Zurcher, Milton L. Boykin, and Hardy L. Merritt, editors

Strategic Nuclear War: What the Superpowers Target and Why
William C. Martel and Paul L. Savage

Soviet Military Psychiatry: The Theory and Practice of Coping with Battle Stress
Richard A. Gabriel

A Portrait of the Israeli Soldier
Reuven Gal

The Other Price of Hitler's War

GERMAN MILITARY AND CIVILIAN LOSSES RESULTING FROM WORLD WAR II

Martin K. Sorge

CONTRIBUTIONS IN MILITARY STUDIES, NUMBER 55

GREENWOOD PRESS
NEW YORK · WESTPORT, CONNECTICUT · LONDON

Library of Congress Cataloging-in-Publication Data

Sorge, Martin K.
   The other price of Hitler's war.

   (Contributions in military studies, ISSN 0883–6884 ;
no. 55)
      Bibliography: p.
      Includes index.
      1. World War, 1939–1945—Germany.   2. World War,
1939–1945—Casualties (Statistics, etc.)   3. World War,
1939–1945—Destruction and pillage—Germany.   I. Title.
II. Series.
D757.S74   1986   940.53′43   86–409
ISBN 0–313–25293–9 (lib. bdg. : alk. paper)

Library of Congress Catalog Card Number: 86–409
ISBN: 0–313–25293–9
ISSN: 0883–6884

First published in 1986

Greenwood Press, Inc.
88 Post Road West, Westport, Connecticut 06881

Printed in the United States of America

The paper used in this book complies with the
Permanent Paper Standard issued by the National
Information Standards Organization (Z39.48–1984).

10 9 8 7 6 5 4 3 2 1

Copyright Acknowledgment

Excerpt from PRUSSIAN NIGHTS by Alexander Solzhenitsyn. Copyright © 1974 by Alexander
Solzhenitsyn. English translation copyright © 1977 by Robert Conquest. Reprinted by
permission of Farrar, Straus and Giroux, Inc., and Claude Durand, Editions YMCA Press,
Paris.

To Manfred Steingräber
and all who fought
and served
and suffered
in Hitler's War

CONTENTS

ILLUSTRATIONS

TABLES

PREFACE

Since the founding of the Federal Republic of Germany in 1949, German-American relations have, on the surface, been perceived as generally positive. They constitute one of the main elements of the North Atlantic community's defense strategy for Western Europe. However, the apparent goodwill between the two countries may have clouded the fact that from the beginning, West Germany's political leaders, from Christian Democrat Konrad Adenauer to Social Democrat Helmut Schmidt, have had real differences on a number of issues with their partners in Washington. Occasionally, unilateral foreign policy changes by a U.S. president have placed the German leaders in a difficult position in Bonn, where bilateral consultations would have been very much preferred.

In recent years, these transatlantic bonds have been subjected to additional strains over the issue of upgrading American missiles on West German soil and Washington's desire to involve the Federal Republic and other NATO (North Atlantic Treaty Organization) partners in the Strategic Defense Initiative (SDI). There also exists in West Germany a lingering awareness that, in spite of that country's overall commitment to remain America's strong ally, a one-sided or at least incomplete image of Germany's past is still being nurtured by many Americans nearly four decades after World War II. This was especially evident from the furor surrounding President Reagan's conciliatory gesture during his recent visit to the German military cemetery in Bitburg, West Germany. Many Germans feel that little is known or much has been forgotten on this side of the Atlantic of the price the German people themselves paid for their twelve years with Hitler.

The purpose of this book is to present, though in an admittedly brief form, an overview of the losses suffered by the Germans in both the military and civilian sectors during and as a result of World War II, through enemy action, as well as at the hands of their own regime.

Statistics of losses cited are for the most part based on official German documents, American and British military histories, and some Soviet sources. They may form the basis for additional research.

It is hoped that this book will contribute to a more balanced and objective view of the German people in the mind of American readers. A more realistic assessment by the latter of Germany's losses incident to World War II will be welcomed there and should contribute to the continuation of a mutually beneficial and positive understanding between the two countries.

ACKNOWLEDGMENTS

I would like to thank Dr. Douglas D. Alder of Utah State University, Logan, Utah, for his input and encouragement throughout the preparation of the manuscript. His manner of liberally offering advice yet allowing me the freedom to present my own ideas on this admittedly emotional subject was instrumental to the form and content of this book.

The Ministry of the Interior of the Federal Republic of Germany rendered valuable assistance in guiding me to other German sources and organizations whose documentary support was essential. Certain ideas for the topic resulted from discussions with German citizens during my several visits to the Federal Republic in recent years and the subsequent exchanges of correspondence with semi-official and federal West German agencies. Translations from German sources unless otherwise indicated were made by me.

I also express appreciation to the personnel of several American and British military history organizations who contributed advice and substance to this effort. Last but not least I would like to thank my wife, our family, and our friends for their understanding, patience, and helpfulness with which they supported me in this endeavor.

INTRODUCTION

With the surrender of the Dönitz government in the early hours of May 7, 1945, at Rheims, France, about one week after Hitler had ended his life in Berlin, the European phase of World War II was officially over. Some isolated *Waffen-SS* units on German soil continued to resist until May 9, and dramatic, sometimes costly raids were staged on mainland harbors by German garrisons left behind on the Channel Islands beyond that date (Whiting 1973, 137–139). But in general, even the most devoted among German soldiers realized that the war had been lost and that further delay in striking the colors was futile. American spearheads had pushed across the Rhine at Remagen on March 7, and major U.S. and British units crossed the river in force before the end of the month at Oppenheim and Xanten, respectively, while Marshal Zhukov's Red Armies had taken Berlin. On April 25, 1945, U.S. and Soviet soldiers had reached the Elbe River near Torgau from opposite directions and had thus cut the corridor of German-controlled territory, sealing the defeat of the Third Reich (Orthbandt 1968, 540).

During the six long years of combat, many millions of lives had been lost. According to Soviet accounts of the Great Patriotic War, Russian casualties alone amounted to 7.5 million soldiers and 12.5 million civilians dead, a total of 20 million (Prokhorov 1980, 350). American losses stood at 1,218,828, of which 407,318 were counted as dead ("World War Two" 1975, 529–530). The British claimed to have lost 555,369 dead and wounded, including colonial troops, in the European theater and Africa (Ropp 1979, 411). Polish losses stood at 320,000; the Yugoslavians claimed 410,000 dead. The French listed 210,671 killed, and Greece 77,700. Of those who had cast their lot with Germany, Italy reported losses of 60,000, Hungary 140,000, Finland 82,000, and Romania 300,000 "World War Two" 1975, 478). Additionally, millions of Jews, and people considered "unwanted" by certain political leaders of the Nazi government, had perished (Stier 1960, 948).

Furthermore, many Germans, themselves opposed to the racial or political aims of the Hitler government, were imprisoned and up to 300,000 paid for their resistance with their lives. Of these, the names of Dr. Goerdeler, Admiral Canaris, and General Oster are just a few. In addition, numerous resisters died at their own hands, especially after the abortive coup of July 20, 1944. Among them was one of Germany's greatest military leaders, General Erwin Rommel.

The bookshelves of the world's libraries are full with volumes detailing the sufferings caused by the war among the erstwhile Allies of East and West. During that conflict, German troops had stood on three continents and had become the enemies of many nations of the earth and their colonial subjects. People in the Western and Communist worlds have been made thoroughly aware of who caused the losses among their own, but there exists far less awareness among them, and especially their youth, of the price Germany paid during, and subsequent to, World War II (Wellner 1982, 265–277). This price, in lives alone, stands at over 9 million, of which 5 million were killed in battles, died as prisoners of war, or simply vanished (Orthbandt 1968, 544).

After the war, the victors went to great lengths to show the world and their prostrate foe the misdeeds of the latter. Germany, in turn, with considerable patience and self-condemnation, accepted its defeat and political reeducation at the hands of her conquerors (von Salomon 1955, 1). It has likewise accepted the trial and punishment of its former leaders (Kiegeland 1979, 513). And the present government of West Germany has continued to pursue and indict those of its citizens who should stand trial for their connections with war crimes.

As the political and military realities of the postwar era sent shivers of the "Red Scare" through the Western world, the American government actively courted the newly created, but reluctant, Federal Republic of Germany in an effort to gain the much-needed muscle of a new German army to shore up the defense of Western Europe and to act as a trip-wire against a Soviet push to the Atlantic (Chamberlin 1963, 221–224). For over thirty years now, the West German *Bundeswehr* has stood shoulder to shoulder with American GIs and British soldiers along the Iron Curtain guarding the mutual security interests of the Western alliance. In fact, in recent years, the position of deputy commander of all Allied forces in Europe has been held by a West German officer (*Der Spiegel* 1984). During these past three decades, a considerable degree of respect and military camaraderie has developed among members of these forces and their dependents, to say nothing of the thousands of German women who became wives of American servicemen after the ban against such marriages was lifted by U.S. military authorities at the close of 1946 (Frederiksen 1953, 136). Under the War Brides Act of December 28, 1945 (Public Law 271), and subsequent legislation, 13,250 German war brides were admitted to the United States by December 30, 1948, with the majority arriving between 1947 and 1949 (U.S. Department of Justice, *Monthly Review* (June 1949): 168). Nearly 2,000 German fiancées of American soldiers entered the United States between 1947 and 1950

(U.S. Department of Justice, Immigration and Naturalization Service, Annual Report, FY 1950, Table 9B).

Thousands of West German officers and technicians have been trained in the United States and both countries have pooled their scientific know-how in military and civilian pursuits, particularly in the exploration of outer space (*Aviation Week & Space Technology* 1975, 223). Joint ventures involved "Project Helios," in which a sun-probing German satellite was launched from Cape Canaveral. More recently, increasingly significant U.S.–West German cooperation has been evident in the Space Shuttle Program. In late 1985, the scientific portion of a mission was actually controlled by a team of West German scientists from a location near Munich.

In spite of these realities, some American literature and media products, as well as motion pictures and television documentaries, have continued to project an image that leans heavily on themes of German guilt and brutality in regard to World War II, thus making it difficult for the American public in general, and their youth in particular, to form a more objective opinion of Germany's role during World War II and especially of the price it paid for that war. Responsible observers on both sides of the Atlantic, including statesmen, educators, and textbook manufacturers, have expressed concern over the permanent negative stereotyping of Germans as a whole.

In the interest of both countries, and especially in view of the reaction to President Reagan's visit to the Bitburg cemetery, a greater realization among the American people of what Germany suffered during World War II appears both timely and needed. This suffering included enormous losses in human lives, both military and civilian, primarily due to enemy action, as well as those caused by its own leadership in retaliation for resistance to the regime. It also came with the dismemberment of eastern areas of Germany and the expulsion of millions of its citizens from their ancestral homelands with attendant heavy loss of life.

This book details Germany's losses relating to World War II—a story that is not adequately known outside of Germany and that has not been written to any degree of completeness for the English-speaking world in general.

Because of this, a considerable amount of material addressing the topic had to be obtained from Germany, although available sources dealing with individual aspects of the theme, published in Great Britain, the United States, and other countries, were carefully perused and used where possible. A computer search of professional and scholarly journals on the subject of German suffering and losses, available in American college libraries, met with generally negative results. Allied unit histories, however, were found to be very useful in compiling German loss figures for individual engagements.

During efforts to locate German sources, the assistance of the West German Interior Ministry proved especially valuable, leading the author to statistics of losses compiled, maintained, and updated by several German agencies, such as the German Red Cross Search Service (Munich); the national organizations of former soldiers of the *Wehrmacht*, the *Waffen-SS*, and the *Afrika Korps*; the National Union for the Care of German War Graves (Kassel); the Federal Military Archives (Freiburg); the Federal Statistical Office (Wiesbaden); and the Munich-based Institute for Current History.

Specific statistics of military loss summaries were based on documents from the office of the *Wehrmacht* historian, where Major Percy E. Schramm, who also held the academic rank of professor of history, compiled the German daily war diary. Later he assisted in the postwar efforts of the U.S. Army's World War II German military studies project, which resulted in the collection of over 200 official reports of former *Wehrmacht* officers. Before proceeding with the actual discussion of the topic, a word concerning the veracity of the German data cited might be in order. Personal research and observations support the truthfulness of reports from field commanders and the reliable assimilation of these reports at Army Group level, prior to their submission to Berlin where they formed the basis for the *Wehrmacht*'s *Kriegstagebuch* (Armed Forces Daily War Diary). Commanders had every reason to be accurate since their own replacements in men and materiel depended on the flow of correct information up-channel. In addition, military personnel officers and clerks at all levels operated within the exacting tradition of standards laid down by the General Staff decades earlier. There appears to be no evidence that statistics were used to cover up errors in tactics or to distort command responsibility for actions. Professor Schramm attested to the stringent procedures in maintaining the *Kriegstagebuch* throughout all echelons of the German military (Detwiler 1979b, 1–14). However, there is at least one report of a major commander's being penalized because his report was "too realistic."

U.S. Army accounts of individual campaigns in North Africa, Italy, France, and, finally, Germany, were informative and are likewise considered reliable. Where statistics were gleaned from major works of individual authors, for example, *The German Army 1933–1945* by Matthew Cooper, and James Lucas's *War on the Eastern Front*, the veracity of their data was crossed-checked where possible. Thus, in spite of the magnitude of the events, it can be said that the loss statistics are useful to anyone desiring to research this subject further.

The Other Price of
Hitler's War

1

LOSSES AMONG REGULAR GROUND FORCES

Ich hat einen Kameraden, einen bessern findst du nit.
Die Trommel schlug zum Streite, er ging an meiner Seite,
Im gleichen Schritt und Tritt, im gleichen Schritt und Tritt.
Eine Kugel kam geflogen, gilt sie mir oder gilt sie dir?
Ihn hat es weggerissen, er liegt zu meinen Füssen,
Als wär's ein Stück von mir, als wär's ein Stück von mir.
Will mir die Hand noch reichen, derweil ich eben lad,
"Kann dir die Hand nicht geben, bleib du im ewigen Leben,
Mein guter Kamerad, mein guter Kamerad!"
(Andersen 1965, 83)

I had a splendid comrade, none better you could find.
The drum beat to the battle, he marched along my side
In perfect harmony, in perfect harmony.
A bullet now came flying, was it meant for him or me?
Him it did tear away. At my own feet he's lying.
As if a part of me, as if a part of me.
He reaches out for me, while I my gun must prime,
"Can hold your hand no longer, stay thou in life eternal
My loyal *Kamerad*, my loyal *Kamerad*!"
(author's translation)

Ludwig Uhland's funeral ode to the fallen warriors of Germany's modern wars carries great pathos. Where military burials were possible, in the combat zones and at home, this song was played in sacred solemnity as the remains of German soldiers were lowered into their graves. It dwells on that deep emotional tie, that *Kameradschaft*, which is a distinct feature of German men at arms, and which in its emotive effect can be compared to the playing of "Taps" over the graves of American servicemen.

Throughout the war, Germany's civilian population was apprised of the costs to the *Wehrmacht* of its early victories and subsequent defeats. General summaries of casualties on the German side were announced by the *Oberkommando der Wehrmacht* (OKW), the Military High Command, in connection with special battle bulletins. In addition, each newspaper carried the obituaries or farewells to men killed in action for their own circle of subscribers. These black-bordered announcements placed there by relatives were usually headed by a small representation of the Iron Cross, and frequently they began with a statement that the husband, father, brother, or uncle had died for the Führer, the German people, and the fatherland. A postwar observer has suggested that the character of the death notices themselves reflected the degree of loyalty of the bereaved to the Hitler government. To a person then living in Germany this appears somewhat speculative, but the confidential memoranda prepared by the German internal security service, the *Sicherheitsdienst*, reflect a decline of patriotic superscriptions and a return to religious themes during the later years of the war.

There is also some evidence that where the majority of death notices had a more religious or resigned tenor, such as in areas where practicing Christians declared their acceptance of divine providence in announcing the death of loved ones, the Party attempted to standardize the headings. "For the Führer and fatherland" was the preferred phrase. But where there had been multiple deaths in one family, the growing grief of the survivors was increasingly competing with the injunction to bear one's fate with dignity (Schütz 1943, 122–124).

In that book, published in England during the height of the war, the author supports the above claims about the character of death notices. Those relatives or wives who were dedicated to the Nazi cause and whose men were members of the Party or the *Waffen-SS* frequently began the obituaries with the phrase "In proud sadness. . . . In the spring of 1942, a wife of an *SS* member announced his death by stating, "Storming at the head of his comrades, my loved husband, . . . in fanatical love to his Führer, suffered a hero's death in the East. . . . A life dedicated to the Führer and the Movement found its crowning" (Schütz 1943, 122).

In the later years, when the tide of battle turned against Germany, there were some delays in official casualty announcements, especially in the case of catastrophically large losses, a practice used by Germany's enemies as well. But to the very end of the hostilities, the sacrifices of men and women at the battlefronts and in the home defense were reported with reasonable candidness.

Indeed, after six years of heavy fighting, hardly a German family escaped the "grim reaper"—not infrequently, more than one member of a family had been lost. In general, such severe losses were carried with an astonishing degree of composure or resignation, possibly developed during the sacrifices required of the German people in World War I, only one generation past, when 1,937,000 of its sons never returned ("Schicksal in Zahlen" 1979, 27).

This is not meant to deny that as World War II continued, bereavement took on a pained numbness. Also, occasionally, a wife would be overcome by the shock of the notification that her husband would never return. Nervous breakdowns would leave permanent marks. Toward the end of the war, casualty notifications increased in number and so did the black-rimmed picture frames in millions of homes. But even in the early days of fighting, during the time of frequent victories for the *Wehrmacht*, men at the front and loved ones at home knew that these victories came at a price, even though the general populace appeared to notice the gains far more than their costs. Especially among the young, there was a great deal of euphoria whenever special bulletins announced new conquests.

Germany had entered the war in 1939 with a field army of 2,321,266 men, plus 426,798 personnel in the *Reichsarbeitsdienst* (Reich Labor Service) and a Reserve Army of 958,040 soldiers, this latter being called the replacement pool. Some 400,000 Air Force and *Waffen-SS* members, as well as 50,000 Navy seamen, brought the total manpower strength of the armed forces to roughly 4,156,000 (Cooper 1978, 164).

Already, beginning in August 1934, German recruits were bound before God by their oath of loyalty to the Head of State and Supreme Commander, Adolf Hitler.

During the ensuing bloodbath, especially when Germany's fortunes were looking bleak, many in the democracies wondered why German troops continued to make such costly sacrifices. Perhaps the oath they had taken provides part of the answer. General Jodl, after the war had ended, commented on his own service under Hitler's command in relation to the oath: "As a soldier, I obeyed, and I believed my honor required me to maintain the obedience I had sworn. ... I have spent these five years working in silence, although I often entirely disagreed" (Demeter 1965, 152–153).

Admiral Dönitz shared these sentiments, telling his commanders that while it was the duty of the German people to choose the government under which they wanted to live, it was the duty of his men, as soldiers, to serve that government.

Besides their sacred promise, which applied equally to officers and enlisted men, there were other factors that kept German soldiers loyal to their cause. Among the officers, for example, there prevailed the long-standing tradition of the *Junker* elite who had served both Prussian kings before 1871 and Germany's emperors since. To bear arms on behalf of the fatherland was considered a most worthy profession and, to many, the only career for which they were trained. Also, the fact that many troops had not accepted the reality of military defeat in World War I made them think that this round would even the score. They felt better led and were certainly better motivated, especially as in addition to the *Waffen-SS* elements, the younger officers, in all branches of the service, frequently identified with the ideal of a Greater Germany in Hitler's "new order." Finally, most soldiers in German uniform did what soldiers in other armies do— they followed orders because they had no viable alternative. Realistically, during the last months of the war, however, some disintegration in morale was observed. The special field gendarmerie was kept busy collecting stragglers behind the front lines and turning them back to units which were being reaugmented, or, in some cases, shooting these men for desertion. Likewise, self-mutilation among the troops became a concern. At least one senior commander on the eastern front found it necessary to exhort his staff and unit commanders to educate their troops against the temptation to leave the front through self-inflicted wounds, and to rigorously order the execution of any found guilty of such act (Förster and Lakowski 1985, 160–161). But in general the performance of German troops bore out General George C. Patton's observation, that they were great soldiers and were sticking to the death and knowing it (Blumenson 1974, 304).

THE *BLITZKRIEG* YEARS

In the six-weeks campaign against the gallant and determined Poles, Germany suffered 10,572 men dead, 3,409 missing, and thousands wounded (Orthbandt 1968, 513). General von Manstein's Southern Army Group made up the bulk of the losses: 505 officers killed, 759 wounded, 42 missing, with noncommissioned officers and other ranks losing 6,049 dead, 30,322 wounded, and several thousand missing (von Manstein 1958, 61). Germany's air force, though possessing air superiority from the beginning, lost nearly 300 planes.

What was more painful and is today, some forty years later, virtually forgotten or simply unknown, is how horribly many of the German soldiers died during the much-heralded *Blitzkrieg* in Poland. For political reasons, the archives containing documentation of combat zone mutilations of wounded Germans were closed for decades following the collapse in 1945. Only recently have these records been made available, on a limited scale, to historians and researchers. A few excerpts from these documents will suffice. During military operations on September 9, 1939, members of a German military band were taken prisoner by Polish forces. Out of a group of over thirty, all but two were shot in cold blood. Sergeant Schloerb, who testified before the *Wehrmacht-Untersuchungstelle*, the military tribunal investigating atrocities in the war zone, survived only by pretending to be dead. In the process, he was severely wounded (de Zayas 1979, 230).

In the same campaign, numerous German prisoners of war, wounded soldiers, and medics trying to assist the latter were likewise shot and mutilated. According to testimony reportedly given under oath, Polish officers were mainly responsible for these acts. Frequently, the victims were killed by a shot in the neck or were bayonetted (Kern 1964, 54). These incidents led to trials of several perpetrators. Where the results left no doubt as to the criminal violation of the rules governing treatment of POWs (prisoners of war), the guilty parties were executed (de Zayas 1979, 178). It should not have surprised the German people later when their own officers were tried for the deaths of Allied POWs and the atrocities committed in Poland and the Soviet Union by the *Einsatzgruppen* (special mission units) under the overall command of Reinhard Heydrich and, later, Heinrich Himmler.

Likewise, Germany's tactical superiority, even in the face of larger enemy forces in the defeat of France in 1940, has clouded its losses in that campaign. They are given as 27,074 killed, with 18,384 missing and over 110,000 wounded (Orthbandt 1968, 178).

Here also, some of its troops were murdered after being taken prisoner. One instance is documented where the crew of a German *Heinkel* bomber, after having crash-landed behind French lines, was killed by French farmers. Those responsible were later brought before German court-martials and punished accordingly (de Zayas 1979, 180). Several other instances where captured German aircrews were physically abused or killed by French, British, or colonial troops indicate the terror that followed bailout over Allied territory. Some of these crews were killed in spite of clear indications that they were surrendering (de Zayas 1979, 181).

Only a few examples are given here, but the amount of reported atrocities on the western front reached a significant number. Particularly violent was the fate of soldiers who were wounded during the assault on Crete. There, about 4,000 German paratroopers and navy personnel died, in addition to members of Alpine units. Of the latter, the 141st Regiment found that all its injured, who had to be left temporarily on the field of battle, had been mutilated and killed, probably by their military opponents, while on other occasions wounded Germans were shot by civilians (Balzer and Kern 1980, 113–115).

The conquest of Crete, though successful, proved to be one of the costliest endeavors for the German command, prompting Hitler to consider it a near Pyrrhic victory and causing him to eliminate the use of major airborne assaults in future campaigns, in spite of General Student's conviction that his *Fallschirmjäger* (paratroopers) could remain a decisive strike force.

Earlier, victory in the race for Norway, which German sailors and airborne and mountain troops won against British invasion forces, did not come cheap. To gain the strategic "land of the midnight sun," many *Landsers* (term for German soldiers, similar to the American "GI") lost their lives. Total casualties during Operation *Weserübung* are given as 5,660, of whom 1,317 were killed and 2,375 lost, mainly when their ships were sunk. The air force saw 200 aircraft put out of action, of which 80 were transports. German naval losses amounted to three cruisers, ten destroyers, six submarines, and one torpedo boat. Several capital ships including the *Gneisenau*, *Scharnhorst*, *Lützow*, *Hipper*, and *Emden*, were damaged (Moulton 1966, 259–260).

In North Africa, after initial successes based on the brilliant leadership of the "Desert Fox," General Erwin Rommel, the *Afrika Korps* had to contend with a two-front war after the Allied landings in Algeria in November 1942. By early May 1943, German forces had been reduced to holding a small area of the Cape Bon peninsula and over 100,000 troops of the once-vaunted *Afrika Korps* passed into Allied captivity (Jackson 1975, 388).

In hostilities against enemies in the West, incidents of willful mistreatment of German prisoners or wounded remained the exception, cruel as they were, rather than the rule. Not so in the East and in the Balkans. The extent of the barbarism inflicted on captured Germans there probably exceeded that in any other theater of war (de Zayas 1979, 273–274). When Hitler set out to rescue his friend, Mussolini, who had gotten himself bogged down against the fierce and heroic Greeks, the Balkans were soon stained red with the blood of German soldiers, sent to make good a promise by the Führer given to the *Duce* earlier, when the latter had allowed the German dictator a free hand in the Austrian *Anschluss* of 1938. Now the Germans had to pull the Italian "chestnuts" out of the fire, losing many men here and legions later before Moscow, which they would reach six weeks behind schedule due to the Balkan intervention. Thus, the *Wehrmacht*, unprepared for the severe winter, was forced to fight a "Napoleonic" campaign within sight of the Kremlin. Some observers feel that the Balkan detour on behalf of the Italians cost Germany the war, in that it irrevocably delayed their assault on the Soviet capital. The toll for the Balkan venture amounted to thousands, of whom 2,559 were killed, with another 3,169 unaccounted for (Orthbandt 1968, 517).

In spite of the casualties associated with these earlier and successful campaigns in Europe and the Mediterranean area, losses of unexpected, gigantic proportions awaited the *Wehrmacht* in connection with Operation Barbarossa, the attack launched by Hitler against the Soviet Union on June 22, 1941. Initially, German forces scored stunning victories, capturing Stalin's legions in one encirclement after another. At Bialystok-Nowogrodek in July 1941 alone, forty Soviet divisions fell into German hands (Orthbandt 1968, 523). These enormous concentrations of Red Army troops in the western Soviet Union weakened the argument that Stalin was totally unprepared for possible operations against Germany.

Throughout his early defeats, however, Stalin had one ace up his sleeve in Richard Sorge, master spy in Tokyo—no evident relation to the author. The Germans thought Sorge worked for them; the Japanese felt that he might work for either side; Stalin knew Sorge was his. Based on the latter's intelligence exploits, the Kremlin leader was aware that Japan would not attack the USSR in Asia, thus freeing most Red Army units for the critical battle before Moscow (Deschner 1968, 314).

From the onset of "Barbarossa," Russian troops defended their soil with determination, driven on by political commissars who shot deserters and laggards. Thus the Germans were made to pay for every advance. But not until their advance was slowed and eventually halted by fresh reserves from Siberia and the increasing mud, snow, and ice of a winter considered severe even by Russian standards did the real bloodletting of the German army in Russia begin. This army had fought its way to the doors of Leningrad and Moscow and past the Black Sea in the South. Now its soldiers were facing their first Russian winter and soon suffered terribly from cold and frostbite, as well as from mounting Soviet counterattacks. At this time, *Wehrmacht* losses for the six-month-long Russian campaign totalled 162,314 dead and 33,331 missing—547,467 had been wounded (Cooper 1978, 71).

Over 23 percent of the 3.2 million-men force that had begun the invasion of the USSR had been put out of action. Truck losses were almost total. Of the 500,000 with which the *Wehrmacht* rolled east, 150,000 had been destroyed and another 275,000 were ready for the repair facility. Even Hitler had to admit that the troops simply could go no farther, and by December 8, 1941, he ordered offensive operations terminated on the central front. Soon temperatures of $-30°$ Celsius added their impact to an ever-growing Soviet resurgence that pushed the German front back, up to 200 miles in some places, causing extremely heavy casualties. From December, 1941, to mid-March 1942, Army Group Center had lost 256,000 men, with 350,000 on the sick rolls, mostly from frostbite. In addition, 55,000 vehicles, 1,800 tanks, 140 heavy guns, and about 10,000 machine guns had also been destroyed (Cooper 1978, 336).

Even the animals fared poorly. General Wagner reported to the Army's supreme command (OKH) that the situation for horses, on which a lion's share of support and supply work depended, was "very serious, with a distressing lack of forage" (Cooper 1978, 334). Over 180,000 horses did in fact succumb to cold temperatures and starvation. Contributing was the fact that German horses froze to death at $-4°$ Fahrenheit. Russian horses, by comparison, could withstand temperatures in excess of $-50°$ Fahrenheit. Before combat ceased on the Eastern front, one and a half million horses, used by the German army, would perish (Caidin 1974, 25–26).

Winter fighting in defensive positions took a much higher toll, per month, than had the summer campaign. Equipment losses almost doubled. When the German army resumed offensive operations in mid-summer 1942, considerably fewer soldiers stood on Russian soil than had entered it a year earlier—2,870,000 compared to 3,200,000.

Many of the men had not only met death through battle, but had experienced stark terror in their last hours. Researchers who have investigated atrocities against German soldiers have found that with the lengthening of the war, serious excesses against Russian soldiers also occurred on the German side. However, they agree that during the early phases of conflict, Soviet political commissars frequently acted as executioners of Germans who had fallen into their hands. In addition, mutilations of wounded seemed to be the order of the day. Discovery of their dead buddies, killed in such manner, hardened the attitude of the German troops in Russia and the commissars' role in all this might be taken into account when considering Hitler's decree that they should not be taken prisoner. This order, however, was not carried out uniformly by regular German troops (Deschner 1968, 309).

From German documents it is evident that many German soldiers met their end by dismemberment, knifing, castration, and execution. In nearly all cases, German doctors performed autopsies and verified the causes of death reported by witnesses. This method of verification could only be used, however, while the German army advanced or recaptured portions of the front held earlier. What happened, once their retreat in Russia became permanent, can only be surmised.

At Broniki, Feodosia in the Crimea and at Grischino, a total of 862 persons were apparently murdered, 596 of them POWs, nurses, and female auxiliaries at Grischino alone (de Zayas 1979, 318). Justification among the Soviets for these atrocities may have been Stalin's edict of November 1941, which ordered the extermination of the Hitler generation (de Zayas 1979, 297).

During the early 1950s, the U.S. army, with the Korean war pitting it against Communist forces for the first time in actual combat, continued to work on providing its troops with updated information on the "peculiarities of Russian warfare." Some of this information was gleaned from volumes of *Wehrmacht* files through which American intelligence personnel were sifting. From these documents it was clear that before Hitler attacked the USSR, the Communist leadership had begun an internal anti-German propaganda effort, right down to the public schools. After June 22, 1941, the Red Army used considerable skill in creating fear and terror among its own troops about what its soldiers could expect if they were taken prisoner by the other side; a tactic used by the Germans when it was their turn to retreat later in the war. Efforts were also made to induce the Germans to desert to the Soviet lines. In the attempt to slow down the German advance, the Red Army resorted to another form of defense as well—psychological warfare, whose key feature was the brutal treatment of German soldiers who were cut off during Soviet counterattacks or who fell into Russian hands because they were wounded and could not be recovered by their own troops in time.

At Melniki on June 25, 1941, two batteries of the German 267th Infantry Division, after being overrun, were bayonetted to the last man. Two months later, another German unit was caught by Soviet tree snipers and lost 100 men. When the Germans counterattacked, they found all their men had been shot through the neck (Detwiler 1979a, D, 11, p. 91).

During the battle of Kursk, a unit of the 320th Infantry Division sliced directly into a superior Soviet counterattack, losing 150 prisoners. From Soviet telephone conversations between two command echelons, monitored by the German side, it became clear that the prisoners' lives would be forfeited:

Regional commander: I have 150 Fritzes [derogatory term for German soldiers] here. What shall I do with them?

Division commander: Keep a few for interrogation, and have the others liquidated.

Later on, other messages from the regimental commander confirmed that the order had been carried out and that even those POWs who had been interrogated had been shot (Detwiler 1979a, D, 11, p. 92).

In several instances, mass graves of executed German soldiers were found on tips from the local population. Many of the dead showed signs of having been severely mutilated. These atrocities were a big reason that an assignment to the eastern front was often dreaded and that both sides became more and more used to brutalities and responded accordingly.

In this regard, it may be appropriate to include the content of Ilya Ehrenburg's flyleaf which, under the title "Kill!" was distributed in great quantity among the Red Army. Its text can be read in Ehrenburg's "Moskau, 1943." The last paragraph of his call against the Germans speaks of them as nonhumans:

> The word *Deutscher* is the worst possible curse word. At the word "German" a rifle fires. We won't talk, we won't get excited. We will kill. If you have lived a day in which you have not at least killed one German, that day is lost for you. . . . If you let a German live, he will hang a Russian man and rape a Russian woman. When you have killed one German, kill another. For us nothing is more funny than German corpses. Don't count the days. Don't count the kilometers. Count only one thing: The Germans you have killed. (de Zayas 1979, 296, 234)

Needless to say, this propaganda had its effect, not only while the war was fought on Russian soil, but to a vengeful extent once the Red Army entered Germany years later.

STALINGRAD

In regular combat, one of the most terrible scenes of bloodletting occurred during the encirclement and subsequent destruction of General Paulus's Sixth Army at Stalingrad. After months of fighting both the Soviet armies and the severe winter conditions, the German troops met their "Waterloo" when Russian forces broke through lines held by Germany's allies to the north. In spite of near superhuman attempts to break the siege from within and without, as well as efforts by the *Luftwaffe* to fly in supplies and lift out the wounded—30,000 were actually evacuated—Hitler's orders to stand and fight to the last man, rather than to accept the principle of mobile defense, cost Germany an entire army. By February 2, 1943, the last German resistance had collapsed. On that day, the temperature registered −39° Fahrenheit. According to several sources, out of the initial 300,000 men, only 92,000 were taken prisoner (Deschner 1968, 321, 297). Of those, only 6,000 survived the horrors of the marches, subsequent transport to Siberia, and their imprisonment, which for 2,000 of them lasted twelve years. Only one man is known to have escaped on foot and reached German lines, prior to the surrender. And even he was killed by mortar fire a day later at a dressing station (Carrell 1964, 623).

General von Manstein paid the following tribute to the Sixth Army: "By their incomparable bravery and devotion to duty, the officers and men of the army raised a memorial to German arms which though not of stone and bronze, will nonetheless survive the ages" (von Manstein 1958, 365).

A similar sentiment was expressed in the *Signal*, the *Wehrmacht* magazine published across Europe in twenty languages. It compared the Sixth Army's stand at the Volga with Leonidas's heroic defense at Thermopylae in 480 B.C. (Mayer 1976, 176–180).

While German troops still held most of the city, their letters home spoke of foreboding doom and desperate hope. Some of those letters that did get out were censored and withheld from the families of the men by the German internal security service.

Excerpts from a few of them illustrate the mood of the men surrounded by Soviet armies. Wrote one *Landser*:

I was horrified when I saw the map. We're quite alone, without any help from the outside. Hitler has left us in the lurch. Whether this letter gets away depends on whether we still hold the airfield. . . . The men in my battery already suspect the truth, but they aren't so exactly informed as I am. So this is what the end looks like. Hannes and I have no intention of going into captivity; yesterday I saw four men who'd been captured, before our infantry re-occupied a strong point. No, we're not going to be captured. When Stalingrad falls you will hear and read about it. Then you will know that I shall not return. (Chaney 1971, 243)

Another soldier wrote:

For a long time to come, perhaps forever, this is to be my last letter. A comrade who has to go to the airfield [probably Gumrak, which fell on January 22] is taking [the letter] along with him, as the last machine to leave the pocket is taking off tomorrow morning. The situation has become quite untenable. The Russians are only two miles from the last spot from which aircraft can operate, and when that's gone not even a mouse will get out, to say nothing of me. Admittedly several hundred thousand others won't escape either, but its precious little consolation to share one's own destruction with other men. (Flower and Reeves 1960, 487)

In November 1942, Colonel-General Zeitzler, later associated with the July 20, 1944, coup attempt, had given the prophetic warning that if the Sixth Army would be lost at Stalingrad, the backbone of the Eastern front would be sacrificed and that the Battle of Stalingrad would be the "turning point of the entire war." No doubt, the troops in the caldron knew that for better or worse, they were a part of history-in-the-making (*Last Letters from Stalingrad*, 1962, 32–38).

This writer was an eyewitness to the announcement in Germany of the loss of the Sixth Army at Stalingrad. It spread like a paralyzing nightmare across the Reich. Mournful strains replaced the regular broadcast fare on the radio. The Stalingrad tragedy left an indelible mark on many German families. They had members of their circle in the Sixth Army. They knew that they would probably not see them again. In addition, many now felt for the first time that regardless of what Dr. Goebbels said, the war could no longer be won and that other tragedies involving severe losses in men and equipment were certain (Deschner 1968, 397). As events would have it, they were proven right. And whereas in previous setbacks German reconsolidations were able to effect eventual and successful counterthrusts, the manpower and materiel for such operations had been left at the Volga.

German tank losses for the first three months of 1943 were 2,529—more than half of all produced in 1942. Equally damaging was the drop in the morale of the once-favored tank units, now badly mauled and neglected. Not until Albert Speer took over the Ministry of Armaments did production begin to improve the front line strength of German armor. Speer performed a near miracle by increasing both tank and armored vehicle output significantly, especially when it is realized that this was done during a time when aerial bombardment at home never ceased. Eventually, in spite of increasing production of tracked vehicles and tanks, the output could no longer keep up with front line demands and the *Wehrmacht* High Command was forced to issue the following exhortation:

The OKW will henceforth often be no longer able to meet demands, however urgent and justifiable, for air, armor and artillery support even when enemy superiority is over-whelming. Any shortage of weapons, therefore, must be made good by strengthening the morale of the troops. (Cooper 1978, 489)

"CITADEL 1943"

The next big defeat for German forces on the Eastern front occurred during the week of July 5–13, 1943, near Kursk, some 450 miles west of Stalingrad. It was to be the last major German offensive in the East and would prove to be an inferno in which much of the remaining German armor was swallowed up in a holocaust of melting steel and fire. The Germans initially acquitted themselves rather well, taking 24,000 Russian prisoners and destroying 1,800 tanks and over a thousand anti-tank guns, but their hope of victory by attrition remained unfulfilled, since the Soviets not only halted the German thrust but in a two-pronged counterattack eliminated the salient and the *Wehrmacht* forces caught in it (Deschner 1968, 322). Prominent Soviet discussions of this, the world's greatest tank battle, ranked it of equal importance with the victory at Stalingrad and chide Western historians for failing, until recently, to recognize its signif-icance in the defeat of the fascist foe (Solovyov 1982, 10).

A German staff surgeon reported his impressions of the battle of Kursk:

We moved straight into the Russians massing for attack. The rest cannot be put into words. Anyone who lived through it can easily become a pacifist, without being criticized. We (as medical personnel) only see the "backside" of the war, but it was so horrible that it exceeded even the ability of thick skinned people to cope. We kept collapsing for all the weakness and overtiredness. In France, we had 240 new dead per day for several days, here we had 1,808. (Paul 1981, 215)

One historian judged Germany's assault, dubbed Operation "Citadel," as having been crucially delayed by Hitler, thus depriving it of the element of surprise. In spite of this possible handicap, a frontal assault was launched against what by then had become the strongest fortress in the world. The Russians had prepared a six-layered defense line backed by 3,305 tanks and 20,220 guns. Against this force, the Germans threw 1,850 tanks and 530 assault guns. The battle became what has been called the "death ride of the panzers." After a cost of 350 tanks and 10,000 troops, the Germans had advanced only 25 miles before the attack was called off by Hitler because of the Allied landings in Sicily. Field Marshal von Manstein was able to prevent a total collapse of the southern front by withdrawing his army in a series of delaying actions. He had buried his own son, a lieutenant in the infantry, earlier and now had to leave 3,330 men behind who had been killed, but he did not abandon over 17,000 wounded who were carried to treatment facilities by their comrades. Nevertheless, the German command could not prevent the Soviets from seizing the initiative after the battle, which the latter retained from then on, until they hoisted the "hammer and sickle" over the *Reichstag* building in Berlin less than two years later (Engelmann 1979, 156).

During the German retreat from Orel near Kursk, only 280 of a 10,000–man unit completed the withdrawal. By now, more and more Russians were facing fewer and fewer Germans. The same was true for the materiel side of the battles on the eastern front.

To gain an appreciation of the magnitude of casualties in Russia, the following figures might prove helpful. In efforts to capture Moscow and in related operations from June 22, 1941, to February 28, 1942, German losses stood at 210,572 dead, 747,761 wounded, and 47,303 missing. Thus nearly one-third of the 3.2 million men engaged in Operation "Barbarossa" had now been put out of action. For every day the *Wehrmacht* was on the offensive in Russia, it lost over 7,000 men. Average losses in defensive operations totalled 2,000 per day. Severe frostbite resulted in nearly 15,000 amputations with over 200,000 total incidents (Anders 1953, 76). By November 1944, thirty months later, total losses of ground forces in the East amounted to 1,419,000 dead and 907,000 missing (Anders 1953, 157). Normally, the number of wounded ran about three times of those killed in action. Thus, by the end of 1944, the Russian campaign had cost the German Army over 2.5 million casualties, not counting the wounded. And yet, another five months of fighting lay ahead before the Allies would break Germany's ability and will to resist.

Although the losses on the eastern front dominated in numbers those suffered elsewhere, German resistance against American and British armies in the West was very costly, mainly due to overwhelming Allied air superiority.

D-DAY AND BEYOND

For a look at German losses in the defensive phase of the war in the West, the official histories of U.S. Army campaigns, from the Allied landings at Normandy on D-Day, June 6, 1944, to the push into Germany's heartland in the spring 1945, prove valuable. These accounts are essentially supported by statistics given in German histories.

Even before the actual invasion of France in the summer 1944, German forces along the Atlantic Wall had been weakened by the seemingly insatiable Russian front, which had consumed legions by September 1943 and had shrunk Germany's eastern armies to 2.5 million troops, in spite of replacements drawn from other combat theaters, including the West. German loss estimates for 1943 alone stood at 2,085,000, which 677,000 were permanent losses (killed, missing, and seriously wounded) (Harrison 1951, 142).

This ratio did not improve before June 1944, resulting in a gap of 535,000 men between losses and replacements. Russia was indeed becoming the cut in Germany's "jugular vein," which even constant transfusions could not overcome. According to OKW statistics, of a total of 3,726,000 casualties, the eastern front accounted for 3,513,000 from June 22, 1941, to December 31, 1943, or over 90 percent (Harrison 1951, 142).

From these figures it is clear that the main strength of the German armies was concentrated far to the East, and that the defenders on the western front were, from the beginning, less than adequate to repel the world's greatest amphibious invasion force, assembled by General Eisenhower as Supreme Commander of *Overlord*.

Through saturation bombing by thousands of planes, as well as naval bombardment, the German defenders lost many options before the first Allied troops waded ashore. Once bridgeheads had been established, Hitler's refusal to release several *Panzer* divisions on time to attack these positions further weakened the defenders. The expenditure ratio of artillery munitions between Allied and German forces was almost 20:1 and accounted for more German reverses and casualties. Thus, in the first week of combat in Normandy, German losses stood at 2,000 officers and 85,000 men, not counting equipment. One week later the totals had risen to 102,360 (Harrison 1951, 181). Even in small-scale engagements, German losses exceeded those of the Allies. In a six-hour battle near Camry on July 29, 1944, 450 Germans were killed and 1,000 prisoners were taken. American losses stood at 50 killed and 60 wounded (Blumenson 1961, 281). This ratio between the two sides created the propensity for even larger German casualties as more Allied forces poured into France and their artillery and tactical air forces combined their fire power. According to a First U.S. Army operational report, before their partial withdrawal from the Argentan-Falaise pocket on August 16, 1944, German troops had been subjected to massed artillery fire and aerial bombardment that created carnage considered to be the greatest in the war. "The roads and fields were littered with thousands of enemy dead and wounded, wrecked and burning vehicles, smashed artillery pieces, trucks overturned and smoldering, dead horses and cattle swelling in the summer's heat" (Blumenson 1961, 557). In addition to 50,000 Germans taken prisoner, 10,000 had been killed in action (Blumenson 1961, 558).

Later that year, German casualties continued to be severe. The 16th Infantry

Division, in a five-day battle, lost 4,000 captured and 2,000 killed out of an original strength of 7,000 (Cole 1950, 204). Occasionally, the tables were turned and Allied losses exceeded those of the Germans as in the Hürtgen forest fighting, during the initial phase of the Ardennes offensive and during Operation *Market Garden*. Yet always the air superiority of the former allowed for continuous pressure against the *Wehrmacht* lines the moment favorable weather conditions permitted the use of American and British tactical air forces. Besides, Germany had now been in war for five years. It had lost 114,215 officers and 3,630,274 men (Cole 1950, 30). By draconic measures, Hitler and his staff had been able to have over 10 million men under arms as late as September 1, 1944, but these figures belied the fact that only a portion of those troops would normally have been rated fit for combat. Many were old, physically weak, and poorly trained (Cole 1950, 30). Among these units was the 70th Infantry Division, nicknamed the ''White Bread Division'' since most of its members suffered from stomach ailments. Notwithstanding its limitations, however, this division held off Montgomery's forces for over a week, either dying in the attempt or being made prisoners (Mitcham 1985, 89).

During July 1944, nearly 200,000 German soldiers were wounded. In August, 60,625 were declared dead with over 400,000 missing. Thus, trying to stem Eisenhower's armies had cost the *Wehrmacht* dearly. In the Lorraine Campaign, General Patton's Third Army suffered 55,182 battle casualties, an amount substantially lower than those of the German forces facing it, which lost 75,000 men taken prisoner alone (Cole 1950, 395).

In the Siegfried Line Campaign, which lasted from September 11 to December 15, 1944, and involved the Allied push to the Roer River, initial German losses did not exceed American casualties. However, as greater strength was added to the attack, German resistance weakened and casualties increased. Before the launching of the Siegfried Campaign, total German losses were estimated at 300,000 men. Allied losses stood at 224,569, about one-tenth of the 2,168,307 who had landed in Normandy (MacDonald 1963, 5). The campaign totals showed 140,000 additional American casualties. German losses are only estimated but are judged considerable since at least 95,000 prisoners were taken (MacDonald 1963, 617). Notwithstanding this tremendous attrition, Hitler was to launch a massive counterattack, the Ardennes offensive, just before Christmas 1944. This attack, the only major one of the entire war in the West since the Allied landings, staggered the American lines. But after initial gains, the Germans had to disengage once weather, Allied air power, and Patton's Third Army relieved the beleaguered Americans to the north. By that time (January 2, 1945), according to all available sources, German losses appear to have been about 60 percent of those committed to the offensive. For example, the 988th *Regiment*, out of a strength of 1,868 officers and men as of December 15, had suffered 190 killed, 561 missing, and 411 sick or wounded by December 28 (Cole 1965, 507).

In the final months of fighting in the West, their defense around the Ludendorff bridge at Remagen cost the Germans 11,700 men taken as prisoners, of a total of 250,000 taken in the Rhineland as a whole, not counting those German officers executed by their own side for failing to blow the bridge (Hechler 1978, 212). By V-E (Victory in Europe) Day, on May 7, 1945, German forces had, since D-Day, inflicted over 766,294 casualties on Allied forces in the West, at a cost of 80,819 killed, 265,526 wounded, 490,624 missing, and 2,057,138 captured for a total of 2,894,000 casualties of which 4,548 were incurred prior to June 6, 1944 (MacDonald 1973, 478).

For a personal look at what *Wehrmacht* troops experienced in facing the enormous Allied advantage in men and equipment, the diary of a German soldier is helpful.

13 September 44. Near Bath a convoy had been shot up by fighter-bombers. We bandage the wounded and send them back. We have to leave the dead lying in the street, for with fighter-bombers overhead any unnecessary movement may be fatal. Some of the dead are so mutilated as to be unrecognizable. One of our mates commits suicide by hanging. . . .
27 September 44. The men are done. They are all old chaps. . . . We have now been two days without food. Three companies attacked Hees. Only a few stragglers came back. . . . Poor Germany! Everybody is under the impression that he is selling his life cheaply.
28 September 44. Yesterday, before we started off, we got canteen supplies: two tubes of toothpaste (not one of us poor swine has a toothbrush on him), one tin of shoe cream (who is still polishing boots?). (Shulman 1966, 211)

As Shulman points out, "The overwhelming weight of defeat in the West and the East was thus finally beginning to bend the discipline of the German soldier. It had not yet broken, but it was being sorely strained" (Shulman 1966, 213). This was even before the *Wehrmacht* units from the West were transferred to the southern sector of the eastern front, thus weakening the German forces even further.

In these days of constant local adjustments or *Frontbegradigungen* (straightening of the defense lines) due to enemy pressure in both East and West, the German leadership implemented even harsher measures to prevent tactical withdrawals from turning into a general retreat. Thus, the will to resist was to be bolstered by Himmler's decree of September 10, 1944, that any soldier who might succeed in deserting to the enemy was exposing his family at home to execution (Shulman 1966, 218). General von Choltitz, the commander of the German garrison of Paris, caused the potential of such a fate for his loved ones by violating Hitler's specific order to defend or destroy Paris. His family was spared only by the delaying tactics of a fellow general, who was a friend of Choltitz.

Other decrees invoked the death penalties for relocations of military units or headquarters to the rear without specific authority from the Führer or Heinrich Himmler. As the situation became more acute, other efforts to maintain combat morale concerned decrees against self-mutilation, more liberal application of the death penalty by the *Feldjägerkommandos* (field gendarmes) in dealing with suspected laggards, and a new order by Field Marshal Wilhelm Keitel who, in the name of the Führer, directed that any soldier allowing himself to be captured without having fought to the last or being wounded would forfeit his honor and any pay due his next-of-kin. Additionally, as already announced by Himmler, his family would be liable for his misdeeds. (Förster and Lakowski 1985, 188). The execution of these edicts, of course, depended on how well the families of implicated soldiers could count on the goodwill and protection of local military and political authorities against those bringing the arrest warrants, and on how conditions in the rear areas permitted the police powers to be exercised. From personal observation and research it is clear that in the hands of desperate leaders these edicts represented a very clear and present danger to any military violators and their families. It certainly was out of these considerations that Field Marshal Rommel chose suicide in exchange for the safety of his wife and son.

ALLIED FIRE POWER

For a technical look at German vulnerability due to enemy action, a study of personnel casualties and damage to equipment offers an indication of German loss rates to American and British fire power (Climo 1959, 1–4). U.S. Army Air Force B–17 bombardments of personnel and soft transport in the open gave an effective area of around 10,000 square feet per 100–pound fragmentation bomb, 30,000 square feet for 250–pound bombs. Personnel standing in the area were affected by 100–pound bombs within an 18,000–square-foot area of each impact.

During the Normandy invasion itself, fire density of 25–pound naval support guns was found to be 0.084 pounds per square yard. Thirteen percent of the defenses were destroyed at this ratio. When thirty-pound shells were used, each impact destroyed 700 square feet of a given target.

A breakdown by position, for example, showed the pre-assault barrage to have had the effect shown in Table 1. Of course, it is possible that some guns listed as destroyed by the preliminary bombardment were in fact destroyed by tanks on the beaches.

In Italy, Allied counterfire using 5.5–inch shells of 100 pounds each on German artillery and *Nebelwerfer* (rocket launcher) positions showed a damage effectiveness of about 61 percent, as indicated in Table 2.

An attack by the Royal Air Force (RAF) on July 18, 1944, with a mix of groundburst 500– and 1,000–pound bombs on a German tank unit in an orchard at Guillerville, with a bomb density of 13.4 per acre, knocked out nine of the twelve armored vehicles. The bombs caused circular craters of thirty yards each. Armored cars and supply vehicles were found in various stages of destruction. The effective area reached to 7,000 square feet per burst. In a four-hour preparatory bombardment, using twenty-five-pound light artillery shells on German slit-trench positions at Geilenkirchen, up to 15 percent of casualties among the

Table 1
Allied Pre-Assault Barrage

Type of Position	Number in Area Area	Effectively Damaged Number	Percentage
Heavy gun positions	11	1.5	14
5.0 cm positions with protection to seawards	6	0	0
Guns in open positions	11	3	27
Pill boxes	24	5	21
Tobruk type positions	34	3	9
Open machine gun and mortar positions	20	2	10
TOTALS	106	14.5	13.7

(Climo 1959, 4)

defenders were achieved with 0.37 pounds of explosives impacting on each square yard, for an affected area of 60 to 100 square feet per round. Of course, the data could only be obtained by postcombat observation and is subject to some variance, yet this clearly proves that the German positions were quite vulnerable to concentrated bombardment or ground fire (Climo 1959, i-ii).

Admittedly, the reliability of these studies is not totally assured since some damage may have been caused during the actual assault, but the difference between the type of ordnance used in the shelling and subsequent ground attack would make a fairly accurate assessment possible.

As American, British, and Soviet forces gained in firepower and increased momentum, even desperate actions by the German defenders were unable to decisively halt their advance, in spite of Hitler's orders that German troops were to stand and hold, to fight to the last breath and bullet. Though some senior commanders tried to save their units from certain annihilation by acting contrary to these orders, their officers' and troops' patriotism, loyalty to the soldier's oath, dedication to duty, and the dire consequences of violating Hitler's personal decrees led to frequent last-ditch stands with subsequent severe losses. These efforts were becoming more frequent as individual cities, mainly in the East, were declared fortresses. The latter were at first bypassed by the Red Army, but later encircled and then besieged. The injunction of holding out to the last man

Table 2
Counterfire Effect

Type of Gun	Damage
88 mm.	Out of action by strike on recuperator from 3 medium rounds on parapet.
88 mm.	Workable until destroyed by crew. 1 heavy round in gun-pit.
88 mm.	Gun undamaged.
↕ 105 mm	Out of action by direct hit on barrel from a field round.
88 mm.	Gun undamaged. Sights and following mechanism damaged by a 155 mm. in gun-pit.
88 mm.	Guns damaged by direct hit on barrel from 75 mm. A.P., and direct hit on recuperator from 75 mm.
88 mm.	Gun out of action by direct hit from a field round.
88 mm.	Gun out of action by strikes on recuperator from a medium round.
138 mm.	Gun out of action by a medium round hit in the gun-pit.
37 mm.	Gun destroyed by direct hit from a medium round.
88 mm.	Minor damage from a heavy round on parapet.
88 mm.	Gun undamaged. Medium round impacting in gun-pit.
88 mm.	Gun damaged by splinter from a medium round impacting in gun-pit.

(Climo 1959, 4)

was rarely followed to letter, but cities such as Königsberg (Kaliningrad), Breslau (Wroclaw), Posen (Poznan), Stettin (Szczecin), Küstrin (Kostrazyn), and Kolberg endured weeks of pounding by Soviet air, artillery, and ground assaults before striking the colors. By that time, both military and civilian survivors had reached their limits and even dedicated fortress commanders had no choice but to spare the few who still remained, and surrender. Even the Reich's capital would be no exception.

THE FALL OF BERLIN

Ever since the Soviet forces had defeated the Sixth Army at Stalingrad and again, after their victory over the German Army Groups Center and South at Kursk six months later, they had only one goal: to evict the *Wehrmacht* from Mother Russia and to raise the Red banner over Berlin.

Soviet troops had fought from the Volga to the Oder, had finally ousted the *Wehrmacht* from Russian soil after four long years of the Great Patriotic War, and had replaced the former occupiers of Bulgaria, Romania, Hungary, Yugoslavia, Poland, and Czechoslovakia (Polevoi, Simonov, and Trachmann 1974, unpaginated).

Once they had reached the German border, "On to Berlin!" had been their battle cry. In a series of defensive maneuvers, several German commanders, often charged with treason by a Führer who had lost touch with the reality of the catastrophe engulfing the Reich, had achieved periodic respites and steadied the Eastern front. But every time the Red Army started a new drive, the German lines were quickly breached. Officers and men of the *Wehrmacht* were becoming more and more aware that the end was near, all the talk of a miraculous victory brought on by the so-called wonder weapons notwithstanding. When marshals Zhukov and Rokossowskij launched their final assault from the banks of the Oder River on the capital of the Reich in April 1945, they were soon able to isolate the city of nearly 4 million inhabitants and its garrison from remnants of other German armies to the south. Still, individual *SS* units, among them the "Charlemagne Division" of French and other European volunteers, fought valiantly right to the last moments (Mabire 1977, 376). Hitler Youth members acquitted themselves well and were decorated personally by their ailing Führer in the garden of the Reich Chancellory on April 20 (Haupt 1970, 127), while General Weidling, the commander of "Fortress Berlin," desperately scraped up whatever units he could from the regular army troops retreating toward the center of Berlin. But after a few weeks, and especially after the news of Hitler's death, he also could not prevent the inevitable.

In those last weeks of fighting, both sides took heavy casualties. There stands today a memorial to the Red Army in East Berlin, to thousands of Russian soldiers who fell during the assault. On the German side, the dead were buried as well as possible, for amid the shelling by Soviet artillery and attacks by the Red air force, the Americans and British did not let up pounding the doomed capital into more rubble. After reaching Berlin's southern suburbs, Marshal Konev's forces encountered a major obstacle to their advance on the city center in the form of the Teltow Canal. "The Germans had prepared strong defenses on its northern bank. Along it were massed large quantities of guns, mortars, tanks and *Panzerfäuste*, the German bazookas" (Chaney 1971, 315).

Bridges had been blown or were ready for demolition. Russian troops, nonetheless, began crossing the canal on April 24, supported by artillery and rocket barrages from their katyusha launchers (little Kates), which the Germans called "Stalin organs" because of the attendant sound before impact. The houses lining the northern side of the canal were pounded by this barrage from heavy guns, which had been massed nearly 1,000 pieces to each mile. One of the German defenders killed in this softening-up shelling was a young man, Dieter Egeler, part of the teenage levy of the Hitler Youth. Armed to the teeth and carrying the fast firing MG 42 (machine gun), he refused to be restrained by his mother and charged from the protection of the apartment cellar to man one of the foxholes on the bank of the canal, just twenty yards from the house where his family and others huddled to await the final assault of the Red Army. Especially the women, by now, had no illusions of what their fate would be should the Russians succeed in forcing the canal. Dieter engaged the Russian infantry which was crossing the waterway in rubber rafts. Each time one of the rafts would be hit, the heavily armed troops would spill into the deep water. But the artillery barrage against the German positions on the embankment took its toll, and a piece of steel tore through Dieter's lungs. Alerted, a neighbor loaded him on a wooden cart and pushed him, under terrific fire of small arms and rockets, to a field hospital in Tempelhof where the youth succumbed. He joined hundreds of soldiers from many nations who found their end defending Berlin. In spite of the hopeless situation, they probably had not needed the grave warning issued by Hitler on April 22, which declared:

Anyone who proposes or even approves measures detrimental to our power of resistance is a traitor! He is to be shot or hanged immediately! This applies even if such measures have allegedly been ordered on the instructions of Reich Minister Dr. Goebbels, the *Gauleiters*, or even in the name of the Führer. (Trevor-Roper 1979, 407)

Berlin was in its last throes, yet the defenders continued to resist. Gradually, they were forced back to the belt-line railroad (*S-Bahn*) and beyond. Each street and house was fought over, as in that city at the Volga so long ago. Here, in Berlin, there were no reinforcements, as STAVKA (Soviet Supreme Command) had been able to throw into the battle for Stalingrad. General Wenck's army was to relieve the city from the West, but it could not break through the pincers the Russians had thrown around it. Soviet troops advanced infiltrating through back yards, cellars, and even sewers. The Germans flooded parts of the subway system where thousands of civilians had sought refuge from the *Götterdämmerung* befalling their city above. The waters hardly stopped the Russians, but they did drown a number of helpless Germans in the tunnels. Other German positions were taken from the rear, and Soviet reconnaissance patrols often climbed church towers behind the defense lines to direct their artillery fire from such excellent vantage points. One of these churches was the Kaiser Wilhelm Memorial Church in the city's center, where German royalty had worshipped during another age. The structure's scars, suffered in the intense battle, are still visible today.

Before General Weidling surrendered what was left of his garrison, Hitler and Eva Braun, after having first killed their dog, "Blondie," chose to die at their own hands rather than be captured by the Russians. The Reich's propaganda minister, Dr. Goebbels, his wife, and their six children, followed the Führer into death. In her last letter to her son by her first marriage (he was serving in the *Luftwaffe* outside of Berlin) Magda Goebbels explained her decision (Trevor-Roper 1979, 408–410):

My beloved son, we have now been here in the Führer's bunker for six days—Papa, your six little brothers and sisters and I—in order to bring our National-Socialist existence to the only possible and honorable conclusion. . . . Our splendid concept is perishing and with it goes everything beautiful, honorable, noble and good that I have known in my life. The world which will succeed the Führer . . . is not worth living in and for this reason I have brought the children too. They are too good for the life that will come after us and a gracious God will understand me if I myself give them release from it. . . .

The children are wonderful. . . . Be proud of us and remember us with pride and pleasure. Everyone must die one day and is it not better to live a fine, honorable, brave but short life than drag out a long life of humiliation? I embrace you with my warmest, most heartfelt and maternal love . . .

> My beloved son
> Live for Germany!
> Your Mother

The bodies of the Goebbels family were found by Major Polevoi of the Red Army. He described the horrible sight: "The bodies of Joseph and Magda were lying on the floor—both had been burned. The children were there, also, and had evidently been poisoned by crushing cyanide capsules between their teeth while they were asleep" (Ryan 1967, 472).

Except for the oldest girl, there did not seem to have been any struggle. Thus had passed from the scene the man who had presented the idea of "total war" to the leadership of the Party some years earlier and who now had paid the ultimate price for that type of war.

At 6 A.M. on May 2, 1945, General Weidling surrendered his remnant of 70,000 men to the Russians. Together with a number of German generals and colonels, he left Berlin a week later for the long trip into Russia. He would not return, dying in a Soviet prison camp in November 1955—ten years after he struck the colors (Toland 1981, 551).

Stalin claimed that this last drive cost the Germans 1 million dead, 800,000 prisoners, 6,000 aircraft, 12,000 tanks, and other great quantities of equipment. Germany probably had less than half of that troop strength left for the defense of Berlin, perhaps 500,000 altogether, in and around the city. But German losses in the "last battle" were significant, especially when one realizes that the defenders had literally been fighting with their backs to the wall.

Civilian losses would take years to tally, since for a long time skeletons were found under ruins, in parks and gardens. According to Cornelius Ryan, nearly

100,000 perished, of which 20,000 died of cardiac arrest and 6,000 by suicide. To the 100,000 killed in the actual assault must be added about 52,000 others, mostly refugees, who were caught in the air raids (Ryan 1967, 490).

Thus ended the defense of Berlin which, in retrospect, appeared hopeless from the beginning, since Soviet forces encircling the city were simply too strong. They had come too far to let the prize elude them and made sure that no relief column would reach the defenders. Yet for the German soldiers who were dying in the rubble and field hospitals of the capital, there was one consolation. They would be buried in German soil. This was not the lot of their buddies who fell before the front moved into Germany proper.

CROSSES OF WOOD

Long before this last major battle, while the German front was being broken in the East, several divisions had been cut off and were forced to go it alone. These units formed themselves into "hedgehogs," trying to extricate themselves from the Soviet tide that surrounded them (Anders 1953, 156). Many of these units failed to be relieved by German counterattacks and eventually disintegrated. They, along with units that still retained organizational integrity, buried their dead along their westward path, only to have these graves totally erased by Soviet tanks and earth-moving equipment during and after the war. A few pictures of cemeteries of individual units are extant (Sag mir, wo die Gräber sind, 1983, 6). But according to the decree of the Communist Party, no trace of the fact that German invaders had trod on Mother Russia's soil was to be left for Russian posterity. Indeed, Soviet officials today declare firmly that nothing exists of the graves of 985,316 German soldiers who fell on Russian soil and were buried there ("Nichts vergessen," 1983, 91–92). Recently, a German news magazine reported that for the first time since the end of World War II, German citizens are allowed to visit a few of the graves containing the remains of German soldiers who died, however, not in combat but in captivity, between 1946 and 1947, a very few of the 1.1 million who never returned to Germany from Russian prison camps. One of these cemeteries now open to visits from Germany is located at Tambow, some 400 kilometers southeast of Moscow. It is a humble place where twelve German POWs are laid to rest. Besides these at Tambow, the USSR acknowledges only 1,253 other such graves in the total geographic confines of the country. What happened to the rest is a concern mainly to their survivors in Germany ("Nichts vergessen," 1983, 91–92). There, the *Volksbund Deutsche Kriegsgräberfürsorge* (National Union for the Care of German War Graves) with headquarters at Kassel, Hesse, has made it its solemn obligation to find, identify, and register the remains of every German soldier who died in World Wars I and II.

A great difference in the care of German war dead exists between those who fell on the eastern and the western fronts. Those who fell in the West were buried by their comrades when possible or, after the battle, by victorious Allied troops. German soldiers in all areas of combat were buried with their graves identified by a simple wooden cross, bearing the name, rank, and dates of birth and death of the casualty.

It is the *Volksbund*'s task to supervise the maintenance of 3.1 million final resting places of German soldiers, including those of some 560,000 Austrians and Tyrolians who died while in the German army during World War II. To amplify the point of Austrians serving in the *Wehrmacht*, it must be recognized that Austria was part of Greater Germany during the war. That there were units made up mainly of Austrians is true, such as the 44th and 45th Infantry Divisions and several Mountain Divisions, but all functioned as an integral part of the German armed forces (Mitcham 1985, 72–73, 335–338). Around 170,800 Austrians were killed in action, 76,200 are still unaccounted for, and 495,047 were wounded. Some 1.2 million Austrians served in the *Wehrmacht*. Of these, 20 percent belonged to the NSDAP (Nazi Party) and thus it can be surmised that at least a part of the Austrian contribution was made on a voluntary basis. Austria's civil population mourned the deaths of 372,000. Her cities were heavily bombed; 88 percent of the housing areas of Wiener-Neustadt were destroyed (Sartorius, August 27, 1984, personal communication).

In the Federal Republic of Germany, 14,000 war cemeteries in over 10,000 cities and communities constitute the last resting places of some 1.2 million combat dead ("Schicksal in Zahlen," 1979, 43–53). The *Volksbund* has brought together over 100,000 West European young people with the intent that reconciliation can and must occur over the graves of their fathers and lead to the prevention of future wars, in harmony with Albert Schweitzer's hope that "the graves of soldiers are the great preachers of peace, whose importance as such will increase with time" (Soltau 1979, 8).

It was in 1950, five years after the war, that West German President Theodor Heuss dedicated the first German memorial cemetery. Through patient efforts subsequently, permission was gained to establish German memorial cemeteries in Belgium and Luxembourg, followed by others in France and Italy. Remains, from the polar regions to North Africa, were exhumed, identified, and permanently interred. By this means, the bodies of 500,000 German soldiers were relocated, 130,000 of these identified for the first time. Even today, skeletons are still being unearthed during construction or plowing in France. Every effort is being made to provide for permanent crosses and plaques. In Europe and North Africa, 366 cemeteries containing the bodies of German soldiers are being maintained (Soltau 1979, 28). The actual numbers of identified German war graves by country in the Western combat zones are given in Table 3.

A completely different situation exists in Eastern Europe and the USSR, as mentioned earlier. In spite of the 1949 Geneva Convention, the provisions of the 20th Conference of the International Red Cross, 1956, as amended in 1977, those of the Helsinki Accords of 1977, and an appeal by Pope Paul VI, virtually no progress has been made as of yet in regard to German war dead in the Soviet Union. Very little has been achieved concerning those in Eastern Europe. In

Table 3
German World War II Graves

Country	Number of Military Graves
Iceland	17
Ireland	128
Great Britain	3,912
Norway	11,404
Sweden	483
Finland	3,002
Denmark	25,332
Portugal	13
Spain	183
France	230,764
Belgium	45,400
Holland	31,513
Switzerland	4
Italy	107,274
Morocco	221
Algeria	481
Tunesia	8,562
Lybia	6,025
Egypt	4,553
Greece	14,370
Austria	14,370

(Schneeberger 1979, 10-11)

these areas combined, over 3 million *Landsers* lost their lives. Specifically, petitions have been filed with the governments of Albania (2,400 German dead), Bulgaria (1,800), Yugoslavia (113,000), Poland (468,000), Romania (38,106), Czechoslovakia (178,000), Hungary (54,000), East Germany (172,000), and the

USSR (2.2 million). These figures include combat deaths as well as deaths of POWs (Schneeberger 1979, 15–18).

Until the German soldiers can be looked on as fellow human beings even in the East, the possibility of acknowledging their families' right to information and the granting of visiting privileges to grave sites that do exist remains clouded indeed.

2

NAVAL LOSSES

After discussing the losses among the regular ground forces, the costs of the war for Germany's navy need to be examined. In 1939, German naval forces found themselves vastly outnumbered by the British fleet, but they had benefited from the more recent commissionings of their capital ships and submarines. Of the latter, though, only twelve were considered combat-ready by the Germans when the war began. The navy, perhaps more so than the other branches of the service, shared Hitler's hope that former German territories, now in Poland, could be regained without the intervention of Britain. Once the latter declared war on September 3, 1939, in the wake of Hitler's refusal to pull back his troops from Poland, the German fleet accepted the reality that her most immediate and serious concern was the Royal Navy.

Initially, German submarines became such a threat to Britain's lifelines that Prime Minister Winston Churchill felt obliged to consider the possibility of a German victory in the war of the Atlantic. However, once sonar equipment and other anti-submarine devices and tactics were perfected by the Allies, the tide turned dramatically and U-boat losses became staggering. In surface operations, German battle cruisers took a heavy toll of the British Home Fleet in spite of the inglorious end of the *Graf Spee* on the Rio de la Plata in 1939. Yet even after the sinking of HMS *Hood*, with the loss of 1,416 men, and the crippling of the *Prince of Wales*—feats that caused considerable optimism among the German people back home—the loss of the *Bismarck* on May 27, 1941, with only 110 survivors out of a crew of 2,300, brought the realization that German sailors were not immune from retribution and that even her most advanced ships could fall victim to persistent attacks by the enemy (Roskill 1961, 415). Other capital ships of the German navy would follow the *Bismarck* to their watery grave. Thus the *Scharnhorst* went down in late December 1943, with 1,968 crew members, of whom only 36 were rescued (Bekker 1974, 361).

From accounts of the few survivors on both ships, the last hours of these giants of the German battle fleet can be reconstructed.

THE *BISMARCK*

The *Bismarck* displaced 46,000 gross register tons (GRT); her hull was protected by a chromium-nickel plating unique in the world at that time. It made her virtually unsinkable and inspired her captain and crew with confidence. Yet only seven days after leaving her port of Kiel on the Baltic coast of Germany, shells would tear into the ship, torpedoes would blow up against her bow, she would endure a hail of bombs, and many of her crew would lie dismembered on her deck, burn in pools of flaming oil, or drown in the throbbing sea around her hull. From the outset, though, her skipper, Captain Lindemann, had no illusions about what the enemy thought of his ship. He expected the British to throw everything in their arsenal at him. "We will win or not return" was his prophetic comment to his officers and men at the start of their mission (Berthold 1981, 7). Actually, the *Bismarck* carried two senior officers—her captain and Admiral Lütjens. There is speculation to this day that had the admiral yielded to the captain after their initial contact with the British fleet, the German ship might have survived and fought on. But it was her purpose to attack transport shipping and not primarily to seek a duel with the British Home Fleet. That is why Lütjens refused Captain Lindemann's request to pursue the stricken *Prince of Wales*. And thus the *Bismarck* became the hunted—not only of the Home Fleet, but of the British Mediterranean Fleet as well. After the German ship was caught, lost, and caught again, a slow dance of death ensued. When one torpedo of many jammed her rudder, the *Bismarck* was condemned to cruise in a great circle, unable to get close to the French coast and under the umbrella of the German air force. At 23:40 hours, May 26, 1941, the pride of the German navy was a sitting duck. Despite his ship's precarious position, her captain refused offers from several of his officers to lower themselves under the water and free the stuck rudder by blowing themselves up against it with explosive charges. Even the attempt to rescue her log book, by catapult plane, failed. With the log book stayed a letter from one of the crew:

Dear Parents, with every one of these hours, which may be my last ones, I think of you, I am with you, I embrace you. Perhaps we'll see each other again and stick this letter into a stove to be burned. But if it turns out otherwise, then bear up the news with the same courage with which I must do it. Now, at this moment, I would like to believe in a 'Wiedersehen' after death. I cling to that hope. Farewell. Yours, Erich. (Berthold 1981, 111)

And while the men hoped against hope, surrounded by carnage, the loud-speaker somehow played the German war hit "*Komm Zurück!*" ("Come back to me!"). The flag still flew, while battery after battery was being knocked out.

Doctors and medics operated through terrible bombardment amid hundreds of dead. Some crew members jumped overboard, and two actually departed without orders, to be picked up later and court-martialed for desertion by a navy tribunal. Finally, Lieutenant Commander Junack decided to give the mortally wounded giant the *coup de grace* by his own hand. He enlisted the help of a few sailors and scuttled the ship. Before releasing them, Junack ordered his men not to reveal how the ship finally sank, should they become prisoners of the Royal Navy. Then he was in the water, floating with several hundred toward the British vessels attempting to rescue their now helpless foes. Many had grabbed the lifelines thrown from the English ships, when suddenly German submarines were discovered. The ropes were cut and the sailors plunged back into the sea, within moments of being rescued. It was the final irony of the death of the *Bismarck* that these U-boats constituted no threat to the British fleet—they had no torpedoes and had travelled two days to reach the sight of the battle. Those German sailors who had managed to get on board British ships were on their way to Canada as POWs (Berthold 1981, 371). Missing among them was Captain Lindemann. After Admiral Lütjens had been killed by a direct hit on the bridge, the captain had maintained control of the ship until her last moments. Then he stood astern, holding on to the hull and refusing the pleadings of some ratings to let him be pulled into the water where he may have had a chance of being rescued. His desperate courage overcame his will to live; he saluted and died with his ship (Berthold 1981, 161).

THE *SCHARNHORST*

The loss of another of Germany's battle cruisers, the *Scharnhorst*, was chronicled by one of her radar officers. The *Scharnhorst*, at the time, was the flagship of the German First Battle Group, stationed at Alta Fjord in northern Norway. Her mission was to interdict the Allied convoys that used the arctic waters to bring supplies to the Soviets via the port of Murmansk. Again, as in the case of the *Bismarck*, the numerical superiority of the Royal Navy proved the doom of the German ship. On December 23, 1943, firing by radar, the British engaged the *Scharnshorst* long before visual contact was made. The weather was utterly severe; waves up to thirty feet high pounded friend and foe alike. The German ship was being shredded by continuous shelling and especially by several torpedo salvos that ripped into her during the 36-minute encounter. Captain Hintze made every effort to keep up the morale and fighting ability of his men, but he also gave orders to free the rafts and other life-saving gear once it became clear that his ship would not escape destruction. Before the order to abandon ship was given, the *Scharnhorst* had become a mass of twisted steel, shattered instruments, and torn, half-melted cables. Her control towers had been knocked out, but as with the *Bismarck*, the crew members whose battle stations still functioned refused to leave. British destroyers picked up some survivors, but both her captain and the admiral on board died before they could be rescued. A Soviet source

differs from German accounts of how the *Scharnhorst*'s top commanders lost
their lives. Both Rear Admiral Bey and Captain Hintze are to have shot themselves rather than voluntarily going down with their ship (Kolyshkin 1985, 218).
Petty Officer Gödde, to whose eventual rescue one is indebted for this eyewitness
description of the death of the *Scharnhorst*, only made it through the ordeal,
literally, by the skin of his teeth. After swimming in the freezing water for some
time, during which the capsizing ship's three turbines continued to turn in a
slow death roll, Gödde was hauled into one of the German rafts bouncing nearby.
When the British finally came alongside to pick him up, he lost his grip four
times for lack of strength and crashed into the sea. Only the fifth time did the
line drop near his mouth—he sank his teeth into it and was hauled on board
(Congdon 1963, 233).

GENERAL FLEET LOSSES

Statistical fleet reports compiled by German naval historians indicate that
virtually every German capital ship was sunk during or at the end of the war—
some with considerable loss of life and, in retrospect, without achieving a sustained, decisive result against the British navy. Of the seventeen major ships,
three battleships, one cruiser, and three light cruisers were sunk during battle.
Of their combined crew strength of over 10,000, most were lost. All but two
other capital ships were either destroyed in air attacks or scuttled by their crews
(Gröner 1976, 14–16).

A further perusal of these reports gives an exact picture of German naval
losses beyond those of the main vessels. Some of its larger ships, especially an
aircraft carrier, never saw service but fell into Russian hands in 1945. Of forty-
three destroyers, twenty-six were sunk (Gröner 1976, 18). Out of 1,669 U-boats
on active duty, Germany lost 967 by May 1945. This number is misleading,
however, since the first figure includes submarines of all readiness conditions,
whereas the losses involved vessels that were combat ready only—the actual
defeat was thus even more severe. Of Germany's merchant raiders, only one
survived (Gröner 1976, 48).

As to total naval losses, the *Oberkommando der Wehrmacht* (OKW) issued
its last official report effective January 31, 1945. Admittedly, this was still three
and one-half months before the end of the fighting, but it does show that in five
years of war 1,486 German naval vessels had been sunk (Historical Division,
1945–1952, 10).

"GREY WOLVES" OR "IRON COFFINS"?

Since the most famous arm of the German navy undoubtedly was the submarine
branch, a closer look at the "grey wolves"—as their commander-in-chief, Admiral Karl Dönitz called them—is in order. The French naval historian, Leonce

Peillard, indicated in his authoritative account of undersea warfare that in the beginning, German submarine operations were carried out on a limited scale. Early successes, such as the sinking of the *Royal Sceptre*, the first of 2,472 merchantmen to be sunk, and the subsequent torpedoing of the aircraft carrier *Courageous*, September 17, 1939, as well as the dramatic sinking of the *Royal Oak* a month later by U–47 under the command of Günther Prien, gave Dönitz cause for guarded optimism. Indeed, during the first four months of the war, his submarines went on to sink forty ships, while losing none of their own (Peillard 1983, 40).

The next test of the "grey wolves" came in support of Germany's reach for Norway. Hampered by faulty magnetic torpedoes, the U-boats were less successful and in fact two out of seven submarines sunk by the British were detected by the premature explosions of their torpedoes. With the widening of naval operations in response to the resupply efforts for Great Britain, U-boats joined the Battle of the Atlantic in June 1940. Remarkable successes were scored against British convoys, but dense mine fields began to take their toll of the submarines. Nevertheless, 1940, after the fall of France, became the "golden age" of the German submarine effort. Over 470 allied ships were sunk at a loss of 31 undersea craft (Peillard 1983, 82–83).

The second phase of the Atlantic battle covered all twelve months of 1941. Single patrols gave way to the "wolf pack" strategy. Although another 432 enemy ships were sunk, 35 U-boats failed to return, and four of their ablest commanders became casualties. Among the enemy losses was the American destroyer *Reuben James*, sunk October 17 after almost a year of American "armed neutrality," which was later changed to the "shoot on sight" order for U.S. naval forces escorting British convoys (Peillard 1983, 95). Thus a de facto state of war between the United States and Germany had come about, while the de jure condition was delayed until after Pearl Harbor.

U-boat operations in the Mediterranean Sea likewise began with success in the sinking of the 22,600–ton aircraft carrier *Ark Royal* by U–81 on November 13, 1941. But before the fighting stopped four and one-half years later, British and German losses in that part of the world would balance each other, with German submarines paying dearly for every success. Within the last six weeks of 1941, seven U-boats out of twenty-five assigned to Mediterranean duty were sunk, in addition to 295,000 tons of German-Italian merchant shipping which were sent to the bottom by the Royal Navy, in cooperation with the Royal Air Force (Peillard 1983, 119).

The third phase of Atlantic operations saw German submarines raid the East Coast of the United States as well as the Caribbean sea lanes. Initially, this operation proved successful. From January to July 1942, three and one-half million GRTs were sunk, at a cost of thirty-two submarines. Then came the "*Laconia* Affair," when the U-boat that had sunk the ship was attacked by an American bomber after having picked up survivors and after having identified itself with a large Red Cross marking. As a direct result of this incident, German submarines were forbidden to rescue survivors, but they still radioed the location of sinking ships in the clear.

During the last five months of 1942, fifty-five more German submarines were sunk, which made an annual toll of eighty. The battles against convoys en route to Murmansk, the major Russian port on the Kola peninsula, took another thirty-eight. Only seventeen replacement boats reached the U-boat command.

Throughout 1943, the Atlantic supply route became the main target of the "wolf packs," but improved detection gear allowed the Allies to identify and engage the submarines at ever-greater distances from their prey. In May 1943, more U-boats were sunk than they sank merchantmen in return. The tide had turned; the commanders knew it and it dawned on the crews as well. During the fifth and last phase of submarine operations in the Atlantic, more sophisticated U-boats took on ever-increasing shipping protected by nearly impenetrable defenses. It became more difficult for the undersea raiders to leave their pens. Many were caught and sunk before reaching the convoys, often after hour-long battles. Some submarines took on Allied aircraft, but in spite of armor-plated conning towers and rapid-fire machine guns, they scored only moderate successes. In June 1943, faced with a loss rate of 30 percent, Admiral Dönitz asked himself the question of whether to cease operations. He said:

If we end the U-boat war, we will allow the enemy to use the forces he now uses against us on other fronts. For example: Should we allow the bomber fleets engaged against us to fly raids against Germany and there cause additional inestimable losses among the German civilian population? Should the submariners condone this and tell wives and children they had to bear this (additional) load? . . . I came to the conclusion that we were faced with the bitter necessity to continue the fight. (Peillard 1983, 319)

In summer 1943, 89 submarines were lost. In attacks on convoys, from January 19 to February 24, 1944, eleven U-boats became iron coffins for their commanders and crews. Likewise, submarine intervention in the Allied invasion of France in June 1944 was neutralized by overwhelming sub-chasing efforts. Between D-Day and August 30, thirty submarines attacked the invasion fleet—a full twenty of them were sunk. Before the year ended, 138 German submarines had been destroyed. Losses even increased during the last months of the war, when six were sunk in January 1945, seventeen in February, sixteen in March, and twenty-nine in April! Within days of Germany's surrender, 221 boats were scuttled by their own crews. This loss was scarcely mitigated by the praise their commander gave his crews in his last message: "Six years of war are behind us. You have fought like lions. Preserve the spirit of the submariners by which you fought bravely and unshaken, for the well-being of our fatherland's future" (Peillard 1983, 375).

ONE WHO SURVIVED

Before leaving the German underseas service, a brief summary of the combat experiences of one of the few U-boat commanders to survive the war appears appropriate for inclusion here. Lieutenant Commander Herbert Werner spent the entire six years of the war in the U-boat service. He lost most of his fellow commanders due to combat. His parents and sister died in the Allied bombing raid on Darmstadt—his girlfriend had died earlier in the ruins of Berlin in yet another air attack. In neither case did Commander Werner know of their deaths until he got home on leave. Thus the trauma was understandably terrible. Other men of his crew would sometimes find the sad news written on a makeshift sign hanging across the bombed-out homes: *"Alle Angehörigen der Familie X sind tot* [all members of the X family have been killed]." Werner himself survived hundreds of underwater explosions; he also escaped death when his submarine was rammed by another during training. His account of what it was like to sink into what he expected to be certain death is given here as an illustration of how many others died after their boats had been ripped open by depth charges.

The boat received a sharp blow. After the command, "All hands to the center station!", I saw some crew members in the torpedo room. I shouted, "All men to the forward section or you will be buried alive!" The boat took on water rapidly. For a moment we were able to get it to the surface. It was my duty to stay with the sinking ship until the rest of the crew had gotten out.

Suddenly a shout from the bridge, "Boat is sinking!" The last man clambered up the ladder, then I felt myself being pulled out of the conning tower by my commander. The crew now floated in the sea. (Werner 1982, 111–112)

This time, Werner had beaten the odds. So many would not, falling toward the ocean floor with ever-increasing velocity. Under water, the batteries' poisonous vapors would often explode, or the fumes would simply eat away the lungs. Of course, at depths greater than the limits of their design, the boats were simply crushed by the weight of the water.

As the bombing of German cities increased, the morale of the submariners was also pushed to the breaking point. Occasionally, Admiral Dönitz would personally advise his captains of the status of their families when raids had been especially devastating. Another source of depression against which the U-boat crews had to fight were SOS messages from sister boats that were sinking. Sometimes a single submarine would be pursued for several days until it was destroyed or, by some means, had eluded its hunters.

Just prior to the invasion of Normandy, the remaining U-boat commanders, including Werner, were ordered to take themselves and their crews on suicide ramming missions in a desperate efforts to lessen the amount of men and material the Allies were landing on the beaches in France. By 1944, the life expectancy of a boat and its crew was down to 100 days. The once-proud service was being turned into cannon fodder. Those who were able to reach Norway were taken prisoner by the British. But when these crews were returned to Germany, they found to their dismay that two more imprisonments awaited them—one by the Americans and another by the French. The latter left the Germans to live in earth mounds or holes in the ground—many who survived six years of combat now died as skeletons from starvation or mistreatment (Werner 1982, 379).

When May 1945 brought an end to the German submarine service, 779 boats had been lost on patrol and others in accidents; 28,000 men went to the bottom with them, 6,000 became prisoners of war. It was a bitter end, especially since their sacrifices now seemed to have been made in vain. For years after the war, the survivors met in commemoration of their wartime service and to lend support to the widows and orphans of those who did not return.

NORTH OF THE ARCTIC CIRCLE

A discussion of the fate of the German navy would not be complete without a look at losses suffered from the Red Fleet. Although less spectacular and more limited in scope than battle losses suffered by German warships in the Atlantic, a painful toll of German coastal shipping along the northern Norwegian sea lanes was exacted by Soviet submarines operating out of the Kola Peninsula. Hundreds of German soldiers being transferred to positions in northern Scandinavia as reinforcements for General Dietl's troops, and who were seeking to capture the port of Murmansk, were lost. Once their transports were sinking, they had only twenty minutes to get picked up by their escort vessels before the numbing effects of the arctic waters claimed them. Soviet naval commander I. Kolyshkin detailed the sinkings of fifty-five transports and escorts and of at least four German submarines. During the period of October 7 to October 31, 1944, the German navy, now seeking to rescue its retreating army comrades, lost thirty-nine transports and fifteen warships, with another twenty-six vessels being damaged (Kolyshkin 1985, 236). These successes earned Soviet submariners several Red Banner awards and created a number of new Heroes of the Soviet Union. Earlier, according to Soviet sources, one of their submarines, under the command of Captain Lunin, scored two torpedo hits on the German battleship *Tirpitz*. This fact, however, is not borne out by German naval historians. Soviet accounts are also careful to point out that the British fleet, which sank the German battleship *Scharnhorst*, was in a favorable position vis-à-vis the German battle group only because it had been able to use the facilities of the Russian port of Polyarnoye.

When the war reached Germany's eastern provinces, the Baltic Sea became a second hunting ground for an improved Soviet submarine force. Its exploits against large German ships, carrying troops and civilian refugees westward, are discussed in chapter 11.

In summary it can be stated that after almost six years of continuous fighting, the German navy had been reduced to a few destroyers, scores of smaller craft,

and 200–plus submarines. It had fought tenaciously, sometimes very success-
fully, but in the end it had to bow to the reality that the combined air and naval
forces of the Western Allies, assisted by those of the emerging Red Fleet, had
proven superior.

3

AIR FORCE LOSSES

In the air, Germany began the war equipped for *Blitzkrieg* campaigns. Its air force was new and powerful. Nevertheless, even in the four-week attack on Poland, combined losses in aircrew, maintenance, and anti-aircraft personnel came to 279 killed, 221 wounded, and 234 missing, for a total of 734 casualties. Over 280 aircraft were lost (Bekker 1983, 52). Before the war's end, and in spite of total Allied air superiority, Germany was able to fly several squadrons of the world's first jet- and rocket-propelled fighter planes. But the far-flung operational demands on the *Luftwaffe* and the gradual, massive build-up of enemy air power were able to weaken it to the point of collapse. Increasingly, her planes were caught on the ground, while waiting for ever dwindling fuel supplies. Nevertheless, of all combat arms, losses among the German air force were probably least severe in perceived impact.

ADLERTAG—EAGLE DAY

The *Luftwaffe* began its operations against British fighter bases in preparation for "Operation Sea Lion" (the planned invasion of England) on August 13, 1940, pursuant to Hitler's Directive No. 17, which clearly specified the targets to be RAF-related (Cooper 1981, 13). Had German leaders not been drawn from their original objective by British attacks on German cities, the plan to take out the RAF fighter planes may well have succeeded. Table 4 presents an overview of *Luftwaffe* casualties on the day that Air Marshal Hermann Göring launched his heaviest attacks on Britain. Loss figures for each unit involved in the day-long assault and the fate of their crews clearly indicate why the German air force could not maintain such an offensive for an indefinite period of time. Later, German changes in tactics gave British fighters their own desperately needed breathing space and enabled the RAF Fighter Command to continue to exact

Table 4
German Toll for "Eagle Day," August 18, 1940

Unit	Type of Aircraft and Number Lost		Fate of Pilot/Crew Members			
	Aircraft	Lost	Killed	Wounded	POW	Rescued
Fighter Wing 2	Me 109	2		1	1	
Fighter Wing 3	Me 109	7	3	1	1	1
Fighter Wing 26	Me 109	3	1	1		
Fighter Wing 27	Me 109	6	3		2	1
Fighter Wing 51	Me 109	3	2			1
Fighter Wing 54	Me 109	3		safe		
Destroyer Wing 26	Me 110	19	16		4	2
Nightfighter Wing 1	Ju 88	1	3			
Bomber Wing 1	He 111	2	2	1	3	
Bomber Wing 2	Do 17	1		1		
Bomber Wing 4	He 111	1		safe		
	Ju 88	2		safe		
Bomber Wing 27	He 111	3	4	3		
Bomber Wing 53	He 111	5	12	2	9	
Bomber Wing 76	Do 17	14	17	4	7	8
	Ju 88	3	5		3	
	He 111	1		safe		
Bomber Wing 77	Ju 87	24	27	3	3	
Bomber Wing 2	Me 110	1	2			
Total		100	97	17	33	12

Source: Compiled from data found in Alfred Price, Battle of Britain: The Hardest Day 18 August 1940. New York: Charles Scribner's Sons, 1979, pp. 222-232.

such a toll from the *Luftwaffe* that the latter broke off sustained operations in the fall 1940. German losses in the Battle of Britain were high. The element that favored the British then as it would the Germans later was the fact that even those German aircrew members who escaped death when their planes were shot down often parachuted into British captivity and were thus lost to future missions. According to an in-depth study of the German air force,

The rate of attrition of experienced leaders was . . . high; in the thirty days of September [1940], the *Luftwaffe* lost four wing commanders, thirteen group commanders, and twenty-eight squadron commanders killed, missing, or made prisoner. One combat wing had lost 40 of its Ju–88s in just 15 days, with 160 trained crewmen. (Cooper 1981, 158)

Hitler was never happy about the war with Britain. This was clearly evident from his half-hearted effort concerning "Sea Lion." He had really hoped to negotiate the English out of the war. Though invasion gear and barges were assembled and German troops may have mounted an invasion even after the air battle for Britain had been broken off, Hitler's heart was not in it and after several days, and some losses to winds and the RAF, he cancelled the entire project. Not all historians, however, agree with this assessment, suggesting that Hitler's perceived benevolent attitude toward England may have been based more on the Führer's pretense than on reality.

Total *Luftwaffe* losses from August 13 to September 15, 1940—the period commonly referred to as the Battle of Britain—amounted to 558 fighters, 348 bombers, and forty-seven dive-bombers, a total of 953 planes, plus hundreds of crew members (Collier 1966, 272). Another 263 aircraft were damaged.

BEYOND THE BATTLE OF BRITAIN

During the next eight months, the German air force participated in several major battles in support of ground troops. By the summer of 1941, total aircrew losses had risen to 18,533 (Cooper 1981, 380). Included in that figure were those killed, wounded, and missing in the bloody airborne invasion of Crete. In that effort alone, 271 aircraft were lost. Subsequently, the *Luftwaffe* began to be more heavily pressed in defense of the homeland. Though at times remarkably successful against bomber formations of both the RAF and the army air forces of the United States, its corresponding losses became increasingly severe.

In an effort to keep Rommel's *Afrika Korps* resupplied, the *Luftwaffe* suffered terrible losses, especially among its slow transport planes. One of these formations was caught over the Mediterranean by a group of American B-25 Marauders which created the "Palm Sunday Massacre," a week before Easter 1943. The "turkey-shoot" of slow-moving Ju–52s sent twenty-five of these planes with over 500 soldiers into the waves of the sea (Collier 1946, 126).

As the fortunes of war turned against the Germans, their air force was not exempt from the conflicting and ever-increasing demands on its planes and pilots.

Although aircraft production per se actually rose to new heights, even during the intensifying aerial bombardment of the homeland, British and American attacks against refineries and transportation arteries took their effect. The major burden of defending the Reich against the Allied bomber swarms fell, of course, to the fighters, including the night fighters. Shortly after the war, General Adolf Galland, one of Germany's fighter aces and major air commanders, traced the fate of this arm of the *Luftwaffe* from beginning to end. As all participants in the bomber offensive against Germany will remember, Messerschmitt 109s, 110s, and Focke-Wulf 190s made most raids against German cities and industrial targets a race with danger and death. But in the end, the general shortages in men and fuel played into the hand of the growing strength of the Allies. Even measures of desperation, shortly before the war's end, as well as the most modern defensive weapons, proved insufficient to wrest the command of the air from the American and British fighter-bombers and thousands of heavy bombers on their runs into Germany's heartland.

According to one source, total *Luftwaffe* losses in all areas of the conflict amounted to 70,000 airmen killed, 25,000 wounded, and some 100,000 aircraft destroyed (Cooper 1981, 377). If one considers casualties among ground support personnel, 250,000 more dead and 230,000 who were seriously wounded must be added. These figures include losses among the many anti-aircraft units, which in Germany were part of the air force. The official *Luftwaffe* War Diaries list 69,623 dead or presumed dead, with 27,294 seriously wounded. Additional losses including those due to accidents stood at 250,000 out of a total of 4 million who wore the air force blue (Cooper 1981, 377).

4

THE FATE OF SPECIAL FORCES

THE *WAFFEN-SS*

Among all the combat arms, relative losses of the *Waffen-SS* were thought to be most severe. This highly motivated force, initially having to fight for acceptance by the regular military services, increasingly bore the brunt of battle. In its role as a "fire brigade," called on to stem enemy breakthroughs or breach strong defenses, its exposure rate was exceedingly high. Because of its zealous identification with Hitler's ideology, it virtually eliminated retreat as a tactical option. Accordingly, the casualties of these German "samurai" were staggering. The average life expectancy of their field commanders was three months, at best. In the battle of Moscow, the *Waffen-SS* lost 43,000 men. The regiment *Der Führer* lost all but thirty-five of its members (Degrelle 1982, 465).

Especially marked by partisans, *Waffen-SS* officers became favorite targets for assassination and mutilation. It might be well to point out here that the most famous *SS* officer killed in this manner, Reinhard Heydrich, *Reichskommissar* for Bohemia and Moravia, was killed not by local Czechs under his administration but by two Czech assassins the RAF dropped into Czechoslovakia from Britain (Graber 1978, 132). The horrible reprisals taken by the *Waffen-SS* in Lidici, following this incident, and later at Oradour, France, in 1944 (also in reponse to partisan provocations), defy rational thought and have permanently blackened the reputation of *Waffen-SS* members as a whole and of Germany in general. The only explanation that might be offered, if at all, is the fact that operations launched in response to guerilla assaults, kidnappings, or murders of individual *SS* members rarely led to the apprehension of the partisans involved and thus resulted in inhuman retribution fueled by a kind of blind rage. As one eyewitness to the march of German units from southern France to the Normandy invasion front stated, "The devil reigned." It is therefore understandable that *SS* units, and partisans fighting in their rear, engaged in a type of brutally escalating warfare in which no quarter was given by either side. Later, during the Battle of the Bulge, when Colonel Jochen Peiper's battle group advanced past the Malmedy area, another unfortunate incident would blacken the history of the Waffen SS—the shooting of over seventy unarmed American GIs by its members. Here, there were no partisans to blame. Rather, a combination of circumstances that are clear to the American side but somewhat clouded in the minds of some Germans, led to the murder of U.S. soldiers, after their surrender. That some SS men were trigger-happy, that the care of POWs was felt to impede progress, and that the offensive was to be Hitler's "last hurrah" in the West may explain, but never excuse, the atrocity.

In spite of the above, *Waffen-SS* members at the end of the war preferred to see themselves in American captivity, which, however, did not always turn out a sure thing. Initially Americans shared their prisoner-of-war guard duties with the Russians. Whenever the latter found SS men among the POWs, a search made easy by the blood group tattooed under the arms of the blackshirts, the Soviets made considerable efforts to have them transferred to their permanent control (Butler 1979, 62).

In recent years there has been a move under way to blame the *Waffen-SS* leadership for the severe casualty rates among their units. The union of former members of the *Waffen-SS* has issued a rebuttal, however, in which SS casualties are shown to be comparable to those of the regular forces. Out of a total of 900,000 *Waffen-SS* troops, 253,000 were lost, or about 29 percent.

A brief review of the losses sustained in various campaigns sheds light on this issue. In 1940, the relatively small number of *Waffen-SS* troops fighting in France suffered 3,430 casualties. In the Balkans, 2,559 dead, 5,820 wounded, and 3,169 missing came from the ranks of the death's head divisions (Butler 1979, 71). Out of a total of 160,405 SS men committed to Operation Barbarossa, the first six months of fighting in Russia had cost them 36,000 casualties (Butler 1979, 92). In only three months of 1943, a year later, 12,000 more were lost on the eastern front. By that time, some divisions were decimated by a 60 percent casualty rate, with over 40 percent of their officers killed or wounded. In the battle of the Kursk salient, that great post-Stalingrad slaughter, over 30,000 SS troops were lost—10,000 within two days. Kursk was a devastating shock and proved that even the *Waffen-SS* could now be mauled (Butler 1979, 113).

Nonetheless, it remained in the thick of fighting until Germany's surrender. Some units even continued to resist after the army had ended hostilities. In at least one instance, regular German troops had to put down such resistance by force of arms during the last days of the Dönitz government (Whiting 1973, 145).

THE *AFRIKA KORPS*

If the myth of blue-eyed, blond German "supermen" ever had any basis in fact, it might have been in the case of the *Afrika Korps*. Only those who could pass stringent health examinations were allowed to volunteer for this elite force, commanded by General Erwin Rommel. Initially he gained stunning victories against the British across northern Africa, prompting Prime Minister Churchill's 1942 House of Commons compliment to his German opponent (Macksey 1968, 7). But then increased strength on the Allied side began to turn the tide against the "Desert Fox." He had stood before the gates of Cairo, almost, and with greater support from Hitler might have cut off England's vital oil supplies from the Middle East. But it was soon the *Afrika Korps'* supply lines that were being cut across the Mediterranean, mainly from Malta, which had been left to the British in a major error of German strategy. From there, a resurging enemy harrassed German and Italian ships and transport planes until Rommel had no choice but to retreat.

During September, nearly one-third of all reinforcements allocated to Rommel's panzer army were sent to the bottom of the Mediterranean by Allied planes and British submarines. In October less than half got through, and not a single oil tanker (Liddell Hart 1971, 299).

The Africa Korps became immobilized for want of fuel, but food shortages and disease also made themselves felt. Rommel himself became ill and had to seek treatment in Germany. When he prematurely returned to Africa, his men had held off the British valiantly, but their strength had dropped significantly. Rommel was well aware of his predicament. In a letter to his wife he confided:

I haven't much hope left. At night I lie with my eyes wide open, unable to sleep for the load that is on my shoulders. In the day I am dead tired. What will happen if things go wrong here? That is the thought that torments me day and night. I can see no way out if that happens. (Liddell Hart 1971, 303)

By this time, Rommel was losing nearly 3,000 men killed in action, 9,000 wounded, and 4,000 missing per month. When Field Marshal Harold Alexander, in a fresh battle, attacked with 230,000 British troops, Rommel opposed him with 80,000 Axis soldiers, of whom only 27,000 were German (Liddell Hart 1971, 298).

Yet when retreat became essential, Hitler would not permit it and demanded, as usual, a "do-or-die stand." Rommel's hands were tied and he vented his frustration in his journal:

A kind of apathy took hold of us as we issued orders for all existing positions to be held on instructions from the highest authority. I forced myself to this action, as I had always demanded unconditional obedience from others and, consequently, wished to apply the same principle to myself. Had I known what was to come, I should have acted differently, because from that time on, we had continually to circumvent orders from the Führer or Duce . . . to save the army from destruction. (*The Rommel Papers* 1953, 321)

By early May 1943, the German *Afrika Korps* was down to 60,000 men with 40,000 Italian allies. British and American forces facing them amounted to

300,000, with fourteen Allied tanks for every one on the German side. By the time General Jürgen von Arnim offered to end German resistance in North Africa, his forces had been squeezed into a small pocket in Tunisia, fighting increased Allied pressure on all sides.

The last message from the German commander stated: "In obedience to our orders, we have shot off our last round. Our capacity to resist has therefore ended. The *Afrika Korps* must live again. *Heil Safari!*" (Jackson 1975, 388). Most German POWs from the *Afrika Korps* ended up in the United States, from where they would return to Germany after the war, whistling such songs as Sammy Stept's 1942 hit, "Don't Sit Under the Apple Tree With Anyone Else But Me."

THE MOUNTAIN TROOPS

Another special service that paid a high price was the Alpine Force. Several divisions from the Austro-Bavarian areas of greater Germany saw action in some of the toughest engagements of the war—from southern Poland to Norway, from the Balkans to Crete and then to the mountains of the Caucasus. Later they fought in the Italian peninsula and finally among their own mountain homes of Kärnten and the Bavarian Alps. The *Gebirgsjäger* slugged it out at altitudes that would make most other men faint from thin air. Their willingness to sacrifice themselves for a greater cause inspired James Lucas, then a member of the Queen's Brigade of the 56th Division fighting in Italy, to write an account of their engagements during World War II.

Their service in Poland was brief but significant. When Russian forces began to move into Poland from the east, the Polish garrison at Lemberg elected to surrender to the German *Jäger* in preference to capture by the Red Army (Lucas 1980, 11). Later, within the Arctic Circle at Narvik in Norway, the mountain troops were so hard pressed that even Hitler gave their commander, General Dietl, the rare permission to withdraw. They were outnumbered, their ranks thinned by the weather as well as the enemy. Only Allied set-backs in France saved these *Gebirgsjäger* from annihilation.

Things went little easier for them in Greece—forcing the Metaxas line cost them 150 lives in four days (Lucas 1980, 31). But their most serious bloodletting occurred during May 1941 on Crete, where German paratroops were already being slaughtered in their assault. It was not until the airborne units were rein-forced by the mountain troops that the tide began to turn. Yet many of the latter did not even get to shore, as one survivor of the relief force reported:

We were aware of the sinister significance of those low, narrow, grey-painted ships that moved toward us. . . . The order came for us to don our life jackets. . . . I was surprised to get out of the battle alive. Our boat suddenly turned over. She had been hit by shells but these had hit high and had exploded in the rigging and masts. . . . We were all flung into the sea. Now that was really frightening, especially when the British ships came steaming toward us. Some of our casualties were caused when *Jäger* were run down by the ships. . . . I hauled myself onto some wreckage. . . . It seemed to me as if I were the only living person in the whole area. There were a lot of German soldiers, chiefly *Gebirgsjäger*, all of whom seemed dead. (Lucas 1980, 47)

During a subsequent nighttime attempt to land the *Jäger*, the British navy again took a heavy toll. The mountain troops on board ship had no way to dig in. They were "sitting ducks," standing or lying on deck amid the rain of shell fragments that filled the air. Many jumped overboard wearing full gear and sank like stones (Lucas 1980, 48). The seaborne invasion proved a failure. Hundreds of men had been killed, with some battalions wiped out to the man. Out of a sea lift of 600 men, only fifty-two reached Crete. Airlifted troops, as well, ran into a hail of fire and were forced to deplane under attack. Not infrequently, their Ju–52 transports crashed into each other before the men got out. In the latter cases, the machines, "with their pilots killed or wounded by machine gunners . . . who aimed deliberately at them, ran out of control to hit other aircraft littering the runway" (Lucas 1980, 50). Bright flames engulfed the *Jäger* in their metal coffins and burned them to death before their buddies could reach them.

Further heavy casualties for very limited objectives were routine in the bloody battle for Crete. All told, the Alpine troops lost fifty-one officers and 1,067 men killed, wounded, or missing (Lucas 1980, 82).

A few weeks later, with the launching of the invasion against the Soviet Union, *Gebirgsjäger* units participated in combat actions that would last four years. In a particularly decisive battle at Uman in early August 1941, the *Gebirgsjäger* corps was victorious but suffered the loss of 145 officers and 4,961 men (Lucas 1980, 126). After the Soviet counterattack during the winter, most German units, including the mountain troops, were severely weakened. Soon the latter were given another "mountain" to climb—in a symbolic and also literal sense. They were to break through to the oil center of Baku on the Caspian Sea and plant the flag of the Third Reich on the highest peak of the Caucasus range, 18,481-foot Mt. Elbrus. Fighting raged at altitudes of over 11,500 feet. Roads were nonexistent; trails were unusable; the weather was hostile; tree trunks were often the only bridges across chasms. The cold was severe enough for tooth fillings to fall out and some *Jäger* died before seeing the enemy, freezing solid while standing erect at guardposts, victims of hypothermia. If wounded, a *Jäger* would enter "a private hell" of suffering. "With light wounds," one veteran reported, "one stayed in the line hoping the injury would not turn septic or gangrenous. . . . It was a matter of honor not to leave the line for superficial wounds" (Lucas 1980, 140). But those who were wounded so badly that walking was impossible suffered excruciatingly.

In addition to the shock of being wounded and then the pain of injury itself there lay ahead often three days of portering. . . . By the time that the wounded man had arrived at the main dressing station his wound would have complicated by cold, lack of correct treatment or simply because he had been dropped by his bearers when they came under . . . attack. Legs shattered by shell fire would have become . . . so putrefied that amputation, usually by the light of a hissing carbide flare, was the only way of saving the soldier's life. (Lucas 1980, 141)

Before long, the tide turned against the *Wehrmacht* at Stalingrad and the *Jäger* began their long retreat across the southern Kuban. Other mountain troops, caught in the wintery wastes of Finland after this former ally pulled out of the war, fought costly rearguard actions to extricate themselves into Norway.

By March 30, 1945, the days of the Third Reich were numbered. The *Gebirgsjäger* who had reached the Caucasus now returned to their own soil. They were unable to stem the Russian forces, whose biggest attack in Austria coincided with May Day. At first the *Jäger* beat them off, clinging to the belief, so widely held by some German troops, that with Hitler dead, they might soon be fighting alongside Patton's tanks to turn back the Red Army from Europe's soil.

A few who left the line now to save wife and child ran the gauntlet of the *SS* mobile courts that summarily sentenced any soldier found away from his unit without valid orders. The trees along the roads of eastern Austria that spring bore mute evidence of the cruelty of those days. On May 3, 1945, the Russian infantry resumed their assault. By that night, the *Jäger* had lost 20 percent of their remaining strength. They held out until May 8, the day of the unconditional surrender. Thereafter, they joined their comrades of the regular forces in the long march to Russian POW camps.

THE "GREEN DEVILS"—AIRBORNE TROOPS

Among Germany's special contingents of armed forces none is known for greater bravery than the *Fallschirmjäger*. Although chronologically behind the Russians in development, Göring's "Green Devils" soon became a formidable airborne force during the first half of the war. Even after the British and Americans raised excellent parachute divisions, German *Fallschirmjäger* continued to hold their own.

Organized under the overall command of *Generalmajor* Kurt Student, they incurred initial casualties at the Vistula River during the Polish campaign. Here, however, they were used in a traditional infantry role. Their first airborne assault took place in connection with Hitler's move against Scandinavia on April 9, 1940. Stiff Norwegian resistance north of Oslo caused the loss of eight out of fifteen Ju–52 transports and a considerable number of dead and wounded among those who had jumped into action. This operation was only partially successful, but it taught the airborne leaders valuable lessons for future deployments. These came within a month when the *Wehrmacht* moved against France through Belgium and Holland. The key fortress of Eben Emael was attacked by men of

"Assault Group Koch," a unit whose existence had been a closely guarded secret. Other paratroopers reached their objectives in newly designed gliders and captured two vital bridges at Vroenhoven and Veldwezelt intact, but they reached a third one, at Kanne, just moments after it was blown up from Eben Emael. At this fortress, the going was bloody and difficult. The defenders called in artillery strikes on their own positions to drive back the Germans. Of eighty-five attackers, six were killed and fifteen wounded before the fortress surrendered (Whiting 1974, 50).

While his commandos battled for specific objectives in Belgium, General Student's major force, augmented by an infantry division, flew to its targets in Holland in an armada of over 400 planes. But the Dutch were ready and the *Fallschirmjäger* got a searing "welcome." Especially bloody was the fight for the Willems bridge spanning the Maas River. Out of 4,000 paratroopers, 180 were dead and hundreds were wounded before the Dutch capitulated. General Student himself, during cease-fire efforts in Rotterdam, was severely injured by a stray bullet.

A year later, the men of Student's growing airborne force wrote their names in blood during Operation *Merkur*, the assault on the island of Crete. It was held by 27,500 British and Commonwealth soldiers aided by 14,000 Greek troops and irregulars. Over 20,000 *Fallschirmjäger* and mountain troops, to be ferried by 600 transport planes and a flotilla of seventy boats, were assigned to take the island. As mentioned earlier in this chapter, the seaborne invasion force carrying some of the alpine units was destroyed by the Royal Navy in spite of gallant defensive efforts by outgunned Italian escort vessels. The paratroopers, at first, had to succeed alone, or die trying. Many did. Fighting was bitter in all sectors and their fate hung in the balance more than once.

When the Allied commander, General Freyberg, evacuated his remaining troops after the week-long battle, he had lost 15,743 men, of whom 1,751 were dead, 1,738 wounded, and 12,254 prisoners of war (Kühn 1985, 361). The Royal Navy, after its one-sided victory over the invasion fleet, sustained 2,000 casualties and the loss of nine warships to the counterstrikes of General von Richthofen's Eighth Air Corps (Feist 1973, 27). Greek losses stood at 5,000 men.

German casualties, proportionately, were staggering. Many paratroopers had been killed before they hit the ground. Those who landed safely faced determined defenders who outnumbered them six to one. When German fortunes were at their lowest point, only massive *Gebirgsjäger* reinforcements, airlifted to the island, saved them and the invasion as a whole. Nonetheless, one-fourth of General Student's airborne troops had died in action. Overall, 297 officers and 4,464 men were dead or wounded, among them a high number of medical personnel (Kühn 1985, 188). It was to be the last large-scale airborne assault launched by Germany for the rest of the war. General Student, although hoping for further opportunities, was deeply moved by the sacrifices of his men. In their honor, a monument was erected near Canea, on which the general paid tribute to "his sons," and their brave enemy. For a detailed listing of casualties by individual companies during Operation *Merkur*, see Kühn, pages 362–363.

During the next two years, the "Green Devils" fought and bled in Russia, where they manned key strongholds on the north central front. The 7th *Fallschirmjäger* Division lost 3,000 men in six weeks of combat. Other airborne forces assisted the *Afrika Korps* in Libya. After the Allied landings in Algeria, paratroopers battled their British counterparts while comrades were left in Tunesia, buried at La Mornaghia (Kühn 1985, 254).

After Allied troops under Field Marshal Montgomery and General Patton had landed in Sicily, the "Green Devils" were again used as a "fire brigade" against British parachute battalions. Later, at Monte Cassino, the *Fallschirmjäger* held off three separate Allied assaults and endured two massive aerial and artillery bombardments before retreating on May 17, 1944. They had inflicted over 100,000 casualties among their opponents, who consisted of American, British, Indian, Polish, and even Brazilian troops. Their own losses can only be surmised, but the German war cemetery near Cassino contains 20,000 graves (Whiting 1974, 144).

Before the end came in 1945, German paratroopers fought several significant battles in France—after the Normandy landings—in the last-ditch stand at Brest, and finally within the last German pocket west of the Rhine at Cleves. Their opposing commanders were united in recognizing the determined and self-sacrificing spirit of the *Fallschirmjäger*. For their part, they had earned six knights' crosses with oak leaves and swords, twenty-five knights' crosses with oak leaves, and 190 regular knight's crosses (Kühn 1985, 369–376). Several distinguished individuals, among them the former world heavyweight champion Max Schmeling, had served in their ranks.

HITLER YOUTH, *VOLKSSTURM*, AND WOMEN AUXILIARIES

Toward the end of the war, regular army commands were assisted, though not always joined, by troops newly called up from two divergent levels of German manpower—the very young of the Hitler Youth, and the nearly 60–year-olds of the *Volkssturm*. Actually, by decree of the Reich government, all males between the ages of sixteen and sixty were called to arms. From those cadres, that of the Hitler Youth faced Patton's Third Army in several battles in France, tried to slow Marshal Zhukov's troops in East Germany as well, and finally lost some 4,500 boys out of 5,000 in the last battle in Berlin. Both it and the *Volkssturm*, which defended German cities from East Prussia and the Rhineland to the German capital, incurred their casualties for two different reasons. The Hitler Youth had a death-defying esprit de corps, whereas the *Volkssturm* was often woefully under-equipped, especially in medium weapons, let alone heavy weapons, and presented no match physically for sustained combat against battle-hardened enemy troops who now fought on the hated foe's own soil. By the end of 1944, the Soviets in fact stood in Germany from East Prussia in the north, to Silesia in the south. The difficulties with the combat effectiveness of the *Volkssturm* whose members, at first, were not attached to regular contingents, led Hitler to issue the following order to the High Command of the armed forces:

> Experience in the East has shown that *Volkssturm*, emergency and reserve units have little fighting value when left to themselves, and can be quickly destroyed. The fighting value of these units, which are for the most part strong in numbers, but weak in the armaments required for modern battle, is immeasurably higher when they go into action with troops of the regular army in the field.
>
> I, therefore, order: where *Volkssturm*, emergency, and reserve units are available, together with regular units, in any battle sector, mixed battle-groups (brigades) will be formed under unified command, so as to give the *Volkssturm*, emergency, and reserve units stiffening and support. (Trevor-Roper 1964, 204)

Initially, of course, the *Volkssturm*, or territorial militia, was meant to be used on a temporary basis—only until regular army units could be rushed to the front to turn back the enemy. Neither this plan nor improved training and weapons became realities due to the ever-worsening military situation.

Due to Hitler's loss of touch with reality he would not accept that the war was lost by the year 1945, and that Germany's grandfathers were hopelessly thrown into the grindstone of Allied armies pushing into the Reich from the West and the Soviet juggernaut advancing from the East.

The *Volkssturm* rested on the historical precedent of militias defending the national interest and territory, as at Kolberg in 1806, Tyrol in 1805 and 1915, and as was envisioned by Britain in 1940, in the face of "Sea Lion." On September 6, 1944, all German males between the ages of sixteen and sixty years became duty-bound to join the defense effort in earnest. *Volkssturm* members were sworn into the service with an oath, before God, that they would be true and obedient to the leader of Greater Germany. They covenanted to fight bravely for their homeland and to die rather than surrender the freedom and future of Germany (Kissel 1962, 32).

Volkssturm units were filled through four call-ups according to their years of birth, the average age of the first levy being fifty-two years old. They were armed with special rifles and machine pistols. However, by March 1945, when over 400,000 rifles had been lost by the regular forces in combat, all serviceable weapons in *Volkssturm* hands were transferred to army units. Yet in spite of Hitler's concerns and their inadequate equipment, certain militia units gave a good account of themselves, as in the case of *Volkssturm* battalion 25/235, formed on October 17, 1944, with 400 men. After a few months of combat it was down to ten men. Sometimes, *Volkssturm* members, who wanted to keep fighting, were abandoned by their regular counterparts. At Küstrin, militia units held out two full months, from January 30 to March 29, 1945. At Kolberg, after a fourteen-day siege, 60 percent of their members were either dead or wounded.

At Breslau, 15,000 *Volkssturm* members were joined by 35,000 regular troops in a hopeless cause. Casualties for these auxiliary units on the eastern front rose to 6,000 dead and 23,000 wounded during a three-month period of intense fighting.

In their efforts on the western front, the *Volkssturm* also had its moments of glory, in spite of the general military collapse. The unit history of the U.S. 100th Infantry Division stated:

> The enemy displayed an unbelievable fanaticism. Boys, old men, even cripples shot at our soldiers. All in all, it took eight days of the heaviest fighting. From one apartment block to the next our troops had to fight their way through the city. It was not until April 13, that the last *SS* man, the last *Volkssturm* member, the last Hitler Youth was beaten down and forced to the ground. (Kissel 1962, 84)

Total losses of the *Volkssturm* can only be reconstructed from a card index of 175,000 names of its members. Besides thousands officially declared dead, mainly in the areas of the western front, 29,687 were still listed as missing in 1963 and must be presumed dead. When the battle for Königsberg (Kaliningrad) was ended, 2,400 *Volkssturm* troops had been killed, while the defense of Breslau (Wroclaw) claimed 1,894 of its members. Thus it can be seen that Germany's People's Militia, in spite of varying degrees of combat effectiveness on the whole, did assist regular forces and paid a considerable toll in blood.

The 470,000 German women, mostly volunteers, who served as nurses and doctors and as regular military auxiliaries, especially in the anti-aircraft defenses, were not immune from being killed in line of their duties. In addition, as the Soviet armies pushed closer to Germany and achieved tactical breakthroughs, German female personnel unable to retreat in time were at the mercy of their captors. Rumors of German women being "spread-eagled" across the front of Soviet tanks rolling toward German positions circulated during the latter phases of the war. Although Hitler had steadfastly refused to draft women into the regular service, since in his mind the sacrifices of the men at the front were equalled by every woman having a child for the good of the fatherland, when the situation for Germany became desperate, permission for some such call-ups was granted to certain party leaders and a limited number of *Fräuleins* along with fifteen-year-old boys, younger than the regular Hitler Youth, were called up to strengthen the home front. It was, indeed, *"das letzte Aufgebot"*—the last levy (Trevor-Roper 1964, 67).

THE ANTI-AIRCRAFT AUXILIARIES

A discussion of the service and losses of auxiliary units would be incomplete without a look at the very young draftees from the ranks of the Hitler Youth, who manned the anti-aircraft guns, searchlight batteries, and air defense communications posts of the German air force and navy. Maintaining fronts reaching from Scandinavia to North Africa, from Moscow to the Atlantic Wall, fielding air forces over enemy territories and the Reich, and serving in the navy on and under the oceans stretched German manpower severely. As Allied air power made itself increasingly felt over the German homeland, new demands to defend the "fatherland" generated yet another type of recruit: the youthful *Flakhelfer*, or anti-aircraft auxiliary.

From their first days of service in February 1943 until the collapse of 1945, nearly 200,000 students served in this capacity. Some of them eventually became regular soldiers once they reached the appropriate age. So far, information about their losses as a whole is not available; however, casualties among members of individual units, named for their locations near cities or Germany's sea coasts, indicate they were considerable. Neither were the losses these boys caused among attacking aircraft insignificant. In the last months of the war, the *Flakhelfer* were also used against Soviet ground forces. While these youths were often the target of Allied fighters or tactical bombers, they would often be forced to witness the bombardment of their own home towns which they served to protect.

One of the young men reported his "baptism of fire" near Braunschweig during the night of April 22, 1944: "It was terrible. Something like last night we have never experienced before. The fear is still in everyone's bones. It was horrible. . . . We did not expect to survive until morning" (Nicolaisen 1985, 18). He then described the battle and loss of a 2–cm gun emplacement resulting in two dead and four seriously injured comrades.

During intervals between daylight raids, the boys continued their education with regular teachers, often to be interrupted by new alerts. From the diary of a *Flakhelfer* one gleans that from January 1944 until March 1945 his unit weathered thirty-three heavy raids during which nineteen heavy bombers were shot down, at a cost of thirteen boys, one of whom was killed accidentally by his buddy. Although their gun emplacements offered relatively small targets, quite a few received direct hits, which sometimes touched off the ammunition for the batteries, such as at Mönkeberg near Kiel. In three raids, eight students from the Kiel Middle School for Boys were killed. The auxiliaries were paid fifty *Pfennige* per day and could be decorated once they had assisted in downing eight enemy planes. Requests by families to have the boys return on leave were rarely approved. The Education Ministry as well as the army, however, was not in favor of the way these youths were being used—it was feared that the interruption of the regular learning process would deprive the military of valuable technical skills among its new crop of draftees. But the boys remained, some being detailed to naval anti-aircraft units. Only when Germany's total defeat was a matter of days away were a large number of these youths allowed to return to their families to avoid capture.

THE MEDICAL CORPS

German medical officers, nurses, and corpsmen were attached to various combat units throughout the war. They served with distinction and often with complete disregard for their own safety. In those combat zones, where the rules of war were reasonably observed by both sides, German medical personnel sometimes elected to stay in place with Allied medics to aid the wounded from both sides rather than to retreat. This occurred, among other places, at Haguenau, France, during the winter 1944. No doubt, hundreds of thousands of German soldiers owe their lives to the exemplary dedication and untiring efforts of their medical service. For a look at one segment of that service, and the attendant dangers associated with an assignment to a German armored force, the report of its medical officer is instructive.

Dr. med. Reiter, brigadier general, assigned to the Fifth Panzer Army from 1944 to 1945, gave an account of his service from Normandy to the Rhineland, during the Battle of the Bulge and, finally, to the end of the war in central Germany. He indicated that military and civilian casualties caused by low-flying aircraft required an ever-forward shifting of medical personnel and also an increase in field surgeons. Equally dangerous to medical troops were air attacks at river crossings, even though the ferrying of wounded was made at points distinctly separate from regular troop crossings. Dr. Reiter stated that his medical vehicles, clearly identified with Red Cross markings, were frequently attacked. Thus, evacuation of wounded became ever more dangerous, in addition to the already difficult problems caused by damage to roads, overpasses, railroads, and aid stations, from regular bombardment. To quote:

Men who had been wounded by low-flying planes often lay without care for long periods in inaccessible terrain. Train loads of wounded men which had been held up on bombed sections of the tracks often remained for hours in unheated cars without further medical care. Attacks made by low-flying aircraft on hospital trains, ambulances and dressing stations, inflicted further wounds or killed already wounded men. Even enemy wounded were killed during these attacks. (Historical Division, 1945–1952, 3)

Dr. Reiter felt that some air attacks may have been made intentionally:

Many cases were reported where ambulances, proceeding singly or in columns, were all attacked on clear days by low-flying planes even though they could visibly be identified. Clearing stations, and in particular, river ferries were also attacked. (Historical Division, 1945–1952, 3)

It was a dark chapter in combat aviation when defenseless wounded and their corpsmen, doctors, and nurses became targets. Dr. Reiter's account was verified by wounded American and British POWs, who themselves were the victims of these attacks.

The author can attest to the fact that as enemy air power increased over German territory, no moving vehicle or train was safe from strafing attacks by American P–51s, P–47s, and P–39s or British fighters. It was open season on German vehicles for fighter escorts, since the *Luftwaffe* had been beaten, and the fighters were no longer needed to protect their 1,000–plane bomber formations.

Dr. Reiter concluded his report by pointing to the devastating effect of Allied air superiority and the adverse weather during the last winter of the war. Although medical personnel and supplies were not lacking, doctors and corpsmen still worked around the clock to the point of utter exhaustion to save the wounded from both sides of the conflict (Historical Division, 1944–1945, 1–5).

5

LOSSES INFLICTED BY PARTISANS

Another dimension of death, briefly alluded to earlier, came from behind German lines. To realize the initial vulnerability and general aversion of German soldiers toward the kind of warfare practiced by irregular troops or partisans, one has to understand the psychology of armed combat as found in the German military tradition. To the average German, trained in a philosophy extolling knighthood and the military profession as an honorable way of life, any contest in which combatants did not face each other openly was less than proper. Open assault, in spite of modern military tactics in which airborne units leap-frogged enemy installations, was still the most morally accepted course. Certainly, under Admiral Canaris of the *Abwehr* (German Military Intelligence), special infiltration units called *Brandenburgers* were used to secure strategic points ahead of the regular columns during the *Blitzkrieg* phase of the war (Höhne 1979, 380). But partisan warfare as practiced against the Germans in all occupied areas, and especially in the Balkans, in the USSR, and later in France, made every German soldier, regardless of his military duties, a prime target for capture, torture, and death. Some of these soldiers were mail carriers, medics, chaplains' assistants, and others serving in support positions. All were the welcome prey of the partisans and many were killed along with thousands of their buddies who actually performed combat functions. To get an understanding of the magnitude of the unconventional threat, a perusal of both German and Soviet documents proves helpful (Cooper 1979, xii-xiii). Severe German countermeasures were launched as a desperate attempt to stabilize the operational rear areas (Armstrong 1964, 154).

Even though reports of German losses caused by partisans differ considerably—the figures range from 300,000 according to Russian sources to about 50,000 given by the Germans—they were not only significant, but fear of partisan activities and subsequent counterinsurgency responses by German forces cast a shadow of lurking terror over duty assignments behind the eastern front, especially along railroad lines leading to the actual combat zones.

In a study of Soviet partisans, code-named "Project Alexander" and funded as a combat documentation effort by the U.S. Air Force, fear inculcated by partisan leaders in their own cadres, as well, is clearly evident. Any partisan who vascillated after joining the movement could see his own family killed by his unit (Armstrong 1964, 154). Little wonder then that even the pre-engagement attitudes on both sides (the German and the partisan) grew increasingly more brutal. As early as 1941, to the Germans, male and female partisans were little more than despicable bandits. To many partisans, the Germans, in turn, were looked on as inhuman beasts, an attitude constantly fostered by the political officers assigned to each partisan unit. Others simply preferred communism to national socialism, though some secretly hated the former as well (Armstrong 1964, 170). During a twelve-month period, from May 1943 to May 1944, out of an estimated 27,000 partisans operating against the Third Panzer Army, only a little over 1,000 deserted to the German units, whereas 12,700 were killed and 9,800 captured (Armstrong 1964, 174). Considering the reality of death sentences against partisans by their own leaders, as well as the uncertain treatment in German hands, even the small number of desertions is noteworthy. It is even more significant in view of the following oath, which each person joining the irregulars had to take:

I, a citizen of the Soviet Union, a true son of the heroic Russian people, swear that I will not lay down my weapons until the Fascist serpent in our land has been destroyed. . . . Blood for blood! Death for death!

I swear to assist the Red Army, and by all possible means to destroy the Hitlerite dogs without regard for myself, or my life.

I swear that I would die in terrible battle rather than surrender myself, my family, and the entire Russian people to the Fascist deceivers.

If, out of fear, weakness, or personal depravity, I should fail to uphold this oath and should betray the interests of my people, may I die a dishonorable death at the hands of my own comrades. (Armstrong 1964, 662)

"Project Alexander" confirmed that Germans were frequently tortured and killed after falling into partisan hands. This practice lasted until the Red Army began to gain the upper hand and the partisans' organizational structure changed to approximately that of a regular combat unit. As the *Wehrmacht* began to retreat, special partisan "reception committees" were anxious to settle accounts with those Russian officers found serving with German units. Propaganda exhorted the partisans to "let the ravens eat the eyes of the German scoundrels! There is only one answer: Death to the Cannibals! They are sowing death, and they shall reap death! Instead of bread, give them bullets!" (Armstrong 1964, 260). They were further enjoined to "avenge the tears and blood of our dear ones . . . to take revenge on the enemy, every day and every hour, to starve him, burn him, shoot him, kill him with a hammer, to destroy the Fascist reptiles day and night, in open combat or from behind'' (Armstrong 1964, 260). No wonder assignments to the eastern front were considered a death sentence by many German soldiers. Only in actual anti-partisan campaigns, such as in ''Operation Hannover'' in the Smolensk region in May 1942, were regular troops at a definite advantage. Casualty figures show 10,500 Soviet losses versus 2,200 on the German side. The unavoidable killing of nonpartisans among the Russian population, of course, would spark new infusions of manpower into the guerilla ranks and further escalated the ruthlessness of the conflict (Armstrong 1964, 446). Toward the end of the war, German operations against large units of partisans frequently took priority in order to give the defense efforts against regular Red Army units at least a chance for success. However, it appears that the partisans' tangible successes were somewhat exaggerated by the Soviet side. This does not detract from the fact that at the peak of the struggle behind the German lines, 250,000 partisans tied up 500,000 men of the German army and special security forces. General Ponomarenko, chief of the Soviet partisan Central Staff, claimed that his forces in Byelorussia alone had killed some 300,000 Germans, blown up over 3,000 bridges, caused an equal number of train derailments, and destroyed thousands of trucks, tanks, and supply depots (Cooper 1979, xii).

Some observers compared the psychological effects of the irregular forces on the German soldiers with the U-boat threat to Allied convoys, always lurking somewhere and striking out of nowhere. Total German casualties credited by the Soviets to their partisans stand at over 1 million. But General Jodl, who might have benefited from such statistics while on trial for his life at Nuremberg, put the number of German soldiers killed by the guerillas at about 20,000. No doubt, the racial and political policies of Hitler and his party functionaries including SS Chief Heinrich Himmler, and the draconian retaliatory measures of the security troops, changed into hatred the sometimes supportive attitude of some Russians in German-held areas of the USSR, especially in the Ukraine and the Baltic republics. Certainly, the implementation of the Nazi scheme of colonizing most of European Russia, albeit nonuniformly, by Himmler's minions as soon as the din of combat had died down caused strong resentment among Russian farmers and townspeople. The program of creating Lebensraum (living space) in the East called for the liquidation of those Slavs considered inferior, to the outer perimeters of the area, the assimilation of acceptable non-German stock and, finally, the settlement of the land by German soldier-settlers and farmer immigrants (Dallin 1981, 27).

In addition, once the roundup and subsequent shooting of Jews began, the feeling toward the Germans by White Russians and Ukrainians shifted to revulsion, further encouraging the emergence of the Soviet partisan movement. For indeed, according to their own official reports submitted in 1943, Einsatzgruppen had liquidated 663,421 Jews in the western USSR and Galicia (Wulf 1960, 26).

By October 1942 the German response to guerilla activity included the burning down of entire villages suspected of harboring, or of sympathizing with, irregulars, and the indiscriminate deportation of entire male populations from towns. Russia's countryside was thus laid waste in what had become a life-and-death struggle. For an appreciation of how the Russians felt about the devastation of their homeland, Ehrenburg's compilations are recommended (Ehrenburg 1945). At the close of the war, even Himmler expressed the sentiment that "perhaps we have overreacted to these bandits, and by this have caused ourselves needless problems" (Cooper 1979, xiii).

German sources collaborate on the brutality of the partisan problem. Farmers, and female workers in German field kitchens, the blacksmith shoeing artillery horses—all could belong to the enemy. Rarely did any German survive capture, and German retaliation was equally swift and final. The partisan was a hero to his country, but to the soldiers he was a lowly killer which justified any means of liquidation (Deschner 1968, 404–407).

Especially horrible were the battles between German troops and their allies on the one hand, and Tito's Communist fighters on the other. Only by pretending to be dead did some wounded Germans survive guerilla ambushes. According to reports, prisoners were often mowed down. Those who still moved were shot in the temple. Mutilations of dead and dying appeared to be routine (Kern 1964, 162). Often, mass graves of entire units whose men had been captured and executed were discovered by troops searching for their buddies. The victims' eyes were stabbed out, noses and tongues cut off, and genitals had been torn off. Some German soldiers were found stripped of all clothes and nailed to truck beds. Croatian troops fighting with the Germans against the partisans suffered a similar fate. Women and children were reported to have participated in the dismemberment of wounded Germans (Kern 1964, 168).

Similar misfortunes befell German troops in Greece as well as in Italy. Accounts of individual and mass killings were given by the very few who survived or by those who observed them from hiding places nearby. In addition to atrocities during the war, mass executions of German POWs by former guerilas, now turned government officials, were reported to have occurred at the end of hostilities. Thousands of *Volksdeutsche* (ethnic Germans) who had lived in Yugoslavia before the war were killed; their deaths testify to what can happen when latent ethnic hatred erupts into open rage.

The bestialities by which German POWs, among them hundreds of nurses and other female personnel, found their end during the last few months of the war cannot be described. Out of a total of 200,000 POWs and 200,000 *Volksdeutsche*, only half survived the partisans' genocide. In one of the so-called atonement marches, 10,000 alone were reported shot, tied together, and thrown in the Danube, or otherwise liquidated. Corpses were mutilated in the most barbaric fashion. Once the Council for the Liberation of Yugoslavia had declared Germans open prey on November 21, 1944, even executions of German children in the hands of partisans occurred. On May 15, 1945, over 300 German men and 700 women were forced to witness the arbitrary execution of an orphan boy,

Walther Minges, who had originally lived in a German community of Romania (Balzer and Kern 1980, 419–428). Truly, partisan warfare with its effect on German troops on the Eastern fronts and in France in general, and on civilians in the Balkans in particular, added a new dimension of terror to the already bloody nature of World War II.

6

THE DEAD, WOUNDED, AND MISSING: A GENERAL SUMMARY

Before turning to the fate of those German soldiers who escaped death by being captured, a look at a brief summary of losses sustained in other categories is instructive. Of course, in the case of the missing, one must realize that this category was made up from personnel of whom some, at least, were captured alive. Many of the missing, however, had been killed, but their actual whereabouts or death could not be confirmed due to the exigencies of the particular combat situation. The German army, all through the war, maintained a monthly report of estimates of personnel and materiel. This report was compiled by the *Wehrmacht* historian, Major Percy Schramm, at army headquarters from data submitted by the various components of the major service branches and marked "Secret Command Matter." After 1944, copies were issued on a strict need-to-know basis and very few officers were privy to its contents. Since the account for April 1945 no longer reached *Wehrmacht* headquarters due to the destruction in Berlin and the severed communication links, the statistics cited are taken from the March 14, 1945, report. It had a closing date of January 31 and represents the final, officially prepared manpower picture of the *Wehrmacht* (Historical Division, 1945–1952, 1).

According to this report, the German army up to this point had sustained the casualties listed in Table 5.

The number of wounded and sick, through enemy action, for that same period stood at 4,429,875, of which 4,188,037 belonged to the army, 25,259 were navy personnel, and 216,579 were on the rolls of the air force.

The statistics for missing personnel, depicted on Table 6, were equally significant. Of these figures, 322,807 were known to be in Anglo-American captivity. Thus, four months before the end of the war, German military casualties reached staggering proportions, as seen in Table 7. Losses of foreign volunteer units (European *Waffen-SS* and other troops fighting in German uniforms) from

Table 5
Total Wehrmacht Losses, September 1, 1939–January 31, 1945: Killed or Died of Wounds

Army (of that)		1,622,561
Eastern Front	1,105,987	
Scandinavia	16,639	
Southwest	50,481	
Southeast	19,235	
West	107,042	
Navy		48,904
Air Forces		138,596
Total <u>Wehrmacht</u>		1,810,061

In the West Since D-Day (June 6, 1944),
German Armed Forces Lost:

Army	66,321	
Air Force	11,066	
Additional deaths due to illness, accidents, suicides and death sentences from January 1, 1939 to January 31, 1945		191,338
Total Deaths		2,001,399

(Historical Division 1945-1952, 3-4)

Western Europe, the Baltic States, and areas of the Soviet Union amounted to 358,742.

These figures omit casualties among para-military units, that is, the Todt Organization which built fortifications and the *Reichsarbeitsdienst* (Reich Labor Service). Their losses are included in civilian population statistics.

Of course, it is necessary to add the casualty figures for the period of February 1 to May 9, 1945, during which some of the bloodiest fighting took place. Major Schramm suggested that the monthly loss rates of the last six months of 1944 be used to complete the count. They are repeated in Table 8.

Using these monthly rates, the total *Wehrmacht* toll reached 2,150,000, of which 1,960,000 were killed in action.

Previous rates for wounded and missing can also be used to calculate ap-

Table 6
Missing German Military Personnel, September 1, 1939–January 31, 1945

Army (of that)		1,646,316
Eastern Front	1,018,365	
Scandinavia	5,157	
Southwest (Africa, Italy)	194,250	
Southeast (Croatia, Serbia,		
Bulgaria, Albania, Greece)	14,805	
West (Holland, Belgium, France)	409,715	
Replacement Army	1,337	
Navy		100,256
Air Forces		156,132
Total Wehrmacht		1,902,704

Note: These figures reflect missing personnel up to and
      including January 1945. The next four months of fighting
      brought additional serious losses in all categories
      (Historical Division 1945-1952, 5).

Table 7
Total Losses of the Wehrmacht, September 1, 1939–January 31, 1945

Causes of Loss	Total	Army	Navy	Air force
Dead Through Enemy Action	1,819,061	1,622,561	48,904	138,596
Other Causes	191,338	not categorized		
Wounded	4,429,875	4,188,037	25,259	216,579
Missing	1,902,704	1,646,316	100,256	156,132
Total	8,333,978	7,456,914	174,419	511,307

(Historical Division 1945-1952, 5)

proximate figures in these categories, but the enormous number of troops passing
into captivity during the final full month of the war and during the first ten days
in May, especially, makes an accurate figure difficult to obtain, since available
statistics exclude Soviet records.

The daily reports of German prisoners of war entering Allied lines in the
western battle areas from D-Day (June 12, 1944) to May 18, 1945, are accessible
and give a vivid picture of the depletion of German manpower. Though these
men escaped death, they were lost to the German effort. Daily numbers of

Table 8
Dead Through Enemy Action, July 1, 1944–December 31, 1944 (monthly average)

```
Regular Army (Field- and Replacement Training
Army, and Waffen-SS) . . . . . . . . . . . . . . . 41,903
     of that in the East . . . . . . . 20,611
     of that in the West . . . . . . . 8,294
     died of wounds. . . . . . . . . . 7,541
Navy . . . . . . . . . . . . . . . . . . . . . . . .  1,975
Air Force. . . . . . . . . . . . . . . . . . . . . .  4,595
  TOTAL. . . . . . . . . . . . . . . . . . . . . . . 48,473
(Historical Division 1945-1952, 3)
```

Table 9
Monthly Totals of German POWs—Western Front

Year: 1944	No. of POWs	Year: 1945	No. of POWs
June	21,195	January	51,071
July	69,309	February	81,238
August	80,015	March	371,861
September	119,374	April	1,878,898
October	48,216	May	2,623,798
November	77,945		
December	57,447	TOTAL . . .	5,480,367

```
Compiled from Allied Forces, Supreme Headquarters G-1,
Daily Report of Enemy Prisoners of War.  June 12, 1944 -
May 18, 1945. Army War College Library, Carlisle Barracks,PA.
```

prisoners taken also reflect the intensity of the battles as well as particular Allied successes, giving a fairly accurate mirror of Germany's fortunes on the western fronts.

In the case of wounded, all figures relate to soldiers whose injuries were serious enough to be treated at military hospitals. One point needs to be made. Even though the total of wounded until January 31, 1945, stood at 4,420,000, many of these involved men who came through aid stations with subsequent

Table 10
Additional Details of Losses by Operational Theater, September 1, 1939–January 31, 1945

Area of Operations	Dead	Wounded
East	1,105,987	3,498,059
North Area (Denmark, Norway Finland)	16,639	60,461
Southwest (Africa, Italy)	50,481	163,602
Southeast (Croatia, Serbia, Bulgaria, Albania, Greece)	19,235	55,059
West (Holland, Belgium, France)	107,042	339,856
Replacement Training Army	---	42,174
Dead of Wounds	295,659	---
Total Members of <u>Wehrmacht</u> killed	1,622,561*	4,188,037*

(Historical Division 1945-1952, 19)

* Obvious differences in columnar entries and totals indicate the
  possibility that totals were derived from additional sources
  not given in this original Table.

wounds, some as high as ten times. Thus, the actual figure of wounded troops was substantially lower. According to another study in this series, 52.4 million wounded and sick saw treatment in German military hospitals between September 1939 and April 1945, with their survival rates declining steadily as the war progressed (van Creveld 1982, 97). Major Schramm gave a figure of 450,000 wounded during the last three months of the war, pushing the number for the entire six years of conflict to 4.9 million. The ratio of killed-in-action compared with wounded was thus 1:2.5, more unfavorable even than for the four years of World War I (Historical Division, 1945–1952, 7).

A discussion of *Wehrmacht* losses would not be complete without a breakdown by geographic areas as listed in Table 10. Not surprisingly, the eastern theater was the bloodiest of all.

As to general officer losses (Germany lost forty-three generals in World War I), World War II statistics show a severe rise. Not counting those whose lives were lost through death sentences (after the July 20, 1944, plot) and suicides in connection with the above, or through utter frustration with the unyielding position of the Führer regarding a flexible defense, 238 generals were lost, of whom 201 belonged to the army and twenty-five to the air force. Twelve navy admirals also died (Historical Division, 1945–1952, 21). Officer losses below the rank of general stood at 71,632 by the end of 1944, or 4 percent of all German troops killed in the war by that time, with the highest percentage of combat deaths occurring during the initial phase of Operation Barbarossa (van Creveld 1982, 156).

A review of the statistics presented in this section shows that for every German soldier who was killed in action or died from wounds, 2.5 men were wounded seriously. From the earlier summary of total casualties, it is evident that approximately one in every five German males was either killed or wounded.

The national substance was severely damaged, though not as devastatingly as that of Russia where the loss of some 7.5 million troops produced a significant reduction in the birth rate for several years after World War II. Nevertheless, Germany's genetic pool had been seriously drained, especially when it is recognized that many of the dead and wounded were in their prime. However, the decline in births due to the war was somewhat mitigated by Hitler's insistence on frequent, brief furloughs for his soldiers ("Schicksal in Zahlen" 1979, 54). Likewise, in line with the importance accorded the German family in national-socialist thought, Hitler ordered, during the early years of the war, that fathers of large families (eight or more children) and only or last surviving sons should be protected from the risk of death in combat. However, as the fortunes of war turned against the Reich, the force of these edicts gradually eroded (Verfügungen/ Anordnungen/Bekanntgaben 1942, vol. 3, pp. 670–676; and 1944 vol. 6, p. 307).

Socially, postwar population figures show a significant decrease in the fertility rates of females for the corresponding age and year groups. Also, millions of women, unmarried because of the shortage of men, obtained a decree after the war that permitted them to use the title *Frau* (Mrs.) instead of *Fräulein* (Miss) which was preferred as a means of identification. Such provision should not be surprising in view of the 1946 census figures which showed the German population in all four occupation zones to comprise 28,546,000 males and 35,952,000 females.

A note on German statistical compilations for this period might be justified. They were as accurate as humanly possible. A century before, Prussia had begun its statistical service under Professor Dieterici. Now, 100 years later, German record keepers faced conditions similar to those at the end of the Thirty Years War, except that the number of people to be accounted for was not in the hundred thousands, but in the millions (Historical Division, 1945–1952, 24).

POSTWAR ACCOUNTING

The task of arriving at precise figures for German manpower losses was indeed staggering. Years after the war ended, there were still discrepancies between several agencies, as is seen below.

According to the official statistics of the German Red Cross in Munich, the number of German soldiers carried in its 1983 files as dead stands at 3,810,000. Over 3,050,000 were members of the armed forces from the areas of the Reich proper, 200,000 were from German minorities of Europe, and 560,000 were German soldiers who called Austria and Italy their home. These figures agree strongly with those given by the government of the Federal Republic (Wittek, personal communication, April 24, 1983). As to civilian losses during and subsequent to World War II, the National Union for the Care of German War Graves lists 500,000 killed from direct hostile action (bombardment and ground combat); 2,251,000 dead from forced expulsion, flight, or deportation; and 300,000 who died as a result of political, racial, or religious persecution—a total of 3,051,500.

The 1958 edition of *Deutschland Heute*, official statistical publication of the Federal Republic, gives the following table of German losses:

1. Losses of the German armed forces, 1939–1945 including those considered to have died while in missing or POW status: 3,050,000 dead

2. Losses of ethnic Germans, not including those from Austria, 1939–1945: 200,000 dead

3. Losses among German civilians through hostile action (mainly air war): 500,000 dead

4. Losses among German civilians from the eastern provinces, through expulsion, including refugees killed by air raids, i.e., at Dresden: 1,550,000 dead

Total German Losses: 5,300,000 dead

(*Deutschland Heute*, 1958, 156)

A compilation of different studies dealing with casualties of the *Wehrmacht* gives a fairly congruent picture, but it also points to the complexity of the task. For comparison, data from fifteen different sources are given in Table 11.

Table 11
German Postwar Statistical Casualty Summaries

Source	Inclusive Dates & Numbers of Casualties		
Daily War Diary of the German Armed Forces. 1961, Frankfurt/ Main, pp. 1508 - 1516.	Sept. 1, 1939 to Jan. 31, 1945 (Note: does not include last 3 months of hostilities).	Dead from hostile action . . . . Dead from accidents, sickness or death sentences . . . . . . Missing.	1,810,061 191,338 1,902,704
Müller-Hillebrand, Major General: Das Heer (The Army), 1933 to 1945. 1969, Frankfurt/ Main, pp. 260-263.	Sept. 1, 1939 to May 9, 1945	Dead . . . . Missing. . . . . *includes POWs who died in captivity Total.	4,500,000* 3,000,000 7,500,000
Ploetz: History of the Second World War. 1960, Bielefeld. Sources: OKW/ OKH and Census Records p. 80-81	Sept. 1, 1939 to May 9, 1945	Dead (Officially). . . . . . . Missing (including POWs) . . . . Total.	2,730,000 4,000,000 6,730,000

68

Table 11 (*continued*)

Source	Period	Category	Number
Zentner, K., Illustrated History of the Second World War. 1963, Munich. Sources: OKW/OKH & Census Records, p. 569	Sept. 1, 1939 to May 9, 1945	Dead	2,730,000
		Missing	1,240,629
		Total	3,970,629
Soversenno Sekretno. Tolko dlja Kommandovanija (Secret Command Matters). 1967, Moscow, p. 660, 707.	Sept. 1, 1939 to June 21, 1941	Dead	100,000
	June 22, 1941 to May 9, 1945	Dead	2,215,000
		Missing	2,207,000
		Total	4,522,000
Keilig, W.: The German Armed Forces 1939-1945. 1956, Bad Nauheim, Doc, 203/11.	Sept. 1, 1939 to Nov. 30, 1944	Dead	1,991,085
		Missing	1,748,778
		Total	3,739,863
Arntz, H.: Human Casualties of the Second World War. 1953, Hamburg, pp. 441-447.	Sept. 1, 1939 to May 9, 1945	Dead	3,050,000
		Ethnic Germans	200,000
		Total	3,250,000

Table 11 (*continued*)

"Fellow Soldier Where are You?" Central Office for Missing Persons. 1965, Kassel, p. 144.	Sept. 1, 1939 to May 9, 1945	Dead (including Austro-Germans). . 3,000,000
		Missing. 1,300,000
		Total. 4,300,000
Public Work Map, 1965 Berlin, p. 51.111	Sept. 1, 1939 to May 9, 1945	Dead 4,000,000
German Red Cross, 1974, Munich.	Sept. 1, 1939 to May 9, 1945	Dead 3,046,500
		Missing. 1,250,000
Germany Today, 1958, Bonn. Bonn.	Sept. 1, 1939 to May 9, 1945	Dead 3,050,000
		Ethnic Germans 200,000
		Germans from Austria and Italy (Tyrol). 560,000
		Total. 3,810,000

70

Table 11 (*continued*)

Grand Larousse Encyclopedia, 1962, Tom, p. 700.	Sept. 1, 1939 to May 9, 1945	Dead 3,900,000
		Austrians. 400,000
		Total. 4,300,000
Encyclopedia Britannica		Dead & Missing 2,850,000
Encyclopedia Americana		Dead 2,250,000
		Missing. 1,500,000
		Total. 3,750,000
Der Neue Brockhaus (German Encyclopedia), 1950, Vol. 5, p. 504		3,500,000

(Wittek 1983, personal communication)

7

THE PLIGHT OF THE PRISONERS OF WAR

Most German soldiers who did not fall in battle or who managed to remain part of units able to maintain their organizational integrity during retreats became prisoners of war. Their number on the eastern front alone has been estimated to exceed 1.8 million (Federal Republic of Germany 1956, 6). Long before the collapse of German resistance on both the eastern and western fronts (including the Italian theater) it had become known what fate would befall German troops captured by the Red Army. Those who would survive the seemingly endless marches and rides in freight trains faced eternal frost and suffering in Siberia's wastelands. The expectation of subhuman conditions in Soviet POW camps caused German units facing certain defeat to operate in a manner that would make their capture by American or British forces at least a possibility.

The terrible aversion of being captured by or turned over to the Soviets is vividly illustrated by the case of Field Marshal Model. After Model had witnessed the destruction of his own army by the Americans and had seen the ever-narrowing gap between him and the Russian armies pushing westward, he declined his intelligence chief's pleas with him to give himself up. "I simply cannot do it," replied Model. He continued, "The Russians have branded me a criminal, and the Americans would be sure to turn me over to them for hanging." His command gone, his troops decimated, Model escaped capture for three days, then led his loyal subordinate into a peaceful, forested location near Duisburg. His last order, after explaining that anything was better than falling into Russian hands, was that he should be buried in this spot. A shot rang out. The general had chosen suicide over anticipated delivery into Soviet hands (Shulman 1966, 286). Later events would prove Model right. In one instance alone, nine German generals captured by the Allies were extradited to Yugoslavia where they where sentenced to death and executed.

This was the time before the outbreak of the Cold War, a time of naiveté in western circles that gave rise to the infamous "Operation Keelhaul" and the slaughter of tens of thousands of Croatian troops by Tito's partisans (Prcela and Guldescu 1970, 420–425). Forcible repatriation by western military authorities of millions of displaced persons from Eastern Europe, as well as Russians who had been under German control, caused the deaths of thousands at the hands of their Communist countrymen. In Stalin's view, any Russian contaminated by German imprisonment might be either a threat to the Soviet state or unworthy to return to it, and some were eliminated as soon as the western troops had moved out of sight (Epstein 1973, 82–85).

Sometimes, German soldiers trying to surrender on the western front were shot down, as well as at Webling, near Dachau, on April 29, 1945, after a firefight with American infantry (Mollo 1980, 30–33). It was hell, and troops on all sides had witnessed atrocities that depressed their own level of humanity to such a degree that only the most objective and astute could retain the feeling of compassion normally prevalent among people.

IN ALLIED HANDS

The treatment of German soldiers captured and retained by the western Allies was relatively humane, but not without excesses, as in the case of camps administered by the French and in the American POW camp at Sinzig near Remagen, Germany, where over 120,000 *Landser* endured severe hardships, 1,213 died, and where in 1985 Remagen's mayor laid the cornerstone for a memorial chapel (Haffke and Koll 1983, 187–190).

Imprisonment by the Allies held a certain, initial fear, even though the treatment improved as prisoners reached their permanent camps (Gansberg 1977, 14–15). Of the 3 million German POWs, 372,000 ended up in camps in the United States. Before they ever got there, they were subjected to frequent interrogations and sometimes beatings by British captors. One of the latter admitted to shooting a prisoner in the head to make others talk (Gansberg 1977, 14). Generally, once in the United States, German prisoners were treated fairly. Many still think of those years as a wholesome experience. Occasionally, the opposite was true as in the case of German prisoners at Ft. Douglas, Utah, on the night of July 9, 1945, when a drunken, German-hating GI "hosed down" their tents with his submachine gun. Eight died and twenty were wounded (Gansberg 1977, 43). Other POWs died as the result of carelessness among their guards. Of fifty-six trying to escape, thirty-four were shot and killed (Gansberg 1977, 44). One who got away was Georg Gaertner. He eluded the authorities, stayed in the United States, married, and finally revealed his identity in September 1985, after his book detailing his life as the Führer's last soldier in America appeared on the market.

There were a few who died at the hands of their fellow prisoners, mainly over ideological differences (Parnell 1981, 27). Fourteen Germans were convicted and hanged for their role in such murders (Gansberg 1977, 52). American reeducation efforts, though technically against the Geneva Convention's injunction against denationalization, were credited with providing a core of supporters for the new postwar Germany.

Another account talks of the looting of German POWs wounded in action (Krammer 1979, 66). Prisoners were also frightened into confessions by having interrogators dressed in KGB (Soviet State Security) uniforms stamp the records of would-be recalcitrants with the letters "NR" (*nach Russland*—to the Soviet Union). American guards were advised not to become friendly with their German charges by being reminded that "the good-looking youth . . . with such charm, was the same murderous maniac who fashioned the booby traps that blew American soldiers into bloody bits. . . . " (Krammer 1979, 25). This did not keep many guards from showing their humane side to the POWs. Where hostile acts or deliberate violations occurred, guards used deadly force. Of the total of 477 Germans who died from various causes, relatively few did so at the hands of the guards.

An example of anti-German sentiments in America was the suggestion to "systematically bleed" the POWs to gain much needed plasma for wounded GIs overseas on the one hand, and the subsequent uproar over the thought of injecting American troops with the "fiendish and ruthless blood of the enemy" on the other (Krammer 1979, 190). The Germans were in enemy country and at least one officer, a Captain Joseph Lane of Camp Cascade, Iowa, made sure in his interview with the *New York Times* that they would not make any mistake about that fact.

I've seen more than 100,000 Germans pass through my cage, and I know these bastards. They're no good. They're treacherous, no morals, no scruples, no religion, no nothing. . . .
I hate them all and my men hate them. We want a peace that will knock them down on their knees and keep them there until they learn better. I don't know what in hell you're going to do about reeducating their officers. My private suggestion is that you just kill them all and save the world a lot of headaches for the next couple of generations. Most of them are just hopeless. (Krammer 1979, 190)

It was fortunate for the Germans that these sentiments were in the minority, or fewer POWs would have seen their country again. Today, at the German war memorial cemetery at Fort McClellan, Alabama, POWs buried there are honored by the members of the U.S. Army and the new *Bundeswehr* (West German Army).

INTO THE GULAG

This last point especially stands in stark contrast to the fate of legions of German men swallowed by Russia's Gulag and for whom conditions in the camps became a terrible ordeal. To appreciate the fate of these captives, a view of their sufferings, as detailed in a 1969 issue of Germany's major news magazine, *Der Spiegel*, is helpful. For German soldiers, capture by Soviet troops proved to be an unbelievable shock which, after weeks of captivity, gave way to physical and spiritual depression—not even strength for prayer was left in the men. Conditions of total helplessness and moral apathy, endless hunger, and exhaustion made many a "Fritz," as the Russians called the Germans, envy their dead comrades.

The total number of German troops who had fallen into Soviet hands by May 8, 1945, reached over 3 million. They lived and died in nearly 3,000 POW camps scattered across the width and breadth of the USSR. Only 1,950,000 returned, some not until 1957, twelve years after the end of the fighting. Virtually no record of their whereabouts exists, since many were buried in mass graves. Until recently, the Federal Republic, though having funded a study of German POWs in Russia, refused to release the results for political reasons. The study revealed that conditions in the camps were utterly horrible—although many German soldiers were surprised to have made it that far since it was generally assumed, especially by officers, that they would be executed after capture.

Once in the camp, the total loss of one's accustomed life style and the subsequent role switching caused severe emotional problems. But the most relentless enemy of all proved to be hunger. Rations were just enough to keep the strong from dying, and some POWs actually learned to regurgitate in order to extend the ecstacy of chewing.

Assignment to work details depended on the firmness of the buttocks—Russian camp doctors, frequently female, made these determinations with experienced fingers. The least firm and sick were granted light labor duties.

Especially feared was dystrophy, from which legions of POWs suffered—with terribly swollen limbs, without the ability to control bodily functions, and unable to stop the slow wasting away until death took them, mostly at sunrise. Poems out of the camps give mute evidence of their absolute suffering and despair. The world in which they once lived and fought was gone forever—there would be no "resurrection." Once they accepted that "their" Germany had surrendered unconditionally, the realization of all their vain sacrifices drove many to despair. Added to the mental weight of this realization were the camp's reeducation programs along the lines of Marxism, and the perpetual presence of Soviet state security informers—fellow prisoners who had agreed to work for the political officers in the camps. Surprisingly, however, the POWs' inner strength appeared to increase once it dawned on them that they might be imprisoned indefinitely. This came about through postcapture sentences, with convictions of up to twenty-five years of forced labor for a variety of reasons.

Even the eventual permission to send and receive mail proved to be a double-edged sword. A joy to some, it could also be used to break a prisoner's will further by removing the letters from the envelopes before delivery. Other POWs received news of the loss of their wives and children as a result of air raids or ground combat. Still, the majority probably tried harder to stay alive where there was news from loved ones who had survived. Yet one-third of all *plennys* (short for *wojemoplenny*, POW in Russian) died in captivity, around 200,000 of them in the Odessa region, another 180,000 around Moscow. For those who had been captured in the early months of the war, a full 95 percent succumbed (*"Zweiter Weltkrieg—Kriegsgefangene"* [Second World War—Prisoners of War] 1969, 84). Of the 91,000 Stalingrad survivors, only 18,000 reached their final camp in Tashkent. Of the 50,000 captured when Army Group Center collapsed in the summer 1944, over 37,000 did not survive the dust and heat through which they were marched. Similar losses in POWs were found in the demise of Army Group South. After marching 190 miles eastward, subsequent to Germany's surrender, 100,000 of them did not reach their camps.

Yet, it must be stated that Russian prisoners of war in German hands had suffered an even higher overall loss rate of 60 percent and were dying like flies of starvation and disease. As a result of court proceedings against persons charged with crimes during the Nazi period, including those committed while in military service, it has been estimated that by May 1, 1944, of 5,163,381 Russian prisoners of war, 2,420,000 had either died of starvation and sickness or had been deliberately executed. By the end of the war, some 2.5 million Red Army soldiers in German hands had perished. This figure does not include those who, after they had vanished from the combat zone to join the partisan movement, were later caught and liquidated on orders peculiar to Operation *Barbarossa* (Streim 1982, 174–178).

Later, Russian workers in the USSR did not have better rations than German prisoners, especially during the winter of 1946–1947. It was a terrible time, with the POWs having to chop out large chunks of frozen potatoes with pick axes in order to have any food at all. Even cannibalism made its debut (*"Zweiter Welt-krieg—Kriegsgefangene"* [Second World War—Prisoners of War] 1969, 86). Bread was almost worshipped. Fantasies about food were the rule. Starving men grazed like sheep over every blade of grass or chewed while dreaming. Dystrophy sufferers were living skeletons; their barracks took on the look of mortuaries. For them, death had lost all terror. Of those who survived, many *plennys* owe their lives to the mercy of Russian civilians who, often secretly, shared their own meager rations.

TWO WHO RETURNED

Accounts of two ex-prisoners who experienced the above conditions first-hand—the story of Siegfried Oelsner and one related by Hans Georg Kemnitzer—give additional insight. Oelsner ended the war as a lieutenant and was originally released from American captivity. He then returned to his mother's home in the East Zone. There he was arrested for working for a western intelligence agency and spent the first two years in *Ljubjanka* prison in Moscow. He then was sentenced to twenty-five years in the Gulag. After serving nine years, Konrad Adenauer, West Germany's first postwar chancellor, secured his release in negotiations with Soviet leaders Bulganin and Khrushchev in 1955 (Oelsner 1981, 290). Oelsner's description of his imprisonment speaks of the crassest of human suffering, of naked fear, of courage, and of self-pity. Especially the torturous interrogations left him close to physical and emotional collapse. The prisoners were not allowed to sleep during the day and were questioned mainly at night. Especially difficult were the sanitary conditions, with 100–liter excrement barrels overflowing constantly. Week-long travel in freight cars, à la "Dr. Zhivago," to Siberia's *"ossobennijie reshimnije lagera"* (special camps) was a severe test. Once there, the greatest danger to the POWs came from the criminal bandit prisoners—the *blatnije*. Reportedly, it was from such utterly hardened criminals that Marshal Kostia Rokossowskij drew his troops, which later battled their way across East Prussia, Pomerania, and Brandenburg under the slogan: "*Sa Kostiju, sa swobodu!*" (For Kostia and for freedom), whereas the rest of the Soviet armies fought under the banner: "For Stalin and for the Motherland!" (Oelsner 1981, 105).

In camps and on work details, POWs were tormented by billions of mosquitoes each summer. It was impossible to defend oneself against them. It was actually easier to rid a camp of informers, who normally met death by drowning in the excrement barrels. During work shifts, POWs were kept in line by guards who resolutely shot anyone who stepped out of formation. Most prisoners in the Gulag soon understood the Russian proverb, that "Mother Russia is large, and Moscow is far away, and here only the bear and the wolf are the public prosecutor" (Oelsner 1981, 147).

Work in the winter was hardest. Often prisoners had to carve the ground up to four meters deep with their axes before sewage lines could be laid. Any lesser effort was foiled by permafrost. One of the worst problems involved the latrines. In the summer they stank infernally; in the winter the frozen pillars of blood, urine, and excrement had to be toppled with a pick axe by POWs called "as-anisators" or latrine wardens. Dual seats in the latrine boards served an important purpose because tiny scraps of paper, carrying messages, were placed in the peaks of one excrement pillar and retrieved with the aid of thin wires by the next user.

In February 1955, *Pravda* reported the opening of diplomatic relations between the Federal Republic and the USSR. When finally released, many German prisoners rolled past the site of their early victories in Russia and past the places where they had buried their fallen comrades. There were no visible signs of any German cemeteries. Once in Poland, they found that in spite of all that the Poles had suffered while occupied by Germany, they were not hostile to the flotsam of their former conquerors.

Arriving in East Berlin, the POWs were now guarded by their own countrymen, the East German *Volkspolizei* (People's Police), a situation that convinced many that their future lay in the West. That is what Siegfried Oelsner did—after his ten-year odyssey through the camps of the Soviet State Security system. He reached Western Germany and obtained the official certificate to draw on the financial assistance available there for all who had survived the Gulag and returned home (Oelsner 1981, 324).

A second account reflects on a POW's experiences under the title *"Nit-schewo."* This Russian word has several meanings, but it is used here to describe the great void—the endless expanse of Russia's East, the lack of control over one's own life, and the disregard for human life in general. Yet it also contains a hope that one's own worst present situation may someday be relegated to that void, and that in spite of humiliation and terror, life may again be worth living. This German prisoner also made the long journey to Siberia, arriving with far fewer than started out with him. Whenever a fellow POW died, the others continued to collect his share of the rations in order to extend their own lives, in spite of severe retributions once the death was discovered (Kemnitzer 1964, 8). When two prisoners jumped train, the rest had to undress and stand in formation in freezing weather while an unsuccessful effort was made to recapture them. Other POWs jumped in front of the wheels of the train when it had completed taking on fuel. As the train rolled farther east, they passed other trains stacked with German reparation materials, often rusting under the open sky. The victor had taken from the vanquished, but then many of the dismantled goods simply sat unused.

Once in Kazakhstan, the POWs found remnants of the Volga-Germans, up-rooted by the Stalin regime in mid–1940 (Kemnitzer 1964, 42). Men had been sent to one region, their wives to another, their children to yet another. In Kazakhstan, camp life was utterly bad. The weather, especially the Buran winds, had no mercy on the ill-protected prisoners. Neither did the camp overseers, who interrogated until their victims either broke down or became insane (Kem-nitzer 1964, 92). Those POWs, who had been the strength of hundreds, gradually collapsed; others were so driven by hunger that they licked the dirty ground where a drop or two of water-like soup had been spilled. Others whined like dogs for a slice of bread, and yet others traded their wedding bands for one *papyrossi* cigarette (Kenmitzer 1964, 112). Some POWs wished they had never been born; others begged their guards to kill them. Those who prayed were taunted by the camp's officers. Some began secret Bible studies, and others, as did Solzhenitsyn later, found Christ for the first time in their lives, a thousand miles from home.

A few German POWs who resisted even the most severe physical and psy-chological tortures defied their captors by singing the "Internationale," the very song that extolled the solidarity of a better life under communism. For those who eventually did return it was agonizing to leave their dying buddies along the route westward. Said one of these who had to stay behind, "You know, in spite of the terrible conditions, there is beauty. God in heaven loves most tenderly those who died, as He once did, on a cross" (Kemnitzer 1964, 266). Those who did make it back gave a solemn vow that they would not forget and that they would tell the world.

There was, however, one exception to the ordeal German POWs in Russian hands were subjected to. Some of their fellow prisoners, mostly high-ranking officers, chose to join the Soviet-sponsored National Committee for a Free Germany. Its members were to serve as the nucleus of a Communist German government, to be installed by Moscow after the defeat of the Third Reich. They were also used in Soviet psychological warfare efforts to get German troops to surrender during the latter phase of the war. Considering the political climate at the time, it may seem surprising that a number of German division commanders, all holding general officer rank, became part of the Committee (Mitcham 1985, 52).

Over 890,000 German prisoners remained in Soviet hands by March 1947. Soviet Foreign Minister V. M. Molotov stated at that time that over 1 million had been released since the war's end, whereas western observers felt only 350,000 were returned (Fehling 1951, 95). TASS, the Soviet news agency, had given an initial figure of 3,180,000 Germans in Russia. Since 1948, the United States had made several inquiries as to the number of German POWs who died in captivity. Reportedly, no satisfactory reply was ever received. Also, as late as 1949, both Britain and France were still detaining large numbers of German POWs as hired workers.

The prisoner of war issue became one of the most divisive ones between the United States and the USSR as a result of Soviet allegations that the Americans had stolen lists of German war dead in order to lay the blame for the disappearance of POWs on the Soviets (Fehling 1951, 133). On May 4, 1950, TASS claimed that 1,939,063 German prisoners had been repatriated and that only 9,719, convicted of serious war crimes, remained in the USSR. John McCloy, American high commissioner for Germany, replied the next day that the figures given by the Soviets were designed for propaganda reasons (Fehling 1951, 137). Even a U.N. resolution adopted by a 43 to 5 vote, charging the Russians with detention of 1.5 million German, Italian, Austrian, and Japanese prisoners, had no effect (Fehling 1951, 172). State Department efforts to improve the situation continued for some time, but it was not until the Adenauer visit to Moscow in 1955, mentioned earlier, that any tangible results were achieved. Of the 130,000 POWs still in Russia at that time, the USSR admitted to the existence of only about 10,000. These 10,000 lives were traded in negotiations for the opening of formal relations between Bonn and Moscow. The complete text of Chancellor Adenauer's discussions with his Soviet counterparts, Mr. Bulganin and Premier Khrushchev, can be found in William Craig's *Enemy at the Gates*, published in 1974.

One last point remains to be mentioned—the plight of the loved ones of those who had been swallowed by the Gulag. No one who has seen the scenes of women meeting train after train of returnees at the main station in Berlin will ever forget. The women faithfully searched the windows of each train, eyes burned out from years of worry, anxiety, and exhaustion. Sorrowful and lonely, they would show the picture of their husband, father, or son to the men returning from the Soviet camps. The men, in turn, stepping from those trains were often shells of their former selves. Prematurely aged from acute suffering, their eyes had sunk into their skull; they were white-haired, their teeth were frequently broken out—such were the survivors of a once-mighty army. There were blessed reunions, but for many the black-rimmed pictures they were clutching would remain the last memento of their dear ones.

PROBING THE *PLENNYS*

In 1983, the twenty-two-volume documentation on the fate of German prisoners of war during World War II was finally offered to the general public. It had taken many years to compile this work, and apparently the political climate in the Federal Republic was considered "safe" enough to release the research. Perhaps the social-democratic (SPD) government of Helmut Schmidt did not want to remind the German people of the suffering of millions of their sons, and thus reopen old wounds and possibly upset former enemies, whereas the Christian Democrats appeared less troubled by such concerns. The exhaustive study covered subjects such as:

1. German soldiers in Yugoslavian captivity, including their treatment by partisans

2. German soldiers accused of misdeeds by the Yugoslav authorities—trials, sentencing, and execution, as well as a record of those who perished while in captivity

3. German prisoners of war in the USSR, their camp life psychology, ranks, structure of inmates, similarities and differences in facing their status, their religious life, efforts at maintaining solidarity, and political education

4. The major issue of hunger for German soldiers in Soviet captivity, the rationing of food, hunger strikes, theft of food, denunciation, types of dystrophy complaints and control of available food stuffs, dysentery and starvation

5. Forced labor as a major issue for German POWs in the USSR, prisoners' work to atone for the damage done to Russia by the German Army, "socialist competition," areas of labor camps (i.e., the Central, Eastern, and Volga regions, the Urals, Western Siberia, Southern Central Asia, and Kazakhstan), and compensation for work performed

6. German soldiers and civilians in Soviet penal camps, their selection for sentencing to those camps, the structure of the penalty camps, including their supervision by the Soviet organ for state security, and location of camps within the Soviet Union, including special camps of Vladimir, Verchneuralsk, Aleksandrovsk, Novocerkassk, and the clinical camp, Kazan

7. Cultural and anti-fascist education within the camps

8. German prisoner deaths and repatriation from Soviet control

9. German prisoners in Polish and Czechoslovakian control, their living conditions, mortality rate, mail privileges, medical care, and work assignments

10. German POWs in American custody in the United States, their living conditions, health, assistance from religious organizations, attempts at reeducation and work schedule

11. German POWs in American custody in Europe, effects of unconditional surrender on German units, forced return of German prisoners to East European powers, aspects of capture, subsequent care, religious life, mortality and illness rates, and discharge of prisoners

12. German POWs in British custody, their treatment in different parts of Europe, reeducation efforts, living conditions, and work assignments in camps in Europe and overseas

13. German POWs under Dutch, French, and Belgian control

14. Spirit and lifestyle of German troops captured by their western adversaries, adult education programs, camp newspapers, public performances, and creativity

15. History of German war prisoners, their statistical administration, visits to camps by International Red Cross representatives, and the fate of female prisoners

16. Recollections and personal diaries of individual prisoners of war (Maschke 1983, 1–8)

From the above listing, it is evident that no effort was spared to delve as deeply and accurately as possible into the conditions that befell several million members of the German armed forces, from high-ranking generals to humble privates. So much for the losses and suffering German soldiers incurred in military operations with their enemies or subsequent thereto.

8

RESISTANCE TO HITLER: A FUTILE SACRIFICE?

Much has been written about the role of the resistance to Hitler during those turbulent war years. Germany did not have a unified resistance movement, but each group of opponents attempted to hinder the Hitler regime in its own way. Communists, trade unionists, social democrats, conservatives, certain Christian leaders, and a number of high military officers were in the ranks of the opposition. All of those who actively, though in deepest secrecy, worked against the Third Reich knew that if discovered, they would have to forfeit their lives for high treason. Although the Federal Republic honors them each July 20, in memory of the von Stauffenberg attempt, there are still Germans who are divided on the issue of whether the conspirators were heroes or traitors. Those who hold the latter opinion are a silent minority; among them are some former officers who helped quell the coup attempt.

The activities of students such as Hans and Sophie Scholl, leaders of the *Weisse Rose* resistance cell at the University of Munich whose beliefs found echoes in several major cities, were sensitively portrayed by Inge Scholl, their sister. The experience of Hans, especially, who came full circle from innocent, youthful, and ardent identification with Hitler to unflinching opposition to the dictator, may have been secretly shared by many students, whose lives consisted of studies intermingled with front line service. The leaders of the Munich cell, who produced and distributed leaflet appeals for Germans to cease tolerating a demonic regime, were arrested and executed in 1943. Their families were likewise taken into custody, according to the dictum that where there was traitor blood, it would be exterminated. Altogether, eight resisters from the Munich group were killed, and eight more from the Hamburg branch (Scholl 1984, 88–92). In 1953 they were eulogized by West Germany's first postwar president, Theodor Heuss. While the students were utterly brave, they did not have the means to actually stop Hitler. Neither did the clergymen of the "emergency league of pastors,'' founded by Berlin theologian Martin Niemöller as early as September 1933. The same held true for those Catholic bishops who addressed Hitler in 1935. If there was a group that had a remote chance of stopping Hitler, it was the military officers, focused around General Ludwig Beck, prewar chief of staff of the German Army, who gradually attracted civilian opponents of the regime as well. The anti-Nazi conspirators were maddened by the British reluctance to take their commitment seriously, borne out by Churchill's remark years later, in the aftermath of the 1944 coup attempt, that Germany's leaders were killing each other.

As to actual attempts on Hitler's life before the last plot, none succeeded, and one cannot escape the conclusion that the Führer lived a charmed life and was destined to play out his singularly crucial role in Germany's tragedy almost to the very last moment. General von Witzleben's plan to arrest Hitler in the fall of 1938 was abandoned because of the Munich Agreement; General von Hammerstein's efforts to do the same three days after the invasion of Poland came to naught when the Führer cancelled the visit to the front. The first plan to actually kill the head of state two months later was dropped in the wake of a bomb blast in Munich's *Bürgerbräukeller*, set off by a distraught individual. By now the civilian counterpart of the military resistance circle had been solidified around Carl Goerdeler, the former mayor of Leipzig. Another attempt on Hitler's life in 1943 failed when a bomb placed on Hitler's plane, after hair-raising efforts just to smuggle it on board, failed to explode. Two assassination efforts in 1944 were frustrated, before the fateful event at the *Wolfsschanze* in East Prussia with its subsequent bloodletting, following the exposure of the conspirators.

Much of what had been set in motion by von Stauffenberg's bomb and the entire *Valkyrie* operation was foiled, after a bizarre chain of events, by the commander of the Berlin Guard Battalion, Major Otto Ernst Remer. Once he was convinced that a putsch against Hitler was under way and that the Führer had survived the attempt on his life, he felt he had no other option but to support those remaining loyal to Hitler (Hoffmann 1979, 479–487). Some of his fellow officers, although understanding his predicament at the time, have nonetheless expressed the wish that, with the hindsight now available to him, Major Remer should no longer justify his actions (Zimmermann 1969, 297). According to reports from the front and within the Reich, the assassination attempt was generally condemned and the execution of the conspirators applauded. For a view at pertinent documents concerning the resistance movement against Hitler, the recently reissued compilations of Bodo Scheurig are recommended. An appreciation of the anxieties, suffering, personal triumphs, and eventual deliverance of individual Christian families in the days of the Third Reich can be gleaned from, among others, the stories of Maria Ziefle (Ziefle 1981) and Beate Wilder-Smith (Wilder-Smith 1982).

The story of the *Weisse Rose*, the Goerderer Circle, the several stillborn officer plots, and the well-known attempt on Hitler's life on July 20, 1944, which proved fatal to a part of the cream of the German officer corps and the country's intellectuals while leaving the object of the bomb blast only slightly wounded, all raise the question: Were the Germans really serious about getting rid of Hitler before the war ended?

This question might be a valid one from people who have never lived in a state with a secret police whose power was practically limitless. Anyone who valued his own life or that of his family and who disagreed with the regime was well-advised to keep his thoughts to himself, for even the children were under obligation to betray any parent who uttered derogatory comments or expressed doubts about the infallibility of the Führer. People who ignored the ban on listening to radio broadcasts from enemy countries often paid for their indiscretion with their freedom. If one supplied friends and acquaintances with the contents of such broadcasts, mainly beamed by the British Broadcasting Corporation, death by beheading could be one's end, as was the fate of seventeen-year-old Helmuth Huebener, a young Mormon in the city of Hamburg (Bracher 1984, 8). Every apartment house had an assigned political warden who reported suspicious citizens to the Party. It is thus understandable why the resistance movement remained on the periphery, or why attempts were called off at the last moment, until Colonel Claus von Stauffenberg took matters into his own hands. When the effort failed, Hitler regarded his own escape from death as the "confirmation of the task imposed upon him by providence." He included vengeance against his would-be successors in that task, "in the National-Socialist manner," which meant that thousands lost their lives. Among them were two field marshals and sixteen generals, including Rommel, von Witzleben, Fellgiebel, von Hase, Hoepner, Olbricht, Oster, Stieff, and von Stülpnagel, some being strangled by piano wire. Colonel von Stauffenberg, Dr. Goerdeler, the next chief of state–to be, and Admiral Canaris, head of the German *Abwehr*, as well as General Fromm also perished in the aftermath. Air force General Schmundt was in the "wolf's lair" when the bomb went off and died from the effects of the blast. Generals von Kluge, Beck, and von Tresckow chose suicide. Erwin Rommel, likewise, was offered the vial since Hitler felt that to expose Germany's most admired general as being connected with the plot would create an untenable crisis. Rommel took the poison to save his wife and son from the concentration camp. He had been won over to the conspiracy but not involved in the assassination plot per se. However, another officer who failed to commit suicide when Hitler survived was found floating in a ditch in France with a self-inflicted but nonfatal wound. On the operating table he mumbled the word "Rommel." That, and an earlier, persuasive bedside visit by one of the conspirators while Rommel was recuperating from wounds received subsequent to the Normandy landings, was enough for the hero of North Africa to be arrested, implicated, and finally to be forced to take his own life (Hoffmann 1979, 518, 529).

After July 20, all members of the armed forces were required to salute in the manner previously used only by Party members—the Hitler salute of the outstretched arm. The surviving staff officers had little choice but to bow to the will of the Führer, whose life had been miraculously preserved. From now on, military officers who became suspect were tried before their own courts of honor. Hitler also shackled the *Wehrmacht*'s leadership during the last months of the war by denying it any kind of tactical freedom. He directed the army to implement a Policy of "scorching Germany to the ground" in front of the advancing enemy. To those who wondered why Germany did not quit when all hope for victory was gone, Hitler's decree of March 18, 1945, is offered as explanation:

> If the war is to be lost, then the nation, too, will be lost. . . . There is no need to consider basic requirements that a people need in order to continue to live a primitive life. On the contrary, it is better ourselves to destroy such things, for this nation will have proved itself the weaker, and the future will belong exclusively to the stronger eastern nations. Those who remain alive after the battles are over are in any case only inferior persons, since the best have fallen. (Guderian 1957, 352)

There was another consideration for sticking to the colors. Even if the army had bolted in response to orders by a successful group of conspirators, there was no promise that the *Waffen-SS* would have allowed itself to be disarmed. Thus the stage would have been set for an internecine bloodbath, while the Reich was pounded day and night from above, and the specter of the demand for unconditional surrender hung over the nation. In addition, the Soviet Union would have been hard-pressed to keep from exploiting the possible confusion and even paralysis among German forces manning the eastern front, and a subsequent collapse of that front could have brought Communist control over Western Europe. This possibility was "even more abhorrent to the senior officers than the continuance of National Socialism as they knew it" (Cooper 1978, 551).

When the July 1944 conspirators finally moved, they may have been deprived of success by a staff officer who noticed the briefcase in which the bomb was concealed and moved it behind the far side of the legs supporting the large briefing table, away from the Führer's person, no doubt unaware of the significance of his action.

After the war, one question was always asked: What would have happened had the assassination succeeded? General Guderian, in his memoirs, admitted that no one could answer that question. "Only one fact seemed beyond dispute: at that time the great proportion of the German people still believed in Adolf Hitler" (Cooper 1978, 551). This statement is not meant to imply that they believed in the evils, which for most surfaced only after the war had ended.

Disaffection grew, but remained limited to the few, nothwithstanding the Allies' attempts to exploit the gradual disillusionment of some of the front-line troops with the Nazi regime, by pointing out that of the 18 million German soldiers, 7 million or 38 percent had been killed, wounded, or taken prisoner, whereas only 2 1/2 percent of the political leadership had become casualties (Dollinger 1967, 13). The younger officers and many of the troops, as well as the civilians who suffered so much, still remembered Hitler's achievements and could not detach themselves from the mystic aura of their leader's invincibility. When Dresden was nearly erased from the map in the world's most terrifying firestorm, their choice was made clear. They stiffened their resolve and, as an American officer had said earlier, they "stuck to it," even unto death.

1. Identified and unidentified German military graves, World Wars I and II. Courtesy of Volksbund Deutsche Kriegsgräberfürsorge e.V.

2. Air raid survivors, Mannheim, 1944. Courtesy of Ullstein Bilderdienst, Berlin.

3. The last farewell to a *Landser* in Russia. Courtesy of Volksbund Deutsche Kriegsgräberfürsorge e.V.

4. Medic in action, "Barbarossa" 1941. Courtesy of Bundesarchiv/Militärarchiv 81–B1.8/3 Ord. IV, Fed. Rep. Germany.

5. *Gebirgsjäger* graves, Caucasus, USSR. Courtesy of Volksbund Deutsche Kriegsgräberfürsorge e.V.

6. Final mission—Burial of Luftwaffe Fighter Ace, Captain Hans-Joachim Marseille, North Africa. Courtesy of Volksbund Deutsche Kriegsgräberfürsorge e.V.

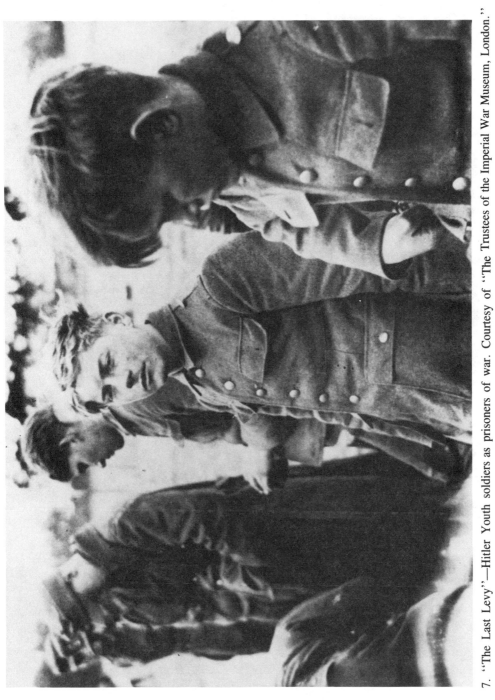

7. "The Last Levy"—Hitler Youth soldiers as prisoners of war. Courtesy of "The Trustees of the Imperial War Museum, London."

8. *Volkssturm* in action—Grandfather and grandson defending their village, East Prussia, 1944. Courtesy of Ullstein Bilderdienst, Berlin.

9. Hitler Youth and *Panzerfaust*, Berlin, 1945. Courtesy of Ullstein Bilderdienst, Berlin.

10. Civilian refugees, Aachen, 1945. Courtesy of Ullstein Bilderdienst, Berlin.

11. "Have you seen him?" Family members looking for news about their loved ones. Courtesy of Archiv des Suchdienstes München, German Red Cross.

12. "Germany kaputt." Hamburg, 1945. Courtesy of Ullstein Bilderdienst, Berlin.

13. "All that remains." I.D. markings from German war dead. Courtesy of Volksbund Deutsche Kriegsgräberfürsorge e.V.

14. German POW graves in USSR (Tambow, USSR). Courtesy of Archiv des Suchdienstes München, German Red Cross.

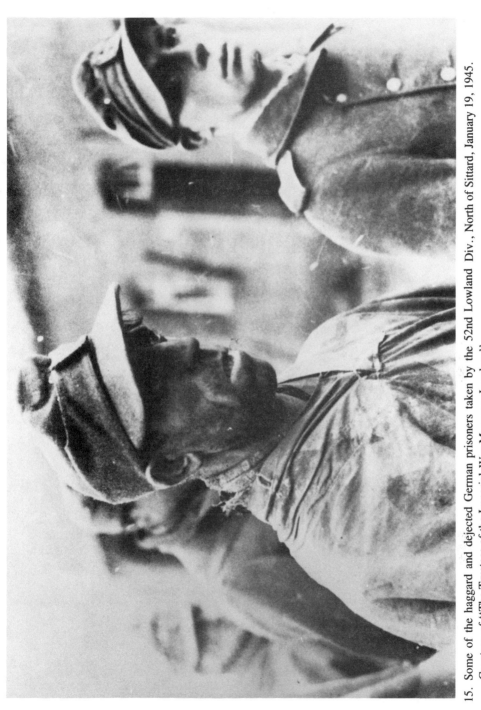

15. Some of the haggard and dejected German prisoners taken by the 52nd Lowland Div., North of Sittard, January 19, 1945. Courtesy of "The Trustees of the Imperial War Museum, London."

9

LOSSES AMONG THE CIVILIAN POPULATION

In spite of the tremendous losses among members of the *Wehrmacht* in combat, after capture, and in the camps, one fact cannot be denied: They at least entered the conflict as armed participants. Not so the German civilians, for whom the suffering of World War II began long before the Royal Air Force started to bomb their cities in 1940.

During the first week of German military action against Poland, nearly 60,000 Germans living in that country were reportedly killed by Poles. After five months, over 12,000 were still left to be identified. Particularly gruesome were the excesses on September 3, 1939, in Bromberg, where apparently hundreds of Germans were shot down, bayonetted, and clubbed to death by soldiers, with the approval of many Polish residents. Entire families passed out of existence. Wounded witnesses who did escape death later testified that Polish militia and regular troops hunted Germans down with a vengeance. Some victims were tied up in such a manner that any attempt to free themselves would result in self-strangulation. Most bodies were covered with leaves, branches, or dirt. As the front came closer, Germans were driven eastward like cattle—clubs and nail-studded boards were used to coerce them, once the people had been placed in camps. Especially terrible were conditions in the internment camp of Beresa-Kartusska (Kern 1964, 23–53.)

Similar atrocities were the subject of investigation by the *Wehrmacht-Unter-suchungstelle*—the military justice investigative unit concerned with human rights violations. It appeared that the reason for acts against the German minority was the fact that they were declared open prey once German troops crossed the Polish frontier. In some instances, dum-dum ammunition was used in the hunt. In another case, the girls of one family were reportedly stripped, beaten, raped, and nailed to tables by their tongues (Kern 1964, 43). This nightmare continued until liberation by German troops. Of course, in the subsequent *Luftwaffe* bombing of Warsaw, heavy casualties among Polish civilians were caused as well.

THE DESTRUCTION OF GERMAN CITIES AND THEIR PEOPLE

In the summer 1940, Prime Minister Churchill gave his support to a proposal of RAF General Arthur Harris, by which the latter felt that pressure could be taken off the RAF Fighter Command, hard-pressed in the Battle of Britain and which, at the same time, could bring Germany to its knees. Harris's plan called for massive raids by hundreds of heavy bombers against the centers of German cities, destroying their industrial capacity while inflicting decisive losses among the workers and other urban dwellers (Barker 1965, 36). As it was, the German air force drew first blood of her own citizens, when it accidentally bombed the city of Freiburg on May 10, 1940. Goebbels blamed the attack on the British, even after the initial confusion about the raid had been cleared up (Irving 1981, 16). But this did not alter the fact that Germany endured four months of RAF attacks against German civilian targets before reprisals against British cities began in earnest (Kurowski 1981, 92, 344). In the resulting war of destruction, German casualties became staggering.

In the counterstrike against Coventry, the effects of which Churchill allegedly could have mitigated since ULTRA, the top secret British intelligence section at Bletchley Park (with the help of Polish specialists), had cracked the German "Enigma" code, 381 civilians lost their lives (Bekker 1968, 180–181). According to Group Captain F. W. Winterbotham, ULTRA had picked up the German target signal for Coventry in the clear, and Churchill had been briefed (Winterbotham 1984, 94–95). Ronald Lewin, on the other hand, vehemently denies that Coventry was sacrificed by the prime minister to safeguard ULTRA's secret from the Germans, and he calls the legend a "monstrous distortion" (Lewin 1978, 103). This latter view is shared by the eminent British historian H. R. Trevor-Roper, who cites the recollections of Churchill's personal secretaries as well as Lewin's research as the basis for his belief. Notwithstanding these latter views, the controversy surrounding Churchill's role in protecting the ULTRA secret has not entirely been laid to rest.

In the first mass raid of the RAF on Cologne during the night of May 30, 1942, in which 1,000 bombers participated, the entire metropolitan area, except for the Cologne cathedral, was razed to the ground, with a loss of 469 lives and the wounding of over 5,000 (Barker 1965, 251–252). Some 13,000 homes were destroyed, 6,000 were damaged, and 45,000 people were made homeless. Thirty-six factories were leveled. In 106 earlier raids against this city, a total of 139 people had lost their lives and 277 had been seriously injured. After the Cologne raid, the RAF dropped leaflets informing the Germans that this was just the opening act of the English campaign of devastation. Encouraged by Churchill's congratulations, "Bomber" Harris went on to select the majority of Germany's cities for a similar fate (Messenger 1984, 78). RAF scientists had earlier worked out improved kill ratios for their bombs by experiments with live tethered goats among which bombs of various fragmentation and explosive capacities were detonated (Irving 1981, 32).

Soon, scores of cities, hundreds of years old, sank into ruin and ashes. All this was happening even before the United States' Eighth and Fifteenth Air Forces complemented the nighttime bombings by the British with daylight raids of their own.

In the process of addressing the House of Commons on June 2, 1942, Churchill stated truthfully that, "as the year progresses, the German cities, harbors and centers of industry will be subjected to a trial the likes of which no country in history has ever experienced" (Paul 1981, 10).

A woman in Berlin, one of those being tried, told her friends:

I believe that I will seek shelter here. Perhaps it is safer in the subway station. But there I am more afraid of the mass of people than of the bombs. If panic breaks out down there, you get trampled to death. I'd rather die among acquaintances. I wonder, what those who come after us will say. I believe that all can count themselves fortunate who did not live during this time when all of Europe was a madhouse. (Paul 1981, 10)

By the end of April 1942, the twenty-pound phosphorous incendiary bombs used in the raids brought serious concern to German air defense officials. If part of the bombs' contents got into foodstuffs, through the burning of grazing areas and ingestion by cattle, serious poisoning of the human digestive tract would occur. Burns from these phosphorus canisters created terrifying pain and injuries or death. Yet people who sought shelter in their bunker-like basements were chastised for staying there while their houses burned down around them. But during the attack and the rain of shrapnel from anti-aircraft shells exploding above, who would go out and risk one's life fighting the fires? Still, numerous canisters were pried loose by alert civil defense wardens and at least some homes were saved from destruction.

In the attack on Lübeck during the night of March 28, 1942, 144 tons of incendiaries and 160 tons of high explosives were dropped during ninety minutes. The miniature holocaust resulted in the destruction of homes, the courthouse, and the Maria Church, with the loss of 320 lives and the wounding of 791. Rostock was hit on April 23. The Heinkel aircraft works received some hits and 100,000 of the 140,000 inhabitants lost their homes. Sixty percent of the town was reduced to ashes, 204 died, and 89 were seriously wounded (Paul 1981, 108).

A month later, about two hours past midnight on May 31, 1942, the first 1,000 bomber raid, as mentioned earlier in this chapter, hit Cologne. Bomber crews, which arrived over the city after most of the fires had been started, were overcome by the sight. After the raid, when the city's homeless formed up for evacuation, they had to promise in writing not to talk about the devastation.

The German author Wolfgang Paul considered the bombing of German cities beyond human comprehension, unless one looked to the Old Testament, where a comparison with Harris's 1,000–bomber force might be found in Job's description of Leviathan:

He esteemeth iron as straw, and brass as rotten wood. The arrow cannot make him flee: slingstones are turned with him into stubble. Darts are counted as stubble: he laugheth at the shaking of a spear. . . .
Out of his mouth go burning lamps, and sparks of fire leap out. Out of his nostrils goeth smoke, as out of a seething pot or caldron. His breath kindleth coals, and a flame goeth out of his mouth. . . . When he raiseth himself up, the mighty are afraid. (Job 41:27–29)

During July, the official map of enemy sorties against the area of Greater Germany showed a temporary easing of attacks. However, Saarbrücken was hit; so was Cologne again, as well as Duisburg, Münster, Frankfurt, Bremen, Emden, Wilhelmshaven, and Flensburg. The Soviet air force penetrated to Königsberg (Paul 1981, 112).

A tabulation of the number of bombs dropped during these raids is shown in Table 12. In Düsseldorf, on the night of September 10, 1942, an attack by 300 bombers in thirty minutes caused eighty dead, numerous wounded, and 17,000 homeless. The fires were extinguished by the Hitler Youth, regular fire brigades, women, and children. Allied POWs and Russian prisoners also helped, as did the day shift workers. The writer's own father was in a similar situation in Berlin; he worked his shift as patent official in the *Reichspatentamt* (Reich Patent Office) during the day, and then manned the 2–cm flak *Fliegerabwehrkanone* (antiaircraft gun) during the night, on the roof of the building.

AREA BOMBING—TERROR BOMBING

During the spring 1943, German cities were subjected to much heavier bombing. On March 6, Essen was hit by a heavy formation, causing 397 dead and 1,440 wounded. Some 3,016 homes were destroyed and 23,000 damaged. These were not single-dwelling homes, but mainly apartment houses. Essen was hit again on April 4, this time also with incendiary bombs which weighed 27 kilograms each and contained a mixture of gasoline, rubber, and viscose, the forerunners of future napalm canisters (Paul 1981, 148).

Wuppertal was next on the list. In the night of May 30, 1943, the city's central area collapsed under a heavy RAF attack of 719 bombers carrying 1,186 high-explosive (HE) bombs, 342,000 incendiaries, and 28,454 phosphorus canisters. People who tried to save themselves got stuck in the asphalt which had softened to a one-foot depth and were burned where they stood. The famous gynecology clinic in Wuppertal-Barmen was hit especially hard. Even though twenty-five women and nursing babies were saved, twenty people died in the laundry. Their

Table 12
Raids on Germany—Aircraft Numbers and Tonnage Dropped, July 1942

City	Number of Planes	High Explosives	Incendiaries	Air Mines	Total
Saarbrücken	23	203	3,350	0	3,553
Cologne	49	382	3,500	19	3,901
Duisburg	379	2,037	40,000	216	42,253
Münster	?	345	8,615	43	9,003
Bremen	50	280	5,720	0	6,000
Wilhelmshaven	73	124	10,000	0	10,124
Hamburg	148	649	22,700	10	23,359
Flensburg	55	139	3,220	0	3,359
Königsberg	72	227	0	0	227
Frankfurt/Main	63	382	8,500	19	8,901
Total	912	4,768	105,605	307	110,680

(Paul 1981, 111-112)

skeletons were not found until 1958. At least 2,450 civilians were killed and 118,000 people lost their homes (Kurowski 1981, 217).

Gradually, German cities saw a new type of architecture, the reinforced flak bunkers, protected by 8.8–cm anti-aircraft guns on the roof while on the inside providing space for thousands of urbanites. Those who could spent more and more time with relatives in the country, in spite of day-long delays in the rail schedule. The German rocket research station, in the raid on Peenemünde, lost hundreds of workers as well as some top scientists as the workers' barracks were the main target of the raid.

During the second half of 1943, Regensburg and Schweinfurt were attacked by American formations. These, however, suffered serious losses to increasingly effective German fighters. During these raids, American and German parachutes hung in the sky like mushrooms after a rain. On July 12 Düsseldorf was bombed; 120,000 people lost their homes. Then came the infamous attack on Hamburg—Operation "Gomorrah." Yet in this case, it was not the Lord in heaven but the RAF who fulfilled His word. An entire 6.5–square-kilometer section of Hamburg was burned out—no one was left alive. Over 50,000 civilians became victims, of whom 10 percent were children. The city became a searing inferno, caused by over 6,000 HE bombs and 748,950 incendiaries (Kurowski 1981, 218).

Table 13
Aerial Bombardment of Major German Cities, July 1943

City	Number of Planes	HE Bombs	Incendiaries	Air Mines	Total
Kiel	510	9,190	190,400	273	199,863
Rostock	160	1,150	108,200	66	109,416
Hamburg	851	6,116	748,950	0	755,006
Bremen	76	160	900	0	1,060
Hannover	89	166	9,000	0	166
Kassel	314	5,356	43,120	0	48,476
Remscheid	30	5,100	42,000	0	47,100
Essen	788	1,787	179,827	802	182,416
Köln	699	1,467	296,799	172	299,438
Aachen	320	581	180,479	23	181,083
Total	3,837	31,073	1,799,675	1,336	1,824,024

(Paul 1981, 156, 157)

From the map published by the OKW, the statistics listed in Table 13 have been compiled. A comparison with the July figure of the previous year shows that the number of sorties as well as the number of bombs had increased significantly.

The RAF's battle against Berlin was launched in earnest on November 18, 1943. Some 2,212 bombers in five major raids converged on the Reich's capital. In the first raid, 1,500 people died; 1,200 in the next. For their suffering and stoical endurance the government rewarded the Berliners with an increase of fifty grams of meat and ten cigarettes per adult per week (Paul 1981, 226). One of the women on the ground during the attack, worn out from hour-long bucket brigade duty and the general horror, thought she had found an answer when she said:

If they destroy our living room, we'll move into the kitchen. If the kitchen goes, we'll move into the hallway. And if the hallways fall into ruins, we'll move into the basement. As long as we can stay . . . a little corner of home is better than a strange place. That's the reason all the "bombed out" return one day, they search through the ruins of their houses. . . . (Paul 1981, 228)

In response to the heavy raids on Germany, *Vergeltungs* or *V-Waffen* (reprisal weapons) were targeted against England. These rockets were unguided and indiscriminately hit residential and industrial areas mainly in the vicinity of London.

Toward the end of 1943, Leipzig was heavily bombed with phosphorous canisters; the water in the mile-long hoses was frozen before it reached the fires. One thousand one hundred and eighty two people lost their lives and 90,000 became homeless—many were missing under the ruins.

By 1944, the will to win was slowly being replaced by the will to endure— the *Durchhaltswille*. Gradually, German civilians were concerning themselves with the possibility that the Russians might not only reach Germany's borders, but actually enter the Reich territory and that the war may not turn out as their leaders had claimed. But it was apathy, not the later terror, that characterized ideas about this subject.

On February 20, 1944, Allied air forces began Operation "Big Week." No longer an uncommon sight, 1,000–plane formations with fighter escort appeared over German cities. A cartoon in a British paper showed RAF and American bomber crews singing, "Night and day, you are the Hun . . . ," a reference to British area bombing by night, the U.S precision bombing by day (Hopkins 1944, 5710). During these raids, Braunschweig, Stuttgart, Leipzig, Regensburg, Augsburg, and Fürth were attacked.

New daylight attacks by the American air forces on Berlin began on March 3, 1944. From then until April 1945, the inhabitants were rarely free from round-the-clock air raids. On March 8, Erckner, a suburb of Berlin, was hit hard and lost over 600 people.

An eyewitness account reported on what it was like on the ground:

The siren wails its high and low pitch. That means full alert. Outside people are scurrying with suitcases and baby carriages, toward the nearest bunkers. The streetcar's brakes screech, attempting to stop the trolley in its tracks. There are traffic jams. Within three minutes, all cars are empty. . . . We are on our way to the cellar. From far comes the deep droning, fearfully strange, portending harm . . . we grab gas masks, steel helmets and wet handkerchiefs. There is no time to be lost. Now they are over us—we say nothing, we do not scream. While bombs are whistling outside, it is as quiet as in a church inside. It rolls, crashes, breaks, trembles. The floor comes up toward us. A hit nearby, burning smoke. One would like to crawl into the earth. Did the neighboring apartment house get it, or was it us?

"Fire in the third floor, everyone to the task!" shouts the air raid warden. We jump up, numb, outside the explosions continue. No one speaks, we grab the pick axe and sand buckets. We clamber to the third floor, but there is no water. The water has been shut off. Always when there is a large scale attack. We dip our buckets in bathtubs and basins filled earlier. Now the sacks of sand cover the phosphorus, but while we extinguish the fire, a new squadron drops its bombs. Into the cellar and get the wet handkerchief— without it, we would suffocate. . . .

Finally it is over. Where the neighboring house stood next-door, there is a pile of rubble. A woman comes running by, screaming—her face in a grimace. She is clutching three empty coat hangers to her breast. Some 48 bombs hit our block. So far we haven't counted the dead. They are still under the rubble, destroyed, we couldn't reach them. Yet what was our task—to show a stiff upper lip. (Paul 1981, 272)

Finally, at the end of March 1944, Air Marshal Harris broke off the RAF attacks on Berlin. Since November 18, 1943, 9,111 aircraft had come to Berlin dropping 16,000 tons of bombs, but the civilian morale held. Neither was there any indication that the Führer had the slightest intentions to capitulate to an enemy who still stood far from the German homeland. Thus, further terrible sacrifices awaited the home front (Paul 1981, 302).

As the collapse drew nearer, however, the *Sicherheitsdienst (SD)* (State Security Service) reports noted increasing church attendance by both Roman Catholics and Protestants—people needed something to cling to to as their outer world began to disintegrate and the possibility of total defeat became a gnawing thought in the minds of more and more people, mostly in secret, to be sure. Especially those who had lost loved ones began to weaken in their iron self-discipline. Sorrow and grief broke through at religious services.

Pastor Kanonikus Anton Pichler wrote:

> Faraway from home, from loved ones,
> Life gave you the hardest test.
> Stars now guard your resting place,
> Where you lie in final sleep.
> Hero both in wounds, and pain,
> True to duty until death.
> I would fashion
> For your wreath, roses and forget-me-nots,
> Much we lost when you were taken,
> We who now stand silently.
> Still we fold our hands in prayer,
> May God's holy will be done.
> My crown to you I proffer,
> Speaks the Lord and lifts the hand;
> You died for the fatherland!
> (Translation mine) (Paul 1981, 325)

On March 12, 1944, began the assault on the German petroleum industry. Although this was a military target, losses of lives among the workers were not insignificant. Large formations of B–17 Flying Fortresses and B–24 Liberators bombed Merseburg, Gelsenkirchen, Magdeburg, Dessau, and Brüx.

On June 21, 1944, Berlin was attacked by 2,500 American planes—in one of the heaviest raids ever. Only the hens kept pecking in the dirt; every other living thing had taken refuge. After this raid, as in others, when large areas caught fire, grey clouds formed which dropped ash onto the living and the dead.

Although Table 14 does not contain numbers of bombs or total tonnage, the

Table 14
Bomber Missions into Germany, July 1944

Target	No. of Planes
Kiel	1,900
Bremen	1,400
Essen	615
Cologne	1,300
Leuna	4,615
Brun	1,125
Stuttgart	1,285
Friedrichshafen	1,366
München	8,020
Linz	600
Wiener-Neustadt	1,350
Total	23,576

(Paul 1981, 342-343)

size of bomber formations attacking individual cities had again increased over the past twelve months.

Throughout Berlin and other cities, ditches covered by earth had been dug to give protection against flying shrapnel from bombs and anti-aircraft shells. Besides the reinforced bunkers below apartment houses, people dug small shelters in their gardens in the suburbs. Others felt more secure in the huge concrete bunkers until one, packed with 20,000, received a direct hit from a new six-ton "earthquake" bomb. All that was left was cement powder, small pieces of clothing, and body parts, soaked through with blood. German cities burned day and night. Miles of burned-out apartment buildings had only the chimneys and the tiled *Kachelofen* (fireplaces) on I-beams left standing; the rest was on the street—the furnishings of those who lay buried in the rubble. Hidden among this destruction were the delayed-fuse bombs—some would explode hours after the raids, others not for days—all terrifying in their unexpected death-dealing roar. To escape this kind of Armageddon, some people fled to the forest, the safest place to be.

The war in the West was now near the German border to where the Allies had pushed the *Wehrmacht* since the St. Lo breakout. By now, the German divisions were a motley lot, thrown together from units that would have been declared unfit for combat duty just a year previously. They included regiments of ulcer patients and others with major health problems. So began a constant competition for the last reserves between the eastern front and the West Wall. In the West, the front line and the home front became one when the U.S. 82nd Airborne Division jumped into the Kleve area. The civilian population beheld with amazement the flood of chocolates, cigarettes, and candy dropped along with American jeeps and paratroopers. The subsequent battle would prove to be the last German victory (Paul 1981, 373).

Later, Aachen became the first major German city to feel the fury of ground combat. The civilian population was already fleeing, when a new fortress commander took charge and halted the disorderly flight.

The beginnings of the ground assault on Germany proper did not slow down the aerial offensive, which now had a new vital target, the Ruhr—Germany's industrial heart. On October 14, 1944, 1,063 bombers and 300 fighters brought destruction to Duisburg. During the succeeding nights, 1,005 RAF planes followed up this raid with 3,937 tons and 2,383 tons respectively. Darmstadt fell victim to an area bombardment—12,000 inhabitants were killed and 70,000 were made homeless. Stuttgart was hit the same night, resulting in 957 dead, 1,000 wounded, and 50,000 made homeless. Raids on several smaller cities dropped 8,310 tons of bombs. Panic and fear now gripped the cities when sirens wailed. The home front threatened to crack under combined hammerblows (Paul 1981, p. 386).

With the German battlefronts under ever-mounting pressure, the government felt forced to abandon its long-standing reluctance against the use of women in combat roles. From now on, even girls would help to man anti-aircraft batteries. Men with arthritis and venereal disease were pressed into service. So were those German soldiers who were found to be trickling into the remaining homeland, whether officially or unofficially. The *Kettenhunde* (literally "chain dogs") or special military gendarmerie were busier than ever arresting and sentencing men in the rear areas.

Germany indeed lay in its death throes. During the first four months of 1945, 500,000 more tons of bombs rained on its cities—over a third of the total for all four years of area bombing. At this point, a new effort to stop the Allied bombers over Germany included suicide missions—by deliberate ramming. On April 7, 1945, 120 *Messerschmitts*, from which virtually all armaments had been removed, took off to intercept 1,300 American B–17s and 800 fighters. Twenty-three bombers were knocked down, but only fifteen of the German fighters returned. Seventy-seven *Luftwaffe* pilots died. The bombing of German cities continued unabated. A summary of raids during the last months of the war is given in Table 15. The Allies wanted to make sure that this time there would not be a "stab-in-the-back" legend to which a second postwar Germany might rally.

Over 119,000 persons were killed in these raids. Some thirty-nine major cities became targets during 1945. One hundred and eighty thousand tons of bombs were dropped in these four months, a staggering one-fifth of the war's total. Berlin lost 49,000 dead in 310 raids during which 47,517 tons of bombs were dropped.

For the war's total, approximately 410,000 civilians were killed, with the missing reaching into the hundreds of thousands. Of the nearly 2 million tons of bombs, about 50 percent were dropped on residential areas, and 12 percent on factories and war-connected industries. Over 3.6 million homes were destroyed, making 7.5 million people homeless (Kurowski 1981, 315).

Where city archives survived the war, the extent of air attacks can be found in diligently kept charts, such as in Ludwigshafen on the Rhine. Here, beginning in 1940, 124 air raids against the town were recorded during the war. These involved 12,771 aircraft, which dropped 39,755 HE bombs and 804,418 incendiaries, causing the damage or destruction of 71,634 homes, and 4,735 casualties, of whom 1,773 were deaths (Breunig, personal communication, September 25, 1985).

BREAKING THE DAMS

In a related effort to cripple, or at least lessen, Germany's industrial capacity midway through the war, the RAF decided to take out the large dams that supplied electricity to many German cities and their industries. This venture received the code name Operation Chastise. On May 15, 1943, with Wing Commander Guy Gibson in the lead, several groups of Lancaster bombers from the RAF's 617 Squadron carrying the "Upkeep" bomb took off for Germany. The weapon they carried had been developed by British scientists, headed by Dr. Barnes Wallis (Euler 1984, 28–46). It had to be dropped at a speed of 352 kilometers per hour from eighteen meters altitude, turning at exactly 500 rotations per minute. It literally rolled on top of the water until it struck the dam. The impact would toss it back a distance, but the inertial centrifugal force would guide it back to the wall of the dam where it settled into the water against the structure and then exploded at about ten meters depth. Thus, the hydraulic force of the water was used in breaching the dam (Kurowski 1981, 213).

The Möhnetal Dam was forced in this manner. From its breach spewed 6,000 cubic meters of water per second into the Möhne and Ruhr valleys, drowning hundreds of civilians, including many foreign women workers. After hitting the

Table 15
Aerial Bombardment of Germany, January 1945–May 1945 (incomplete)

Date	Target	Number of Planes		Tons Dropped
Jan. 6	Hannover	561	RAF	2,365
Jan. 6	Cologne	149	RAF	1,092
Jan. 15	Leuna Works	509	RAF	2,181
Jan. 17	Magdeburg	291	RAF	1,060
Feb. 3	Berlin	937	USAAF	2,264
Feb. 13	Dresden	773	RAF	2,659
Feb. 14	Dresden	311	USAAF	771
Feb. 14	Chemnitz	294	USAAF	718
Feb. 16	Regensburg	263	USAAF	559
Feb. 20	Nuremberg	439	USAAF	2,000
Feb. 24	Pforzheim	369	RAF	1,551
Mar. 10	Scholven-Buer	153	RAF	755
Mar. 11	Essen	1,055	RAF	4,700
Mar. 12	Dortmund	1,107	RAF	4,851
Mar. 30	Hamburg/Bremen	345	USAAF	2,849
Apr. 14	Kiel	298	RAF	1,905
Apr. 15	Potsdam	364	RAF	1,751
Apr. 25	Wangerooge	415	RAF	2,176
Apr. 25	Berchtesgaden	318	RAF	1,181
Total		8,951		37,388

(Kurowski 1981, 343-4)

dams in the Ruhr, Gibson took his remaining aircraft for a run on the Edertal Dam in Hesse. Here 205 million cubic meters of water drowned forty-seven persons, their corpses floating through the city of Kassel (Sweetman 1982, 155–156) The raids were not without cost to the RAF and other Commonwealth crews. Of 133 airmen engaged in the operation, fifty-three were killed and three were captured (Sweetman 1982, 205).

"GOMORRAH"—THE HAMBURG INFERNO

Another catastrophic event in the annals of the air war against Germany involved the destruction of the old Hanseatic port of Hamburg. This city, especially, bore the brunt of Harris's Bomber Command on the nights of July 24–25, 1943, when successive waves of British bombers, guided by pathfinder aircraft and disorienting the German defenses by the use of "window" (strips of metallic chaff), devastated the metropolis. Nearly 10,000 tons of incendiaries and high explosives turned the urban area into the greatest man-made holocaust the world had known up to that point. The firestorm uprooted trees, ripped roofs off buildings, and incinerated its residents. Several authors, mostly British, have given a graphic account of the disaster. So did Hamburg's police president, *SS* Major General Kehrl, in his official report, causing Albert Speer, Germany's armaments chief, to declare that more raids like the one on Hamburg could paralyze the entire war effort.

When one examines the British preparations for the attack it is clear that the destruction of workers and their dwellings was a paramount goal. It was part of the effort to smash the civilian support that enabled the war to continue. Aptly called Operation "Gomorrah," its mechanics were honed to a fine edge to provide the maximum destructive power by staggering four raids to achieve the initial damage to the city and, subsequently, kill the rescue teams, thousands strong, who would converge from all over northern Germany to put out the fires and save those still living. Before July 24, 1943, Hamburg had withstood 100 raids, but none in which over 700 heavy bombers combined in four waves to deliver 30,000 HE bombs, 3 million stick incendiaries, and 80,000 pounds of liquid phosphorus to create an inferno. In a ten-day period, six square miles of homes, offices, and factories were devastated. Over 750,000 people were made homeless; 70,000 died, many in horrible agony (Caidin 1960, 20). One survivor stated, "I saw people killed by falling bricks and heard the screams of others dying in the fire. I dragged my best friend from a burning building and she died in my arms. I saw others who went stark mad. The shock to my nerves and to my soul, one can never erase" (Caidin 1960, 9). The police president reported after the holocaust:

Its horror is revealed in the howling and raging of the firestorms, the hellish noise of exploding bombs and the death cries of martyred human beings as well as in the big silence after the raids. . . .

No flight of imagination will ever succeed in measuring and describing the gruesome scenes of horror in the many buried air raid shelters. Posterity can only bow its head in horror of the fate of these innocents. . . . (Caidin 1960, 9)

In the fires, the normally beneficial home storage of coal and coke actually served to fuel the flames which reached a height of three miles above the ground, a speed of 150 miles per hour, and temperatures of 800 ° Celsius or 1,472 ° Fahrenheit! Tar boiled, trapping those who sought safety outside of the buildings, and frying people into little stumps, the so-called *Bombenbrandschrumpfleichen* or "corpses shrivelled by the heat of burning bombs." Glass and metal were twisted and melted together (Caidin 1960, 93). The famous Hagenbeck Zoo and its animals were destroyed. As anticipated, all public utilities, including many water lines, were knocked out in the first raid. Still, the rescue teams, by superhuman efforts, extinguished many fires in that first night, until the water pressure ebbed to a trickle. Then, in the midst of the rescue effort, at 2:40 P.M. on July 25, the second attack began, this one by the U.S. Army Air Forces (USAAF). The following night, another section of Hamburg ceased to exist under a bomb carpet laid by the RAF. This raid's firestorm was fed by cooler air from out of town; its center became a one-and-a-quarter-square-mile torch fed by hurricane-strength winds. Thousands, near insane from panic, threw themselves into the many canals that intersected the city. They held their children only high enough out of the water to avoid drowning them. Yet many died from thermal radiation reaching their lungs, although they were up to their necks in water. Later, their corpses floated through the waterways, on fire! On land, the living and dying burned together. It was a scene of abject savagery. Still, Sir Arthur Harris sent in more planes to flatten any suburban areas that showed signs of sustaining life. On the night of July 29–30, 726 four-engine bomber released another 2,382 tons over the dying city (Caidin 1960, 112).

Doctors and nurses ministered to all they could, themselves numb from disbelief and fatigue. Only during the last raid, on August 2, did the weather finally come to the rescue of the stricken city, bringing clouds and rain and thus aiding the firefighters and defenders. Even so, relief teams had to water down parts of Hamburg until early October, so intense had been the heat of the caldron.

Another quote from General Kehrl sheds light on the extent of the postraid recovery operations:

Rapid disposal of all bodies was a matter of great urgency as putrefaction set in quickly owing to the great heat, and epidemics were therefore to be expected. . . . The magnitude of the task may be inferred from the fact that even today (three months later) recovery of bodies is not completed. . . . (Caidin 1960, 125)

The overall report of the U.S. Strategic Bombing Survey (USSBS) corroborates German statements, indicating that" . . . the raids on Hamburg in July-August 1943 were among the most devastating of the war" (USSBS 1945, 72). It cited Hamburg as an outstanding example where a series of raids destroyed 55 to 60 percent of the city, did damage to thirty square miles and completely burned out 12.5 square miles, wiped out 300,000 dwelling units, and made 750,000 people homeless. German estimates range from 60,000 to 100,000 persons killed, many of them in shelters where they were reached by carbon monoxide.... But the total destruction, 75 to 80 per cent, was due to fires, particularly those in which the so-called firestorm phenomenon was observed. (USSBS 1945, 92)

Among the many causes of death, shock accounted for over 12 percent of fatalities in persons hospitalized as a result of burns or injuries (USSBS 1945, 132).

There can be no doubt that the attack on Hamburg was so catastrophic that a duplication against other cities would have dictated a major shift in German war policy. As mentioned earlier, Albert Speer felt impelled to tell the Führer that "a rapid repetition of this type of attack upon another six German towns would inevitably cripple the will to sustain armament manufacture and war production" and that "a continuation of these attacks might bring about a rapid end to the war" (Speer 1971, 370).

At RAF Bomber Command headquarters at High Wycombe, Harris had his staff compile his famous Blue Book, which listed the most important German cities marked for annihilation by his growing force of Lancaster bombers. This book was shown to some 5,000 influential visitors in hopes of achieving two goals—to prove the viability of his strategy and to assure continued support for the same (Harris 197?). Harris's book contained aerial photographs of German cities before RAF attacks, with subsequent plastic overlays in blue for areas destroyed. Soon, blue became the dominant color for the inner areas of most major German towns. No unbiased observer could deny that the bombing had assumed indiscriminate proportions.

Already during these mid-World War II raids, RAF leaders recognized that notwithstanding the destructiveness of high explosive (HE) bombs, they were not outstandingly cost-effective, for one had to cube the explosive force of the bomb in order to square the area affected by devastation. By modifying the fuses, however, which allowed the bombs to penetrate to the lower levels of the apartment buildings before detonating, and mixing HE and incendiary payloads to create the kind of tinderbox material for subsequent fires, much greater damage could be achieved. Resulting firestorms created aerial pollution, which, though on an admittedly smaller scale from that being currently envisioned as a by-product of a nuclear exchange, brought on unusual sunsets in the vicinities of burning cities and beyond (Powers 1984, 53).

Equally effective in destructive extent were British air mines and layer bombs, which assured penetration into reinforced basements of multi-storied apartments. Frequently, the air mines set up a vacuum that could pull the lungs out of people unfortunate enough to be in the vicinity of the detonation. Others, victims of intense heat, simply turned to hollow forms of white ash that collapsed into puffs of smoke when would-be rescuers uncovered them beneath the burned-out buildings. During night raids, German cities glowed in an eerie daylight, so bright was the cumulative effect of the fires. Due to the massive assaults, efforts of municipal fire departments were reduced to marginal success because of the rapid loss of water pressure. Unexploded bombs or "time" bombs added to the danger of these rescue efforts.

Through all these attacks, the German home front generally held together. Great examples of bravery and neighborly assistance became routine. Those who were torn from this life could no longer resist; those who survived yet another day felt that their greatest gift to the departed was to show an unflinching determination, a dig-deeper-and-harder attitude, to carry on. Often, the fires from the night bombings still smoldered when American planes leveled what remained. In addition, the H2X radar bombing device now deprived the civilians below of the normally welcome and protective element of heavy cloud cover (Craven and Cate 1951, 720–723). The number of killed and wounded steadily rose, and these casualties were often among the very young, the very old, and the female adults, since most eligible men had long been pressed into service at Germany's foreign fronts. For a detailed look at the civilian response and reaction to the bombing, the amplified version of the USSBS (MacIsaac 1976) is an excellent source.

THE DEATH OF DRESDEN

What many observers consider the worst attack of the war involved the city of Dresden on February 12–14, 1945, only seven weeks before the collapse of the Third Reich. Today, there are some who say that the reason for the burning out of that century-old center of culture, and the fire deaths of what initially were thought to be a quarter of a million civilians, many of them refugees fleeing the Soviet onslaught in the East, was an ultra-secret decision by the Western allies to slow up the advance of the Red Army, which could have used an undamaged metropolis like Dresden to its advantage. More likely, the published reason for delivering a major blow into the German rear area, precisely to aid the Soviet advance, lay at the heart of the attack. Certainly, Stalin had asked for just such a strike and the Allies had earlier promised one. Soviet historians, however, maintain that Russian commanders never specified that Dresden should be a target. Regardless of the ultimate reason, the fact remains that by the time the raid was made, Germany was essentially beaten. Of course, because of the personality of Hitler, who held supreme control over military and diplomatic actions, no sincere overtures at ending the fighting could be anticipated. In the attack on Dresden, Allied airmen and their combined leadership caused unimaginable damage and suffering. Initially, it was thought that their "conventional" attacks killed as many German civilians as the atomic bombs of Nagasaki and Hiroshima combined (Irving 1981, 8).

Both German and Allied sources verify the extent of physical damage, but over the years adjustments in the actual casualty estimates have been forthcoming. According to the most current figures, based on recently found official German reports for the period after the raids, approximately 35,000 people died in the Allied holocaust; tens of thousands were wounded (Bergander 1985, 263–268). This figure may approach reality. Its veracity might be inferred from intentions, voiced shortly after the catastrophe by Goebbels, to execute 40,000 Allied and Soviet flyers in German hands in retaliation (Bergander 1985, 263). As to factors bearing on the decision to bomb the city in the first place, the process of selecting Dresden as a target appears to have been rather foggy. Reflecting on Irving's exhaustive search of RAF files and Whitehall papers, including the account of Churchill's discussion with his air chief, Lord Portal, leaves one with the uneasy feeling that since virtually all German cities had been devastated and Dresden, up to now, had only been nicked, it was time that she, too, should be razed. Besides, Churchill apparently wanted to "baste" the Germans "in their retreat from Breslau" (Messenger 1984, 185). Thus, the old capital of Saxony could follow scores of sister cities into oblivion. Bergander somewhat agrees with this assessment, pointing out that the city would become an inevitable target, contrary to the thinking of its residents and political leadership (Bergander 1985, 132–144).

As it turned out, Dresden was void of defenses. Her entire flak batteries had been relocated elsewhere or shipped to the Russian front. Her fighter protection, because of hesitation in higher command channels, sat out the first attack on the ground and did not engage successive waves with any effect. Dresden was thus essentially an open city—and the master-bombers (pathfinders) were able to mark the target at will. As to strategic importance, even British pilots then and Allied historians since have failed to see such, though the USSBS makes an effort to link the city to some military purpose of benefit to the crumbling Reich. Some bomber crews actually felt remorse while consigning the beautiful city, which, incidentally, housed 26,000 Allied prisoners of war, to its fate. British POWs killed in an earlier raid had been buried with full military honors (Irving 1981, 87). Air Marshal Harris stated later that the attack on Dresden "was considered of military necessity by persons far more important than I" (Irving 1981, 87). While the crews talked to each other over their radios, unmolested by any fighters or flak, Dresden's inferno began below them. The first bombs exploded at 10:15 P.M. on February 13. As with Hamburg, the staggered arrival of bomber swarms assured that Dresden's own rescue units, as well as those coming in from the still-free area of central Germany, would be caught in a hail of bombs and bullets as they began their extremely dangerous work of trying to save lives. Not one member of several rescue companies survived. A bombadier of the 635th Lancaster Squadron who saw how column after column of Red Cross and protection units were moving to their rendezvous with death recalled that "it was the only time I felt pity for the Germans. But my pity lasted only a few seconds; it was our task to strike the enemy and to annihilate him" (Irving 1981, 162). The 650,000 incendiaries alone created a firestorm that would guide the planes for 300 kilometers. In addition, 1,477.7 tons of high explosives, among them 529 4,000–pound air mines, were dropped (Bergander 1985, 163).

The crews would get only a little rest back in England before a new target would tear them from their sleep: Chemnitz! This time the briefing officers indicated that the true nature of the attack would again be civilian targets! (Irving 1981, 178).

VENGEANCE OR RESTRAINT

By the end of hostilities in early May 1945, most German metropolitan areas resembled ghost towns. Many wounded soldiers, pressed into home service, left wives and children in the morning, only to learn upon returning from work that evening that the apartment house in which their loved ones had been left earlier had suffered bomb damage during the day. Sometimes the fate of their family was uncertain until the rubble had been cleared.

It is understandable that under these conditions the civilians themselves, now victims of years of aerial bombardment, were increasingly hard-pressed to refrain from lynching any crew members who, after bailing out, fell into their hands. Times had changed from the early part of the war, when in both England and Germany downed airmen were generally treated properly by their intended victims. As the bombing of Germany reached ever new intensities, people on the ground felt it more difficult to restrain themselves. Still, in the frequent capture of Allied airmen, relatively few atrocities against the flyers were committed by German civilians. This writer himself had the opportunity to observe American airmen being marched through a city in central Germany. None of the people watching the procession took any overt hostile action against the POWs, a different posture to be sure from the humiliation dealt U.S. aircrews captured during the recent war in Southeast Asia. This is not to say that excesses did not occur or that the Nazi Party counseled restraint toward downed airmen, especially in the aftermath of major raids. To the contrary, it saw in the issue an opportunity to rouse and at the same time unite the civilian population against the *Terrorflieger* (terror flyers). Goebbels, especially, by the summer of 1944 felt that downed Allied airmen who had engaged in low-level strafing runs against civilians had forfeited their right to the customary protection accorded POWs under the laws of international warfare and suggested that his view was being increasingly shared by the *Wehrmacht* and the population in general (Kesaris 1980, 104). In the main, however, the cooler heads of the German military authorities prevailed, and it was they who took charge of the captured flyers as soon as possible. However, after the air war had reached new ferocity, Hitler became dangerously critical of *Luftwaffe* personnel who were saving downed airmen from being lynched by civilians (Irving 1977, 780).

A recently completed study of Allied prisoners of war, including downed airmen, in German hands suggests that incidents of violent death among aircrews following bailout were higher than commonly thought. This was true especially among fighter pilots who had strafed farmers in fields, civilian cars, passenger trains, and occasionally even children, as well as by mistake, later in the war, their own buddies who, as POWs, were being marched from the approaching battlefronts. Captured bomber crews whose aircraft and flying suits sported such mottos as "Murder, Inc." or similar logos also fanned the flames of revenge among the civilians on the ground. Occasional escapes by Allied flyers, of which the one from *Luftwaffestammlager* (*Luftstalag*) III (air force POW camp) near Sagan in February 1944 was the most famous and, subsequently, the most tragic, brought the fate of the former into greater jeopardy. Nonetheless, numerous flyers credited the civilians who first took them into custody with saving their lives. To these Germans and the restraining voices within the *Luftwaffe* and the German High Command, which at times even included Göring and Hitler, belonged some credit that at war's end, about 99 percent of Allied POWs were able to return home (Foy 1984, 22, 23, 28, 115, 156).

VOICES IN THE WILDERNESS

It is to the credit of civilized man, that during this rain of death, unleashed against Germany, a few voices were heard on the Allied side questioning this genocidal warfare. At first, concern was expressed only about neutrals which became victims of Allied bombing. These voices seemed to be confined to those activists who wrote, after U.S. bombers had attacked Rotterdam on March 31, 1943, causing up to 3,000 casualties among the Dutch:

The more we speed up and increase the scope of our bombings in Europe, the more these innocent bystanders will suffer—and the more difficult they will find it to believe that we are really approaching them in the spirit of good will and Christian fellowship. They must find it very hard—those who survive—to have us tell them, as they behold the mangled bodies of their dead, that it hurts us more than them to do this, but that we must do it for their own good in order to eventually free those of them who are left, from the tyranny under which they live. (Villard 1945, 483)

In this same article, mention is made of a group of Englishmen who petitioned their government and the RAF to stop bombing civilians in Europe, expressing horror at the very heavy toll in civilian lives due to Harris's 1,000–plane raid on Cologne, which they considered an "inhuman and un-English" practice of making war on civilians. Even the Bishop of Coventry deplored the gloating over RAF raids on Germany, as leading to the moral deterioration of the British people (Villard 1945, 484).

Toward the latter phase of the war, when the defeat of Germany was only a matter of weeks away, numerous reporters entering the country expressed shock at the destruction they found. Said S. L. Solon, *News Chronicle* war correspondent on March 14, 1945: "When the sun grows cold and the last cities on a crumbling earth are dying ruins, I suppose that the surviving remnants of human life will live as they live today in the bowels of Cologne" (Brittain 1946, 880).

These sentiments were echoed by a shocked reporter on the *Evening Standard* describing her view of another German city: "I could not recognize much of the old city for all its picturesqueness has been bombed to fragments. It is as though some giant has crashed his foot down. . . . Nuremberg has been wiped from the face of the earth" (Brittain 1946, 880).

The American newspaper *Stars and Stripes* reported the aftermath of the attack on Dresden through the words of a British POW who worked there:

Reports from Dresden police that 300,000 died as a result of the bombing did not include deaths among the 1,000,000 evacuees from the Breslau area trying to escape the Russians. There were no records of them. . . . They had to pitchfork shriveled bodies onto trucks and wagons and cart them to shallow graves on the outskirts of the city. But after two weeks of work, the job became too much to cope with and they found other means to gather up the dead. They burned bodies in a great heap in the center of the city, but the most effective way, for sanitary reasons, was to take flame throwers and burn the dead as they lay in the ruins. (Brittain 1946, 880)

Vera Brittain, shortly after the war, stated:

The ruthless mass bombing of congested cities is as great a threat to the integrity of the human spirit as anything which has yet occurred on this planet. . . . The true and terrible significance of obliteration bombing, like the mass extermination of the Jews by the Nazis, lies in its utter denial of the sacredness of human life. By denying the divine spark in man, it denies the God in whose image it was made. . . . There is no military or political advantage which can justify this blasphemy. (Brittain 1946, 881)

TARGET BERLIN

Before leaving the subject of bombing, mention must be made of the fate that Berlin, as the capital of Germany, had to endure. It was the most bombed city in all of Germany, the British coming promptly at 8:00 in the evening with their first Mosquito bombers and the Americans giving the Berliners a pounding during the day.

This writer lived through one of the major daylight raids:

Early in 1945, upon returning from Silesia to our home in Berlin, we suffered a major raid. I had been listening to the Flak-Funk [the anti-aircraft network] on my little crystal detector set. Sometimes one could also pick up the British Broadcasting Corporation [BBC] which was beaming toward Berlin, but it was forbidden to listen to it on the pains of death. So whenever the BBC came across the airwaves, one quickly jarred the wire of the set to get away from it and never mentioned it to anyone that the signal had strayed to one's set.

Anyway, on this beautiful February morning, several heavy formations of bombers had flown into central Germany. But they had not dropped their bombs, which was always cause for suspicion of a surprise raid on us. And sure enough, very soon the announcement came that the bombers had turned north. Since we were in Tempelhof which is in South

Berlin, we would be the first to see them or get hit. Soon I could hear the drone of the multi-engine aircraft—and as I darted onto our balcony, facing the beautiful Wulfila-Ufer and the Teltow Canal, I could see the contrails high against the sky. I had just enough time to call to my mother and grandmother, "There they are!", and to grab my assigned briefcase with the family documents (everyone had a special responsibility to safeguard certain important family items and take them to the reinforced basement bunker) and then it happened. There was a brilliant flash in the sky as the lead elements of several formations opened their bomb-bay doors, catching the sun like many mirrors. Then came a roar, similar to a thousand trains moving through the air. Those were the bombs beginning to cascade to earth—I got pretty scared and raced down the several flights of stairs to the basement. On the first landing, I saw my mother and grandmother embracing each other, but I was just jumping past them, several steps at a time, really quite terrified—the roar became louder and louder and when I reached the basement, the bombs started to hit.

Although our air raid alert system was excellent—we normally had at least 20 minutes of warning or more—this day there seemed to be a surprise factor and it appeared that none of the people darting into the cellar had the benefit of any warning. Women ran in with their hair pinned up, mop buckets and brooms in hand, children and one or two men—some were screaming in terror. The bombs were laid in carpet fashion. The earth shook and shook. The first thing in the cellar that went out was the light, then the dust from the paint on the ceiling and walls came down—then people were praying. I tried to get underneath an old couch—I thought if the building collapsed, the springs of the couch would give me some air space in which to breathe.

It was some time before the "all clear" came. We were still alive! As we slowly made a cautious move out of the cellar we were shocked by the darkness. Two hours earlier it was a beautiful summer day. Now we couldn't see the sun. All there was to see was a putrid looking greenish blue sky, with scraps of burned cloth and paper floating through the air. It was dark in the middle of the day. The first thought that came to my mind was, "the Americans have used poison gas!" Later we learned that they had bombed a chemical factory across the canal. Our own street had suffered some roof damage. Windows were long gone and had been replaced by cardboard and small squares of plexiglass. We were glad to be alive, but still in a state of shock. That afternoon, my friend's father, a captain in the army, on convalescent leave, returned from the city center. I saw him first and said: "Did you know we almost got it today?" He took it very calmly—suggesting that as long as the houses were still standing, it couldn't have been too bad. He survived the war, but his wife, my friend's mother, poisoned herself and her son before the Russians arrived weeks later. The medics tried to save them both, but only with my friend was the stomach pump successful. That was one of the most devastating raids I can remember. (Personal journal, author)

On February 3, 1945, Berlin was attacked by 937 bombers, accompanied by 613 *Mustang* and *Thunderbolt* fighters. In fifty-seven minutes, 2,264 tons of bombs rained on the city, killing 22,000 inhabitants. What to them was a disaster proved salvation to one of Germany's important resistance leaders, Fabian von Schlabrendorff. He was next to be sentenced by Hitler's notorious hanging judge, Roland Freisler, but was spared when the building that housed the German People's Court received a direct hit, killing Freisler and destroying von Schlabrendorff's dossier (Böddeker 1985, 47).

ASSESSING THE DAMAGE

Before the shooting actually ended, a group of American evaluators moved into Germany to look at the effects of the Allied bombardment. Later, their findings were published as the *United States Strategic Bombing Survey*, mentioned earlier.

The investigation team found that 2.5 million workers had been tied up clearing away the debris, reconstructing the essential plants, and helping in the dispersal of other industries to less-endangered locations. In addition, 1 million had been employed making an ever-greater number of anti-aircraft guns and related equipment. Another million workers attempted to produce those civilian goods that were being wiped out by the bombing (USSBS 1945, 38).

Attacks against the German transportation system necessitated continuous repairs—and all of these factors drew much needed manpower away from the actual front. Enormous amounts of goods and military equipment produced at the risk of the workers' lives never reached their destination but were smashed on the way, as barges, trains, and trucks were destroyed by Allied fighters and fighter-bombers.

According to the USSBS, the RAF and USAAF combined bomb weight dropped on Germany came to 2,697,473 tons, delivered in 1,442,280 sorties, at a cost of 21,914 bombers. Between them, the Western allies claimed to have destroyed over 57,000 German planes (USSBS 1945, Table 1).

As to attacks on German cities, the Survey noted that almost one-fourth of all bomb tonnage was targeted against large cities. In terms of damage caused, these air raids surpassed all others, whether they were launched against manufacturing plants, the oil refineries, V-weapons launching sites, military targets, or the transportation network (USSBS 1945, 71).

As mentioned, the RAF specialized in area raids, while General Spaatz of the USAAF rejected this type of indiscriminate attack directed mainly against civilians. The Americans held to daylight precision bombing. Nevertheless, tens of thousands of civilians died in these raids as well. According to the Survey:

During the period from October 1939 to May 1945, the Allied Air Forces, primarily the RAF, dropped over one-half million tons of high explosives, incendiaries, and fragmentation bombs in such area raids on the 61 German cities having a population of 100,000 or more. These cities included 25,000,000 people, 21 percent of the Reich's population, and had a labor force of 4,858,900.

All attacks are estimated to have totally destroyed or heavily damaged 3,600,000 dwelling units, accounting for some 20 percent of Germany's total residential units, and to have rendered homeless 7,500,000 people. They killed about 300,000 people and injured some 780,000. (USSBS 1945, 72)

Other loss figures compiled years later would differ somewhat from those above. According to East German statistics, 410,000 German civilians lost their lives, 650,000 were wounded, and over 13 million were made homeless. Of over 1.2 million tons dropped by the Allies on Germany, 55.8 percent reportedly fell on cities and transportation centers, with 131 major cities suffering large-scale raids. Overall losses of living quarters were listed as 4.1 million (Groehler 1981, 509).

The USSBS also contains statistics on the effectiveness of the different bombs, which ranged from 500 to 22,000 pounds. The latter ones were used against submarine pens and flak bunkers in the cities. But for residential areas, incendiaries were found to have been 4.8 times more effective than the high-explosive kinds. Besides Hamburg and Dresden, the Survey shows that firestorms also consumed the inner cities of Kassel and Darmstadt. Visitors to these cities today may not realize that the large avenues and spacious exhibition parks in the city centers are the results of wastelands caused by human-made holocausts over forty years ago.

The investigators also probed into the effect of the bombings on German morale, and the will to continue the war. Thousands of interviews during the summer 1945 and analyses of German private mail, and questionnaires completed by foreign workers who had experienced the Allied raids, revealed that in addition to far-reaching suffering among civilians, nearly 20 million lost their essential utility services such as gas, water, and electricity and another 5 million were evacuated from their homes. The raids also drove a wedge between the people and the propaganda of the Party. The interviews disclosed that those who had been bombed were more likely to become apathetic and war-weary than those who had escaped bombardment, but that the former stiffened their will in different ways. Night attacks were dreaded more than those during the day. In Munich, the authorities found that when the citizens could plainly see the huge bomber swarms flying in perfect formation over their city and dropping their bombs without the slightest interference by the *Luftwaffe*, people reacted with a mixture of fear and anger (USSBS 1945, 97). Raids causing the loss of schools and children's recreational facilities also created major anxiety and depression in many mothers since the children would now be taken from their homes to live and attend schools in the countryside under the Party-sponsored *Kinderlandverschickung*, the evacuation program for German youth. This effort to provide academic and political training while preserving the German genetic pool no doubt saved the lives of thousands of youngsters, who otherwise would have been subjected to additional months or even years of heavy bombardment. Altogether, some 2.5 million German youths were evacuated into 9,000 camps, often as entire grades, along with their teachers (Dabel 1981, 14). While the latter remained responsible for academic instruction, senior Hitler Youth members oversaw the actual administration of the camps.

One debilitating effect of the raids was the gradual numbness and decline in productivity from the loss of sleep caused by round-the-clock alerts. Men who served in vital defense jobs at the home front often would work two shifts, one doing their regular work and the other as crew members of anti-aircraft batteries. Not infrequently, children would simply remain in the cellars in makeshift bunk beds for days at a time. Nervous disorders became quite common from strain and exhaustion. Nearby explosions caused dysfunctions of people's facial muscles and attendant jerking of the head. Seeing one's city ablaze in the night, when fires lit up the sky so brightly that people could read the newspaper at midnight, while others desperately tried to save their lives and a few valuables from the flames, was traumatic. Equally shocking was getting out on the street after the "all clear," following a daytime raid, and seeing a big empty space where hours before had stood a large apartment building. The sight of the mangled bodies of one's neighbors and the body parts of flyers dangling from the rain gutters likewise had their effect. But the Survey seems to agree with other observers in Germany that increased terror bombing reinforced the will to "show them," no matter how real the disaffection of the people vis-à-vis their political leadership had become. Dr. Goebbels indeed used some heavy raids to make his most impassioned speeches across the nation. Germany's air force chief, Hermann Göring, who had agreed to be called "Meier" should any enemy plane reach Berlin, became the butt of innocent, but nonetheless confidential, jokes.

The Survey gave high marks to the efficiency of German civil defense. The 1.4 million tons of bombs dropped on Germany proper tested the air raid protection services to the utmost. According to the German Air Ministry, by January 1945 250,253 civilians had been killed by the bombs, 305,455 required hospitalization, and nearly 800,000 buildings had been destroyed or seriously damaged (USSBS 1945, 101).

Where possible, the rescue teams, dispersed all across Germany, did what they could to alleviate the suffering and lessen the losses. Where raids had caused catastrophic damage, regular army troops were assigned to aid the victims. In retrospect, it is doubtful that the German people ever experienced more unity than during those years when the wailing sound of the sirens announced the coming death from the skies.

The OKH listed overall losses of both sexes due to bombing attacks at about 800,000, including foreign workers. According to American statistics, U.S. and British aircrew losses in attacks on Germany proper stood at 158,546. Thus for every Allied flyer killed, five German civilians had died or had been wounded on the ground. Even though a comparison of the losses of German civilians versus those of the German armed forces shows a ratio of 1:4, there were brief periods during which civilian casualties were actually higher than those at the front—a witness to the effects of total war on the home front (Kurowski 1981, 41).

IN THE CROSS FIRE

By the end of 1944 and for four months of 1945, those civilians who had survived the bombing of their homes faced a new danger—ground assault.

As American and British armor, paratroopers, and infantry crossed the Rhine and moved eastward and Red Army forces raced for Berlin from the East, many

German towns and villages became hotly contested in house-to-house fighting. In the East, millions of Germans and other nationals fleeing from the Russian troops were jamming the roads while being subjected to strafing from the air or direct attack from tank columns overtaking their treks. On the other hand, many cities were declared fortresses by the Führer or the local party functionaries. Their citizens could not leave easily and lived weeks in the twilight zone between life and death, becoming the bystander victims in the savage ground action that characterized Germany's eastern defense and also, occasionally, erupted in the West. Added to this danger was the certain shelling of their farms and dwellings if Allied observer planes spotted German military traffic in their vicinity. Not a few German families lost their lives or were wounded as their places were caught in the cross fire of enemy attacks and friendly counterattacks. German civilians became quite hostile to their own soldiers when the latter tried to make their houses into defense posts. And, as was standard operational procedure in any combat zone, a civilian who tried to save his home by hoisting the white flag faced death by a firing squad or hanging, as a deterrent to other would-be quitters, as long as some organized German resistance was still on the scene (Irving 1977, 774). Many civilians seeking medical help would brave the clearings in streets and squares during temporary lulls in fighting to reach makeshift hospitals or field clinics. Some lost their lives upon the initial attack on German soil, as at Aachen; others died as a result of shelling and small arms fire just a few days prior to Germany's surrender.

The city of Aachen also bore the sad distinction of being the only major German town to have its Allied-appointed mayor murdered by a Werewolf assassination team that had been dropped behind American lines from a captured B–17. Dr. Franz Oppenhoff, who had reluctantly accepted the post, realizing full well that Berlin would put a price on his head, died on Palm Sunday weekend in March of 1945 (Whiting 1972, 138–139).

THE STAR OF DAVID

In addition to those civilians killed through actual combat during the six years of war, one particular group of German citizens was subjected to suffering and death at the hands of their own authorities. These were the German Jews who were living within the confines of the Reich. Though some may have initially discounted Hitler's pronouncements in *Mein Kampf* as so much election oratory, the *Kristallnacht* (Night of [broken] crystals) of November 9, 1938, made them painfully aware that the Nazis might be trusted to translate their Führer's ideology into terrifying reality. During the six years from Hitler's assumption of power in January 1933 to the outbreak of the war, about half of Germany's 522,000 Jews emigrated (Bauer 1982, 109). They were indeed fortunate.

It is estimated that 350,000 Jews remained in the area of Greater Germany, which now included Austria. Once the *Wehrmacht* moved east, the fate of Germany's own Jews was largely overshadowed by the deliberate extermination campaign carried out by the *Einsatzgruppen* (special mission units) against Jews in Poland and later in the USSR, as well as the deportation of Jews from those areas of Western Europe now under the control of Germany. Within Germany proper, Jews were placed into ten concentration camps, which were not extermination facilities per se but in which precious few were found alive when freed by Allied troops in 1945. At Bergen-Belsen, which was liberated by British soldiers on April 15, 1945, 37,000 had died. Another 14,000 perished in the weeks following, victims of starvation and typhoid (Bauer 1982, 329). President Ronald Reagan chose the site of this former camp to pay tribute to those who perished there and to remind the world's conscience of what had happened some forty years ago. Altogether, Jewish researchers give the total number of German Jews lost in the Holocaust as 125,000, in addition to 65,000 more who died in Austria (Bauer 1982, 335).

The persecution and subsequent removal of almost all Jews from public life through incarceration and eventual death was something they themselves could hardly fathom. After all, many influential citizens of the German Reich were Jewish. Yet there were warnings of what was to come.

Those who heeded them left and deprived Germany of many leading scientists, who, instead of being available for the fatherland's war effort, offered their services to the Allies.

In 1979, a German journalist, after investigating the losses accrued to Germany as a result of the heinous persecution of Jews under the Nazis, succinctly concluded that in driving Germany's Jews into exile, and later into the death camps, Hitler lost the very scientists who might have given him victory through their giftedness in nuclear research. The eventual victory of the United States was significantly enhanced by these Jews working for their newly adopted country, although no atomic weapons were dropped on Germany. It has been pointed out that "there can be no doubt that the Nazi persecution . . . crucially contributed . . . to create the situation where the necessary means were provided to make a substantial start on the Manhattan Project . . . " and that

both the United States' possession of atom bombs before the end of the Second World War and the failure to develop nuclear weapons in Hitler's Germany were an inevitable consequence . . . of Nazi racial persecution. (Engelmann 1984, 198, 205)

But not only that. The list of Jewish artists, intellectuals, playwrights, musicians, and medical researchers who left Germany or were imprisoned and succumbed contains many of the country's leadership in these fields. Hitler got his wish, and the present Federal Republic is less fortunate because of it. In addition, the "cleansing" of Germany and German-held areas meant that the *Wehrmacht* was deprived of the manpower to fill several additional divisions and lost those forces, used to make Germany and Europe "*Judenfrei*," for the war effort. It has been estimated that 336,000 Jews and non-Aryans could have been drafted from the area of Greater Germany (Engelmann 1984, 130). In

World War I, 100,000 Jews fought for the Kaiser, 17.7 percent of German Jewry. Half of them were decorated for their service.

That Germany's legation chief in Paris, Ernst vom Rath, was killed by a Jewish assassin (Herschel Grynszpan) did not help their situation, which was growing more ominous from month to month. After Rath died, the pogrom on November 9, 1938, was an omen of things to come. Ninety-one Jews were killed, 30,000 were arrested, 267 synagogues were burned, and 7,000 Jewish shops and homes were looted. To rub salt into their wounds, Germany's Jews were forced to pay billions to the state for the damage caused them at the hands of frenzied anti-Semites.

The latter's attitude was summed up by the historian Hans Buchheim after the war:

The Jews were not considered human. . . . The Jew was not merely an enemy to be fought or a despised person who, though he could be murdered, was still a human being. The Jew was considered a bacillus that spread sickness among the people. He . . . was to be exterminated. (Federal Republic of Germany 1980, 72)

Lost to Germany were such outstanding men (not all Jewish) as Albert Einstein, conductor Otto Klemperer, authors Thomas Mann and Bruno Frank, and the composer Kurt Weill. Besides, Germans were deprived of the services of over 5,000 Jewish physicians.

Beginning in 1941, Germany's Jews were arrested in a heartless manner, their property confiscated or destroyed. They were loaded into moving vans and locked in cattle trains which rolled eastward with 1,000 to 1,500 unfortunates each. German women, who were known to have Jewish boyfriends were shamelessly humiliated. The wearing of the yellow star badge had been mandatory since 1934. Some removed it at the peril of arrest, so they could occasionally blend into the normal life of their cities (Schoenberner 1981, 313).

Max Ludwig gave a particularly touching account of the removal of Jews from Heidelberg and the surrounding areas. Before Hitler's *Machtergreifung* (assumption of power) on January 30, 1933, 1,240 persons of Jewish lineage lived in Heidelberg. Of these, 827 emigrated; two returned, 320 were deported, and only thirty-three survived. Survivors came solely from the Theresienstadt concentration camp, where some had arrived as late as February 1945. In the Baden and Palatinate districts, the first deportations began on October 22, 1940 (Ludwig 1965, 8). On that date, 6,504 Jews, ages one to ninety, were removed to France, where they suffered exceedingly at a camp near Gurs. From there they were later shipped to what for all would be their final destination—Auschwitz, Maidanek, or Treblinka. Nearly 2,000 did not make this journey. They had perished in France. Some, however, had been able to emigrate before being shipped to the camps in Poland. Ludwig's account includes a by-name roster of all Jews deported from this area and their last address and fate.

The insidiousness of Hitler's racial purge reached into the very schoolrooms of the nation, where Party members in full uniform oversaw the compilation of family genealogies by students. Prior to their actual removal, German Jews were also required to take on the additional names of Israel or Sarah and to have their official identity cards and birth records annotated accordingly. German parish records for that period give mute evidence of this practice.

Although the Jews were the major German minority decimated by the Nazi regime, smaller groups of Germans considered an impurity to the Aryan stock were also arrested. These included the Gypsies, of whom 400 were sent to Dachau as early as 1936 (Wytwycky 1980, 30). Eventually, most of the 30,000 German Gypsies found their way into camps where 15,000 succumbed from disease, overwork, or plain abuse. Additionally, some 80,000 German citizens who were either chronically sick, habitually criminal, homosexual, or mentally ill died under the euthanasia program, though it was "officially" terminated in 1941 after protest from Germany's Christian leadership (Bauer 1982, 208).

Once the Federal Republic came into being, it was determined to atone in some way for what had happened. According to its Finance Ministry—in contrast to the East German government which has refused to pay any restitution payments—total West German payments in its *Wiedergutmachungs* (restitution) program, by which it seeks to mitigate the human and material losses caused by the Hitler regime, reached 70 billion DM (deutsche mark) as of 1984. This figure includes payments to those who have been victimized by the Holocaust terror, either as survivors or as relatives of the dead. Additional payments of 15 billion DM are expected to be made. Authority for these expenditures rests on two laws, the *Bundesentschädigungsgesetz* (BEG) and the *Bundesrückerstattungsgesetz* (BRÜG). The former deals with indemnification claims, while the latter seeks to restore losses. Israel's share from payments under these laws has been about 40 percent, in addition to 3.45 billion DM free drawing rights under the Luxembourg Treaty or Shilumim Agreement, negotiated by Konrad Adenauer with his Israeli counterparts following the war, as a German "debt of honor" (Balabkins 1971, 140–143).

This moral obligation to make up for the past has been accepted by all major West German political parties. Beyond the official efforts at restitution, private reconciliation efforts toward Israel were initiated by young Germans in 1963 at the Ein Charod Kibbutz. Since that time, thousands of West German youth have lived and worked as labor missionaries on Israel's collective community farms in a gesture of goodwill and support. In addition to these voluntary goodwill efforts, claims for indemnification against the private sector of West Germany's economy have and are being entertained in German courts. For example, as late as January 1986, the major firm of Feldmühle AG, a member of the Flick concern, was asked to pay 5 million deutsche mark (DM) to Jews who had been forced to work in its former munitions plants during the war years.

10

THE GREAT RAPE

Some years after the war, a cartoon circulated in West German papers, depicting the giant *Siegesengel* (victory angel) statue in Berlin, which had at its top a female angel with outstretched wings and arms—and a Soviet soldier standing at its base, demanding, in broken German, "Frau, Komm!" (Woman, Come!). Although the cartoon was meant to evoke smiles among its viewers, it brought back to millions of German women the most dreaded two words most of them had ever heard, words uttered countless times by insatiable enemy troops as they pushed their way across eastern Germany.

The first Soviet conquest of a German village occurred on October 22, 1944, at Nemmersdorf, near Goldap, in East Prussia. Before a counterattack temporarily threw back the invaders, members of a Soviet Guard Division, fired by the call to "repay" the Germans, had apparently raped, mutilated, and killed all females of the village. Older people were sawed in half or nailed to barn doors. French POWs and Polish workers found in the village were castrated or had their genitals cut off (Deschner 1968, 579). This Ghengis Khan–like terror lasted only a brief time since the Russians were unable to hold the village, but it served as a torch in the night to enrage the German defenders and to paralyze German women who found themselves in the path of the Red Army with gripping fear.

It convinced those among the Germans who had not been able to believe reports of similar atrocities as told by Hungarians and Romanians earlier. To have believed them would have meant to accept a nightmare's becoming a reality. Of course, these same Germans probably had not realized that millions of Russian civilians had perished when the *Wehrmacht* struck across Russia. That Soviet troops did not wait until they got to Germany to indulge in these excesses, though on a smaller scale, was attested to by Milovan Djilas, a Yugoslavian freedom fighter against German forces in the Balkans. He described Tito to have been

well-satisfied with the support of the Red Army, except on the issue of behavior
of Soviet troops toward civilians and the attitudes of their commanders, who
were resentful of Yugoslav admonitions or else oblivious to them. Djilas reported
that

All . . . went on simmering and the simmering grew worse with each new and more drastic
case. The city committee informed us that at Cukarica, on the outskirts of Belgrade,
Soviet soldiers had raped and slashed open a pharmacist to whose funeral five thousand
came as a demonstration. (Djilas 1977, 420)

Finally, the Yugoslavs and their "Politburo," including Tito and Djilas, had
a formal talk with General Korneyev, the Russian commander. After Djilas lost
his patience and compared the proper conduct of British officers, who were also
helping the Yugoslavs against the Germans, with the behavior of the Red Army,
the Soviet general broke off the meeting in anger. Djilas's remarks, however,
were duly reported to Stalin who, at a dinner in Moscow later, had the Yugoslav
do penance for his assertions. As soon as the toast and subsequent jests had put
the guests at ease, Stalin "remembered" to liquidate his dispute with Djilas.
He half-jokingly insisted that the Yugoslav drink a small glass of vodka to the
Red Army. Against his better judgment (Djilas did not drink hard liquor), the
latter obeyed and drank it to the last drop. Then he explained to Stalin the basis
of his earlier remarks. Stalin interrupted him with these words:

Yes, you have, of course, read Dostoevsky? Do you see what a complicated thing is
man's soul, man's psyche? Well then, imagine a man who had fought from Stalingrad
to Belgrade—over thousands of kilometers of his own devastated land, across the dead
bodies of comrades and dearest ones! How can such a man react normally? And what is
so awful in his having fun with a woman, after such horrors? . . . We opened up our
penitentiaries and stuck everybody in the army. The Red Army is not ideal. The important
thing is that it fights Germans—and it is fighting them well, while the rest doesn't matter.
(Djilas 1977, 435)

This incident involving two Communist leaders appears to weaken the claims
of some Soviet apologists that the rape and attendant butchery of German women
was based on the sole motive of revenge for German atrocities.

A *Volkssturm* member gave a sworn statement of what he saw after Nemmersdorf was temporarily retaken:

We found in the living quarters a total of 72 women, including youth, and a 74 year
old man, all dead, almost all killed in bestial fashion, except for those shot in the neck.
Among the dead were infants whose heads had been crushed by a hard object.

In a room we found an old woman dead, still in sitting position. She had lost half of
her head, which appeared to have been chopped off with an axe or spade.

Those corpses we had to carry to the village cemetery, where they were left, because
an international medical commission had been called to look at the dead. . . . Other people
were found murdered at the outskirts, killed by shooting, beating, and even crucifixion.

After burial, the belated commission required their exhumation. According to the medical findings, every female, including girls as young as eight, had been raped. (Nawratil 1982, 27)

Yet the world press showed little interest in non-German outrages, including the liquidation of French prisoners of war who had been working near Nemmersdorf.

An immediate effect of the Nemmersdorf tragedy was to increase the stream of refugees on the roads leading west, thus denying them to German units heading for the front. Volumes of documents in German federal archives testify to the suffering of the civilian population in the wake of the Russian advance.

In preparation for his well-researched and documented best-seller about the final days of Berlin, *The Last Battle*, Cornelius Ryan interviewed 271 Germans, of whom 167 were Berliners, to give an insight into the stark terror of this dimension of the German atonement. His volume, by the way, is dedicated to a young Berliner who, born during the last months of the war, was later machine-gunned at the infamous wall that would divide the former Reich capital. But in April and May 1945 Berlin was in its own death throes. As soon as the immediate danger of German retaliation was past, Russian troops made reality of what most other armies hardly dared to dream. These troops had come cheering and winning and also dying from their last jumping-off point, the Oder River, and now Berlin, the capital of their arch foe, lay at their feet and at their mercy. Hitler's Order of the Day, issued at the time of the final Soviet assault, exhorted the German troops to give their last strength in halting the enemy who, in the Führer's mind, would murder old men and children and reduce women and girls to army camp whores. The troops were ordered to swear a solemn oath to defend, not what by now might be an empty concept of fatherland, but their homes, wives, and children (Ryan 1967, 347). The Red Armies were reaching Berlin and the word to the women was to remain in their cellars and bunkers. Amid the craters from bombs and artillery shells, and general havoc, but also among spring blossoms on trees and in gardens, came the first encounters with Russian troops. The few men who, for various reasons, were with their families sought to protect their wives by either standing between them and their assailants or threatening to commit suicide. In virtually all cases, these efforts resulted in the death of the men, while the women were raped anyway—often entire squads would satisfy themselves with one woman. True, the actual front-line units or shock troops behaved properly much of the time, but those who followed had no such inhibitions. One of their victims was Ursula Koster. As told to Ryan, she was sleeping in the cellar with her parents, her six-year-old twin daughters, and her seven-month-old boy when four Russian soldiers beat the door down with their rifle butts. After shoving her parents and children at gunpoint into another room, they all assaulted her. Next morning, two more came—filthy, clothes gritty—and each raped her. After that, Ursula grabbed her children and made for a bathtub in which she hid out (Ryan 1967, 455).

Another young Berlin woman, Juliane Bochnik, who had hidden under a sofa to escape the Russians, was betrayed by a "frightened" older person after her father had refused to reveal her location, even at gunpoint. She was dragged out and stripped by a clean-cut young officer. She kept begging him to leave her alone and finally he consented to abandon his prey. Two of her friends, after being raped, had taken poison, but were saved by medical personnel (Ryan 1967, 457). Some men, by various designs, hid their daughters or wives, some leading the female occupants of entire apartment blocks from cellar to attic, always ahead of the pursuing troops. Women discolored their hair, smeared their faces with soot, carried pistols between their legs, and hid in the big standard cans of the Berlin sanitation department. Some rapings had unusual effects. Especially among officers, remorse and return to decency the day after would often result in food parcels' being sent to their victims. Some girls were saved from the final act by having lost so much weight that their bodies lacked female charm. Sometimes, other soldiers were also beaten off by the first conquerors—while the terrified women begged for mercy or poison capsules. In the Pankow district of Berlin, the suicide rate, mainly of women, for a three-week period rose to 215. Some girls suffered mass rapes, up to thirty times. If they did not hemorrhage or face death from internal injuries, they were among the lucky ones because others were shot after drunken troops had satisfied their lust (Ryan 1967, 458). Thus, the sexual assault often ended with the death of the victims. An earthly hell truly had descended upon the women of eastern Germany. Their screaming was heard throughout the nights as they were gathered up and abused (Ryan 1967, 458).

Alexander Solzhenitsyn wrote about the rape of German women in his poem, *Prussian Nights*. As a young artillery captain, he experienced firsthand the holocaust that was played upon the conquered:

> A moaning, by the walls half muffled:
>   The mother's wounded, still alive.
> The little daughter's on the mattress,
>   Dead. How many have been on it?
>   A platoon, a company perhaps?
> A girl's been turned into a woman,
>   A woman turned into a corpse.
> It's all come down to simple phrases:
>   Do not forget! Do not forgive!
> Blood for blood! A tooth for a tooth!
>   The mother begs, "Töte mich, Soldat!"
> (Solzhenitsyn 1977, 37, 39)

The last words of the German women in his moving account are a plea for the Russian soldier to kill her.

When German women tried to get help and protection from Russian officers, they would often be told that it was just revenge for what their men had done in Russia. From all accounts, however, it appears that the frenzy to which the

Soviet troops had been whipped up was founded not so much on actual sexual misdeeds of ordinary German troops against Russian women (the penalty for rape in the German army was death), but on a combination of atrocities by the *Einsatzgruppen*, the general destruction of life and property incident to combat, and the voluminous stream of propaganda to "kill, kill, kill!"

Not totally uncommon were some ironic twists in all of this. There were some women in Berlin whose political persuasions clearly lay with the Red Army— at least they were Marxists who somehow had escaped the *Geheime Staatspolizei* (Gestapo). These were also assaulted, a rather rude and contrary greeting from those whose cause they had tried to further at a great risk to themselves.

Alexander Werth, who spent the war with the Red Army while working for a Western newspaper, discussed this morbid topic with a Russian officer. The latter explained the misdeeds of his soldiers as follows:

> In Poland, a few regrettable things happened from time to time, but on the whole, a fairly strict discipline was maintained as regards rape. . . .
>
> But the looting and raping in a big way did not start until our soldiers got to Germany. Our fellows were so sex-starved that they often raped old women of sixty and seventy, or even eighty—much to those grandmothers' surprise, if not downright delight. But I admit it was a nasty business, and the record of the Kazakhs and other Asiatic troops was particularly bad. (Werth 1964, 964)

This officer's statement squares pretty well with other observations. Although the Soviets are very defensive about the issue, their historians admit that the troops had gotten somewhat out of control. Certain "orders of the day" by senior commanders show that the misconduct was having a detrimental effect on the combat-effectiveness of the troops, even in victory. Likewise, concern over the consequences of their soldiers' actions in connection with Soviet plans for setting up a viable communist German state in the territory now being overrun by the Red Army led to a call for caution and moderation, expressed in a *Red Star* editorial in February 1945, still three months before the fall of Berlin. Stalin himself began to draw the line between the Hitlerites and the rest of the German people. Following suit, the Communist Party's Central Committee called for an end to Ehrenburg's passionate anti-German diatribes to the troops, realizing that such exhortations were becoming counterproductive. Nonetheless, of all the terrible truths that German men and women and even children witnessed as the war came home to them, none was more terrifying than this inglorious chapter in their defeat.

11

THE MOURNFUL TREK

In spite of the fear based on this undeniable evidence of brutal treatment by the coming avengers, some Germans could not bring themselves to leave their ancestral homes. Others, seeing the futility of fleeing the invaders' wrath, were satisfied to meet their end on familiar ground. Still others felt that they must add their individual efforts to resist the enemy and, if that proved in vain, to render as much aid to their vanquished neighbors as possible, provided, of course, they themselves survived. Furthermore, in virtually every eastern province, the local *Gauleiter*s (regional party chiefs) refused to permit even a cursory preparation for evacuation, much less an actual departure. On pain of death, no one was allowed to leave, or even talk about it; to do so would have meant admitting the possibility that the Russians might come that far. That would have undermined the home front for sure! When the disaster struck and all the dams of the *Wehrmacht* broke, millions became hostages in the gigantic final battles on their own soil, while the party functionaries frequently escaped with the only vehicles full of fuel. Some were later caught by the Allies and returned to the power that now controlled their former domain. Sometimes, their life ended at the gallows of those who had replaced them (Thorwald 1979b, 41).

EAST PRUSSIA

An account of what it was like to be overrun by Soviet troops is provided by Count Hans von Lehndorff, the sole survivor of five brothers who met their death either in combat, at the hands of Russian soldiers, or in the purge of anti-Hitler groups following the abortive coup of July 20, 1944. The count related the last weeks of the defense of East Prussia and his role in relieving the sufferings of hundreds of his countrymen caught in the cross fire of armies and the subsequent nightmare of plunder, rape, and indiscriminate killings.

Von Lehndorff's abiding faith in God carried him through the weeks of anxiety and the savagery of conquest and allowed him to cope with what for so many was an utterly hopeless situation. Together with a large German army contingent and numerous civilians, he experienced the enemy first in Königsberg, the capital of East Prussia. For days the city, which had been declared a fortress, was subjected to artillery shelling and bombardment from the now-quite-active and numerically superior Soviet air force. Von Lehndorff divided his time between his work as a surgeon and being spiritual leader of this medical team. Once the Russians reached his hospital, the same scenes reported earlier repeated themselves; the more intense, the more alcohol the troops found. On April 11, 1945, about one month before the Third Reich struck the colors, von Lehndorff wrote:

Just as we feared, the Russians had found some alcohol. . . . Then something like a tide of rats flowed over us, worse than all the plagues of Egypt together. Not a moment went by but that I had the barrel of a pistol rammed against my back or my stomach, and a grimacing mask yelling at me for "Sulfidin!" So nearly all these devils must have got venereal disease. . . .

On every side we heard the despairing screams of women: "Shoot me then! Shoot me!" But the tormentors preferred a wrestling match to any actual use of their firearms. Soon none of the women had any strength left for resistance. In a few hours a change came over them; their spirit died, one heard hysterical laughter, which made the Russians madder than ever. . . . When the tumult subsided, four women were dead. (von Lehndorff 1963, 59)

It wasn't long thereafter that another horseman of the apocalypse made his appearance among the Germans left behind: hunger. It turned many into skeletons in the upper part of their bodies, with heavily water-swollen legs below. Most had to be left to their fate since they were too far gone for amputations. Then came the typhus which decimated those still alive and took Dr. von Lehndorff's able and highly valued assistant. Those who still had the strength attempted by every means to move westward. Without papers, many were caught and shipped to collection camps for Germans, to be deported to the Soviet Union. From the camps they traveled for weeks across Russia. When they reached their destination, a high percentage of each railroad car's passengers had succumbed. During von Lehndorff's second escape from his captors, he reached his own home and found that both his mother and brother had been shot, together with sixteen other persons of the village. "Why did God let the Russians into Germany?" he questioned. Once the Poles replaced the Russians as the new landlords, many Germans changed their ethnicity to that of "Masuren." It gave them a better chance to stay alive since the Masuren people had had ties with the Poles earlier. When von Lehndorff finally reached the freedom of Germany proper, he felt like a new person. He was one of the few to have survived the East Prussian passion.

Another catastrophe of massive proportions involving German refugees had occurred about the same time as von Lehndorff experienced the siege of Königsberg. As the Russian troops accelerated their drive for the Oder, considerable forces of the German Battle Group North were bypassed and compressed along a thin stretch of ground from Königsberg to Danzig. Into this stretch of German-held territory, hundreds of thousands of German civilians had streamed with thousands of seriously wounded German soldiers and members of the European *SS* division "Charlemagne."

When the last attack was made on the East Prussian capital in April 1945, all but 100,000 civilians either had been rescued or were dead. After a hopeless defense, General Lasch, the fortress commander, gave up the fight. He did so to lessen the suffering of his civilian refugees, trapped in the city. For this action, General Lasch was sentenced to death by hanging (in absentia) on orders of Hitler, who also had his family arrested under the next-of-kin rule decreed earlier. Yet all survived and lived to see the general return from Soviet captivity in 1955 (Böddeker 1985, 163). Once the capital changed hands, the people left in Königsberg took the brunt of another type of pain. Those who survived were often driven together and shipped to Siberia, where in Camp 1083 near Tscheljabinsk they spent years making bricks. This camp was home to hundreds of East Prussian women and girls. Those who returned to Germany continued to meet periodically to commemorate their time in Russia (Marienfeld 1981, 7–8).

Those fortunate enough to have reached the ice of the Frisches Haff (an enclosed body of water on East Prussia's Baltic seacoast) on their way to evacuation by sea now faced the terror of strafing and bombing attacks while on the ice. Many broke through the surface when their horses were shot and fell—so close to possible rescue.

The refugees who did get out had to thank General Hossbach's dwindling Fourth Army for a desperate rearguard action fought on their behalf. An example of what they had escaped was found at Metgethen, a small village west of Königsberg. Again, German troops, in a rare recovery of lost territory, found virtually no sign of life (Franken 1978, 86).

In Metgethen's tennis field, twenty-nine German soldiers had been dynamited. These and other atrocities involving female victims were verified by an international commission and deplored by Yuri Uspenski, lieutenant of the Second Guards Artillery Division, whose diary was found on his body weeks later.

One should take revenge, but not with the penis, rather with weapons. The rape of girls—it is not justifiable. . . . The soldiers have done a lot. But this behavior is now being countered. Yet enough has been done to have the Germans cross themselves a hundred years from now in memory of the winter of 44/45. (Franken 1978, 87)

Sometimes, Russian officers warned the first German women they met of the troops who were following. But often the T–34 tanks simply cut off the horse-drawn columns with their refugee women, children, and aged and tore them to pieces, leaving the survivors to be plundered by the mounted infantry. Occasionally, men found in the flotsam were lined up and shot.

Of the 2,653,000 Germans in the East Prussian region, 277,000 froze, starved, drowned, were torn by bombs or tank treads, died outright, or took their own lives (Franken 1978, 29). Shortly after Christmas 1944, the Reich defense commissioner declared that East Prussia would not be evacuated, even at that late date. Two weeks later the Russian grand offensive began. Frost and tanks found the strong and weak alike. Survivors endured many acts of violence. Individual women were raped so often that they lost consciousness; young girls' intestines were torn open, with venereal disease the certain keepsake of some survivors (Franken 1978, 45).

When German units in East Prussia made a last effort to cut through to the West and open a path for the refugees, who were now driven by blind panic, they found the attempt most difficult. Those civilians who fell behind were at the mercy of troops who were told not to show any compassion. Still, the White Russian and Ukrainian troops were rather decent. Others did not bother to restrain themselves. Women were violated, regardless of whether they were of German, Polish, or Baltic nationality (Franken 1978, 65).

Those still fleeing passed hundreds of dead by the sides of the roads—infants wrapped in newspaper, old people sitting where they had died. Women tried desperately to save their little ones, warming milk in their own mouths and forcing it into the babies, as birds do with their young.

As in East Prussia, the collapse of the German front created suffering, hardship, and terror in other areas which were part of eastern Germany. Pomerania, West Prussia, and Silesia all lay in the path of the advancing Red Armies, and the latter two bordered lands that had been occupied by German troops. *Sudetenland* Germans and Germans in Czechoslovakia proper would experience a similar fate later. Colonel General Guderian, head of Germany's armored forces, had spoken the truth when he stated, "The eastern front is like a house of cards, a collapse anywhere will bring the whole of it down" (Franken 1978, 7). Soldiers rushing home on leave to assist their families in fleeing westward were often greeted with disbelief by the loved ones they meant to save. The furlough was called *Sonderurlaub zwecks Sicherung der bürgerlichen Existenz* (special leave to safeguard the family's existence). As late as October 1944, civilians still believed in the "Eastwall" defense system which they thought would stop the strongest Russian attacks. Besides, no one was allowed to leave unless authorized by the local district's party leader. Premature pull-ups of one's belongings carried the death penalty. Even slaughtering animals bigger than fowl could cost one's head, because it might trigger a general feeling that evacuation was imminent. Still, in most cases, those who came from the front were convincing. Even Polish and Russian workers helped to prepare German families for departure, if often in secret. Just as during the advance of Northern troops in the American Civil War slaves frequently remained loyal to their white families, so some of the foreign workers preferred to stay with those who had been their masters rather than to be liberated by their countrymen.

However, farther east the retreat of the German civilians had actually begun, and none too soon. General I.D. Cherniakhovskij's Order of the Day was clear and to the point:

> There will be no mercy—for no one, as there was none for us. It is pointless to ask our troops to exercise mercy. They are inflamed by hatred and demand revenge. The land of the fascists must be made a desert. . . . (Franken 1978, 19)

A few months later, the general, who commanded the Third Byelorussian Front, woud die at Mehlsack, East Prussia, leading his troops who were carrying out his decree.

POMERANIA

Before long it was Pomerania's turn. As in East Prussia, evacuation here was forbidden until the very last moment. This policy cost over 300,000 people their lives even though they had the easiest route of escape to the West. It was also within sight of this province's shores that several rescue ships were torpedoed with such terrible casualties—15,791 dead altogether (Haupt 1970, 95).

Naval and passenger vessels carried over 2.6 million people from shores and ports, some even after the capitulation on May 7, 1945. Those refugees who chose the land route lost 15.5 percent of their number. As in East Prussia, many of the ones left behind in Pomerania were gathered up by the Russians and deported to the USSR (Franken 1978, 108).

SILESIA

The Red Army's invasion of Silesia brought similar scenes to this province. Again, the captured German soldier and civilian was at the mercy of the good, the bad, or the unpredictable. In Domslau, about 100 wounded Germans were forced to kneel in the snow before being executed. Overall, in Silesia 674,000 people lost their lives; 1.5 million were overrun; 1.6 million escaped into Czechoslovakia and other areas. Out of 4,254 Silesian villages, 2,553 experienced murder, 2,626 experienced rape, and 3,183 became locations for forcible deportation. Suicides occurred in 1,077 towns. Of course, one must recall that the Red Army had passed Auschwitz and Maidanek en route to Silesia (Franken 1978, 125).

The following report of a young woman illustrated the conditions many civilians had to endure:

> Please, mommy, don't be frightened, but I don't have Gabi with me, also I have a frozen arm. Otherwise, I would have carried Gabi further [Gabi is her little daughter].

But I could not have found a coffin for her, even here, because there hardly are any, and she would have been covered up quickly here as well.

Once she was dead, I could not carry her much farther. I could not stand it any longer and wrapped her up and laid her deep in the snow near the road behind Kauth. There Gabi was not alone, for thousands of other women came that way with their children and laid their dead there also, because no wagons or cars travel there which might harm them after death.

Gabi was dead, right suddenly, even though I had wrapped her in two blankets. But she was only four months old, and fifty children of two and three years old died. It was so terribly cold and stormed so icily, and it snowed, and we had nothing warm, no milk, nothing. I tried to nurse Gabi behind a house, but she would not take the breast, because it was so cold. Many women tried it, but froze their breasts. That must be terrible and the puss oozes! . . . One woman lost all three children. This young woman tried all night to get a glass of warm milk for her child. In vain. . . .

I cried and cried for misery and several times I wanted to lie down in the snow and die. And my arm grew evermore stiff. When it became day I saw dead children again. Perhaps some left their children alive in order to save themselves. We just stumbled along. The chilly wind blew. I no longer felt my feet. Finally, we got to a place where there were people, they had opened doors and some of us could thaw out. They warmed some milk for the children. But when I unwrapped Gabi and was so happy to give her something to drink, she was so quiet, and the woman next to me said, "She is gone. . . ."
(Franken 1978, 131)

Sometimes Russian tank crews jumped out of their vehicles, showing kindness to children. The youngest were spared; all else were open prey.

Indeed, the "last days" appeared to have come to Silesia. In Grünberg, of the 4,000 who remained, over 500 took their lives within the first two weeks after being overrun. The dead were left to bloat because the authorities thought this would deter further suicides. Truly, these Germans suffered terrible retribution for Hitler's war on Russia.

Of 300 *Arbeitsdienst* (work service) maidens caught by Soviet troops at Neisse, all were reportedly raped—many were seriously injured and some were killed. Their clothing was torn, they were violated while other soldiers threatened them with automatic weapons. The girls begged to be spared and later fought with hands and feet against their assailants. When rescued by a German counterattack, the survivors acted like patients in a mental institution (Franken 1978, 161).

During the last year of the war, the Reich's patent office was relocated from the heavily bombed capital of Berlin to the quiet town of Striegau, about thirty miles southwest of Breslau. The author's father, a member of the staff, barely escaped with his life after trying to rescue some personal effects while Soviet tanks were already battling the town's defenders. Little did he know what German troops would find upon recapturing the city a month later. Striegau's original population numbered 17,000. In mid-March of 1945, after one month of Soviet occupation, only thirty people had survived death or expulsion. Because of the severity of destruction, the German side catalogued the obvious atrocities, which included evidence of mass rape. Here as elsewhere, mothers and daughters voluntarily chose death rather than endure the nightmare any longer. Amazingly, municipal gas supplies continued to function and many chose this means of ending their life; hanging was a second method.

About one such mass suicide of women in Striegau, the lone survivor reported to the son of one of the victims:

> On February 13 [1945] we remained in our basement until 8 P.M. without being molested. Then we heard steps, we barely dared to breathe from sheer fright. Four soldiers appeared who behaved properly at first, but then became intimate. Soon the word was, "Frau, komm mit!" [Woman, come along!] You can imagine what happened to us next. We were raped all night long. When I returned to the basement, I found a married couple dead, they had refused to allow their daughter-in-law and grand-daughter to go along. About 10 A.M. we went to fix some food. Then it began anew. We screamed, we begged them to leave us in peace, but they showed no mercy. We resolved to end our lives. . . . Everyone had a knife and a piece of rope. Frau P. was first. Young Frau K. hanged her daughter and then herself. Her dear mother did the same with her sister. Now only two of us remained. I asked her to fix my rope for I was too upset to do it. Then we embraced one more time and kicked the luggage away on which we had stood. I, however, could touch the floor with my toes, her mother [Frau K.'s] had made the rope too long. I tried over and over—I wanted to die. I looked to the right and to the left, we hung in a row. They were well off, they were dead. As for me, I had no choice but to free myself from the rope. (Böddeker 1985, 113) (Translation mine)

Further to the East, Breslau's resistance, Silesia's capital, cost the lives of 40,000 civilians and thousands of soldiers. For eighty-three days the city had endured massive artillery, rocket, and aerial attacks.

After the battle died down, the new masters arrived—the Poles. Years before, the Nazis had made the Jews wear the Star of David; now the Germans had to wear white armbands and lost their civil liberties.

THE SUDETENLAND

The final chapter in Germany's eastern passion was to be written in Czechoslovakia. It would be a cruel harvest, compared with which other excesses might still seem rational, if such were possible.

On May 5, 1945, the hour of revenge for Lidice came. And yet, as mentioned, the men who had killed Reinhard Heydrich had not been local Czechs but were dropped into the country by the British. German-Czech relations, per se, had not been extremely hostile; in fact, Czechs were exempt from serving in the German army, but their excellent munitions and armaments industry was placed under Nazi control and made to support the German war effort. It was Heydrich's style of administration that resulted in Beneš's request and the British Cabinet's approval to kill him, lest the Czechs accept German occupation too passively. But now the partisan radio carried only one slogan: "Smrt Nencum!" (Death to the Germans!). Prague's fearful spring had started. The beautiful city was turned into a boiling caldron in which reason was drowned in blood (Nawratil 1982, 59–60).

The degree of vehemence with which the Czechs temporarily turned against the Germans might be partly explained as a desire to settle accounts of long-held animosities. Retaliation for years of German domination no doubt was a leading theme. A special massacre occurred on July 31, 1945—nearly three months after the war had ended—on the Elbe bridge at Aussig. Hundreds of German shift workers were thrown into the river on their return from work, because of an explosion that allegedly was caused by some of their fellow workers. According to well-placed sources, between 1,000 and 2,000 lost their lives or were wounded. Total casualties of the general program against Germans in Czechoslovakia reached 230,000.

Finally, a word about German minorities in the Balkan countries, where many had lived for a century and more, appears appropriate. As a direct result of the war and the subsequent persecution, 100,000 Romanian Germans lost their lives. Some 40,000 Hungarian Germans shared this fate. In Yugoslavia, 135,000 were killed, mainly because they were landed or otherwise became targets for real or imagined grievances.

EVACUATION BY SEA

Admiral Dönitz, Chief of German Naval Operations, who after Hitler's suicide would briefly head the remnants of the Third Reich, had been able to gather all available ships to effect a massive rescue operation not unlike that of the British some five years earlier at Dunkirk. His hope was to extricate 2.2 million East Germans from certain capture and to provide a pool of manpower for a future West German state which he felt would emerge from the ruins. However, in spite of his navy's efforts, it was impossible to keep Soviet submarines from penetrating shipping lanes close to the German Baltic coast. In several attacks on German ships, nearly 20,000 refugees and wounded soldiers perished in the icy January waters of the Baltic Sea, sometimes within sight of land (de Zayas 1979, 94–95). The most costly sinking, virtually unknown in Western annals until recently, was the loss of the *Wilhelm Gustloff*. Displacing over 25,484 tons, she had been used for transatlantic traffic before the war and subsequently was one of the "Strength Through Joy" vessels of the Third Reich's recreational program for workers. On January 30, 1945, she was heading west with 5,004 passengers. At six minutes past nine in the evening, Captain Third Class Alexander Marinesko of the Soviet Baltic Submarine Command fired two torpedoes into her. Within minutes, all but 904 people on board had met a tragic death in the icy deep (Dobson et al. 1979, 140–141). Besides the *Wilhelm Gustloff*, several other large ships were sunk in a similar manner with great loss of life. One was the *General von Steuben*, which went down on February 10 with 3,000 seriously wounded troops. Only 300 were rescued (Haupt 1970, 21).

By mid-February, 680,000 refugees were waiting on the narrow strips of land, still in German hands, to be sea-lifted to Schleswig-Holstein or Denmark. Near-miracles and ceaseless efforts by the German navy caused many tens of thousands to be evacuated. But it could not prevent a third major disaster when the *Goya*, loaded with 5,385 soldiers and civilians, was torn in two by Soviet torpedoes. Less than 200 survivors were picked up from the icy sea (Kieser 1984, 290).

12

THE EXPELLEES

> We expellees renounce any desire for revenge and retaliation. We
> take this solemn and sacred stand in memory of the boundless
> suffering to which mankind has been subjected, especially during
> the last decade. With all our strength we will support every effort
> which has as its goal the creation of a united Europe in which all
> peoples may live without fear and coercion. We will take part, with
> earnest and tireless labor, in the rebuilding of Germany and Europe.
> We have lost our homeland. Homeless people are strangers upon
> the earth. God gave all men their respective homelands. To separate
> them from their homes by force means to kill them spiritually. We
> have suffered and experienced this fate. Therefore we feel called
> upon to insist that the right to one's homeland as one of mankind's
> basic, God-given rights be duly recognized and translated into reality.
>
> From The Charter of German Expellees,
> August 5, 1950

Even after the cessation of hostilities, the fate of the German population that
remained in the eastern areas of the Reich proved to be dismal. Tens of thousands
were simply snatched up and sent to labor camps deep inside the USSR, and
millions were forcibly expelled. For years after World War II, they arrived in
West Germany with little more than their clothes on their backs. An amazing
feat was performed by West German authorities to assimilate these masses of
people into the economic and social fiber of the Federal Republic.

As mentioned in Chapter 7, the first deportations of Germans occurred as
early as 1940, when the latter were moved from East Volhynia to Siberia and
Central Asia, shortly before Hitler's invasion of Russia. Once the war began,
additional forced resettlements were ordered in the case of the Volga Germans

and those living in the Crimea and the Caucasus regions. As with the first group, these people also were relocated to Siberia and to the Kazakh Socialist Republic. About September 1942 the British government gave its first approval to the eventual expulsion of the Sudeten Germans by the Czechs, after the hoped-for Allied victory. Roosevelt's concurrence followed in May 1943. A month later, the Soviet ambassador to the Czech government-in-exile gave his consent as well. As the tide of war turned against Germany in the East, some groups of ethnic Germans living in Eastern Europe moved west with the retreating *Wehrmacht*. Those who delayed their departure often found themselves deported to the USSR, as in the case of some Germans in Hungary, Transylvania, and Yugoslavia. As mentioned in the previous chapter, once East German provinces fell under the control of the Red Army, deportations began from these areas as well. As the USSR annexed the northern part of East Prussia and made it the Kaliningrad Military District, and Poland extended political control over German lands east of the Oder/Neisse line, millions of Germans who had survived the war faced forcible removal. The groundwork for their expulsion had been laid earlier in a number of conferences beginning with Teheran in late 1943, where Roosevelt and Churchill discussed a new western frontier for Poland. On December 15, 1944, in the House of Commons the British prime minister approved the westward expansion of Poland at the expense of German territories, and the elimination of Germans from these territories. At Yalta in February 1945, Stalin, Churchill and Roosevelt ratified the earlier decision, although postponing the final settlement of Poland's western frontier (Federal Republic of Germany 1953, 109).

During this same month, the Poles began to take over German property. In May 1945, Czech premier Beneš confiscated goods and farms in the Sudetenland. In the summer of that year, the U.N. Charter noted that German expellees were denied international aid which was available to millions of homeless from other nations. In the fall 1945, expulsion from Poland, Czechoslovakia, and Hungary began in earnest, with transport on foot, by trains, and other means, and lasting for several years thereafter. With the aid of the British and American military governments in the Western Zones, German administrative bodies in the *Länder* (states) of the future Federal Republic implemented procedures and laws to handle the millions of homeless and helpless coming into their areas.

Whereas U.S. Secretary of State James Byrnes's major foreign-policy speech at Stuttgart in 1946 gave hope to a possible, eventual return of some of Germany's eastern areas, Stalin declared Poland's western frontier as final. By the end of 1948, the realities of the Cold War had brought considerable change in the outlook of the American and British governments toward the entire German question. Permission for the formation of organizations of expellees from the East was granted. When the Federal Republic came into being in 1949, these refugees were granted equal status with local West German citizens. The U.S. Congress that same year formed a committee on the subject of German refugees and a year later presented its findings to the House of Representatives. As a result, 54,744 Germans were admitted to the United States under special visas, their passage paid by the U.S. government (Federal Republic of Germany 1953, 111).

Before the issue of the expellees receded from the front pages of Germany's papers, Queen Juliana of the Netherlands pleaded with President Eisenhower to assist the millions who had been driven from their homes in the East (Federal Republic of Germany 1953, 112).

For years, visitors to Germany could see the *Sammellager* (collection camps), some truly wretched, in which so many waited for a new, and hopefully better, life. Aid, especially from America, lessened their suffering, as did numerous drives conducted by Allied military chaplains for toys and food for the youngsters in the camps. Here lies one of the reasons for the genuine pro-American sentiment found among people from Silesia, Pomerania, East Prussia, and the Sudetenland.

THE OFFICIAL RECORD

The magnitude of the refugee problem and challenge can best be comprehended by looking at the detailed tables published by the West German Statistical Office in 1968. Table 16 reflects the extent of this almost inconceivable human tragedy on the basis of the size of German populations as of 1939 in areas affected by the expulsions. Table 17 shows the second dimension of the expellee dilemma.

THE HUMAN SUFFERING

Informative as these statistics are, they can only convey the trauma in part. A look at one major group of victims of the expulsion, the Germans in Czechoslovakia, translates the dimension of the tragedy into personal terms.

Since Caesar's time, the area called the Sudetenland had been under Germanic influence. When the Sudeten Germans passed under the Czech flag after World War I, they constituted the second largest ethnic group in the new country called Czechoslovakia. Already in those days, at a rally in Prague, fifty-four Germans were killed and 107 wounded (App 1979, 5). The Sudeten Germans identified themselves less with the Czechs than with Germany. That is why the *Wehrmacht* was welcomed enthusiastically when it entered the Sudetenland in 1938. Even A.J.P. Taylor suggested that its return to German control was proper, since the 8,719 square miles with almost 3 million people had been previously linked to German sovereignty for several centuries (Taylor 1962, 213). During the war, Czechs worked for Germany but, as mentioned earlier, were not conscripted into the military.

It is noteworthy in this regard that Churchill, as prime minister, felt that German casualties would be sufficient to make room for other Germans to be expelled to what would remain of Germany. Later, when out of office, he called the expulsion "a tragedy on a prodigious scale" (App 1979, 31).

Table 16
Expulsion and Assimilation—German Population in the Territories of Eastern Germany and Eastern and Southeastern Europe Affected by Expulsion in 1939 (in millions)

Territory	Reichs-and Volksdeutsche
East German Territories under	
Foreign Administration	
Silesia	4,6
AD Breslau (2,0)	
AD Liegnitz (1,1)	
AD Oppeln (1,5)	
Brandenburg	0,6
Pomerania	1,9
AD Stettin (0,7)	
AD Köslin (0,7)	
AD Grenzmark, Posen-West Prussia (0,5)	
East Prussia	2,5
AD Königsberg (1,1)	
AD Gumbinnen (0,6)	
AD Allenstein (0,6)	
AD West Prussia (0,3)	
Total:	9,6
Eastern and South-Eastern Europe	
Danzig	0,4
Baltic States	0,3
Poland	1,0
Posen-Pommerellen (0,3)	
East Upper Silesia (0,2)	
Central and East Poland (0,5)	
Czechoslovakia	3,5
Bohemia (2,2)	
Austrian Silesia/Moravia (1,1)	
Slovakia and Carpathian Ukraine (0,2)	

Table 16 (*continued*)

Hungary		0,6
Yugoslavia		0,7
Romania		0,8
	Total:	7,3
Expulsion Territories Grand Total:		16,9

(FRG 1953, 3)

While still in England, General Sergej Ingr, commander of the Czech-Slovak forces abroad, reportedly stated:

When our day comes, the whole nation will apply the old Hussite battle cry: "Beat them, kill them, leave none alive!" Every one should look around now for appropriate weapons to harm the Germans most. If there is no firearm at hand, any other kind of weapon that cuts or stabs or hits should be prepared and hidden. (App 1979, 33)

Clearly, the elimination of the Sudeten Germans from within the national boundaries of postwar Czechoslovakia was planned in advance. When it broke upon them, the populations of whole villages were forced to assemble on a minute's notice and were moved to concentration camps or driven on foot to the borders of Austria or of East or West Germany. They had to live on 750 calories per day (App 1979, p. 36).

This type of persecution did not escape the notice of U.S. envoy Robert Murphy, who cabled the State Department on October 13, 1945, pointing to the suffering of the Sudeten Germans. Likewise, the U.S. Senate got involved when the plight of Dr. Herbert Stahl (an American citizen but ethnic German, whose farm had been confiscated) became known to Senator Hruska (U.S. Congressional Record 1976, 4758–4759). Senator Langer of North Dakota earlier had pled for immigration quotas to help Sudeten Germans enter the United States.

The final act of this episode was the Czech government's decree of May 8, 1946, which declared any crimes committed by Czechs and Slovaks against Germans and Magyars between September 1938 and October 28, 1945, as not eligible for prosecution (App 1979, 44).

In the United States, the reality of the tragedy is shown by a comparison of two editions of an American publication, *Webster's Geographical Dictionary*. The 1969 edition lists the area and German population of the Sudetenland, giving the geographic features with their German names, and the population at war's

Table 17
Expellees by Territories of Origin and Assimilation on October 29, 1946, and on September 13, 1950 (in thousands)

Territory of Origin (Territory of domicile on 1.9.1939)	Expellees					
	on 29 October 1946		in the Soviet Occ. Zone	in the 4 Zones and Berlin together	on 13 Sept. 1950	
	in the Federal Republic	in Berlin			in the Federal Republic	in West Berlin
East German Territories under Foreign Administration						
Silesia	1,623	27	1,049	2,699	2,053	37
Brandenburg	78	16	230	323	131	22
Pomerania	658	24	504	1,186	891	32
East Prussia	922	25	491	1,438	1,347	28
TOTAL	3,281	92	2,273 [2,274]	5,646	4,423 [4,422]	118 [119]

Table 17 (continued)

Saar Territory	39	0	5	45	47	0
Foreign Countries						
Danzig	141	5	72	218	225	5
Soviet Union	124	3	57	184	158	3
Poland	283	9	246	538	410	10
Czechoslovakia	1,559	4	841	2,404	1,912	6
Hungary	138	0	4	142	178	0
Yugoslavia	98	1	24	123	147	0
Romania	108	1	57	166	149	1
Austria	85	1	11	97	111	2
Other Foreign Countries	109	4	15	128	117	3
TOTAL	2,642[2,645]	28	1,327	3,997[4,000]	3,407	30
GRAND TOTAL	5,963[5,965]	120	3,605[3,606]	9,688[9,691]	7,876[7,876]	148

Note: Figures in brackets are author's corrections to obvious addition errors in the original tables.

(FRG, 1953, p. 3)

139

end as 2,945,261, living on over 8,000 square miles (*Webster's Geographical Dictionary* 1969, 1090). The 1972 edition omits all reference to German terms of the Sudetenland and, more disturbingly, gives no trace of the nearly 3 million people cited just three years before (*Webster's Geographical Dictionary* 1972, 1157).

What happened to them? Some 1,183,000 reached the former U.S. Zone, 750,000 entered East Germany, and 400,000 were initially unaccounted for, but 241,000 are now listed as having been killed during the expulsion or as having died from deprivations caused by the forced exodus.

Although the above account focuses on only one segment of the expellees, the experiences of those driven from Poland, East Prussia, and Hungary were similar. Most of the 14 million Germans who were evicted from their homes have accepted their fate. They are aging, and according to a recent survey conducted by the University of Tübingen, their children no longer identify with the homeland of their parents. Even of the latter at least initially, some did not feel as accepted in their new home as statistics would have one believe. The term *Rucksack Germans*, coined in the early stages of the assimiliation process, had a derogatory connotation that was not easy to forget. Yet, undoubtedly, the story of the settling of the refugees in their new homes, including the considerable financial support furnished by West German agencies, is a success story. But even this positive fact cannot erase the memories of the lands of the eastern provinces. Only time will tell whether the German names of Breslau, Stettin, and Königsberg will reappear on the map of Europe. In view of the realities of the postwar world, West Germany's president, Walter Scheel, felt that "any such hopes had become illusions" (Federal Republic of Germany 1980, 160).

Thus, the loss of East Prussia, West Prussia, Pomerania, Silesia, and also the Sudetenland was accepted by the social-democratic government of West Germany in the 1970s (Federal Republic of Germany 1971, 8). Chancellor Willy Brandt himself traveled to Poland and Prague and signed the respective treaties. In the treaties, both signatories agreed to look at the past suffering with regret but no longer in a spirit of accusation (Federal Republic of Germany 1974b, 15, 42–47). The right for citizens wishing to seek new residences in either country was guaranteed. However, in spite of the conciliatory language of the protocols, the older refugees knew that the signing of the treaties spelled the death knell to any dreams they might have had, for over three decades, to return to their former homelands. The Christian Democratic Union/Christian Social Union (CDU/CSU) Parliamentary party issued a statement on the topic in which it cautioned against premature commitments involving a final settlement (Federal Republic of Germany 1971, 139). But it did not block the ratification of the treaties in the *Bundestag* (parliament). Thus it is virtually certain that any chance for regaining the eastern provinces by negotiations has been forfeited. Nevertheless, the issue of the lost provinces has not yet been laid to rest. During 1985, many people in West Germany commemorated the events surrounding the end of World War II, forty years ago. As with other functions in this regard, meetings of expellee groups were attended by high-ranking officials of the federal government, including Chancellor Helmut Kohl. It was evident from their speeches that these leaders took great pains to convey the West German government's unchanged empathy for the refugees, while at the same time avoiding any indication that the government envisioned a restitution of the lost territories in the near future. Communist commentaries in this regard, especially those from Moscow, have expressed concern that a spirit of revanchism, possibly originating with some militant expellees, might be creeping back into West German politics. This has been emphatically denied by Bonn. It is clear, however, that even four decades after the expulsions, the matter continues to be a sensitive issue between all parties concerned.

Not only the loss of the East which, if applied to North America, would amount to the separation of the entire eastern seaboard from the continental United States, but the division of rump Germany was a direct result of the war and has caused many painful wounds among the German people. Along the borders between West and East Germany, and the Berlin Wall, scores of Germans have bled to death after being shot or lacerated by mines and automatic devices. The scars of the division run deep and have added to the great sum of physical and psychological suffering incurred by Germany. The country's plight is nowhere as starkly visible as in the former capital of all Germany—where a monument sculptured by an artist in the West shows two kneeling figures reaching out for each other, but unable to touch—the story of the two Germanys since World War II.

13

THE TRIALS

Conditions in postwar Germany were marked by several issues that reached into the rebuilding process like the fingers from an eerie past. One of the most emotional of these was the arrest, arraignment, prosecution, and conviction of persons charged by the Allies with having committed crimes against humanity and the rules of war (U.S. Office of the Chief Counsel for Prosecution of Axis Criminality 1947, iii, 189–190). Considering the terrible losses suffered by the Allies, especially the USSR, in stopping Hitler, and the monstrous dimensions of certain Nazi policies, it came as no surprise that the victors would bring the Nazi leadership to trial.

JUDGMENT AT NUREMBERG

The most famous of the indictments, of course, brought the surviving leaders of the Third Reich to Nuremberg where, in 1946, U.S. Chief Prosecutor Robert H. Jackson led the other victorious countries in charging twelve men, as well as several organizations of the defunct Third Reich, with war crimes. Each day, over the Allied-controlled radio, the German people were informed of the latest charges against their former leaders. Certainly not all felt or could bring themselves to believe that these men were, in every instance, guilty as charged. Some even doubted that the Allies had the right to prosecute just them since, in the German public's mind, the victors had been guilty themselves of at least some war crimes.

One British historian, upon being granted access to the private files and papers of Justice Jackson, has discussed formerly secret information surrounding the trial. Jackson's personal commitment to his assignment, though never faltering, was put under severe stress before he left the United States, when he found that his government had agreed to allow the deportation of millions of Germans as forced laborers as part of the reparations plan. Most of the members of national socialist organizations, even in the "fellow traveler" category, were declared eligible for this fate, and a great number of Germans were, in fact, as already noted, moved to Russia for that purpose. Jackson feared that the entire matter would "compromise the moral position of the United States, which America had espoused and maintained during the entire war" (Irving 1983, 18).

Some people in Washington among them Senator Fulbright, had expressed the opinion that the Allies should simply classify the guilty and execute all those in the top category without the bother of a trial. Even the British, at the time, in spite of their usual adherence to due process, were discussing the liquidation of top German leaders without trial. But Jackson, though willing to strip the accused of the protection normally accorded POWs, wanted to adhere to America's legal philosophy of innocence until guilt was proven. The Soviet and French judges found this not only foreign, but strangely amusing.

The first charge made was that of aggressive war, waged by Germany, after the Soviet delegate demanded its exclusive connection with Germany. Otherwise, Russia's actions in Poland and Finland could have been used by the defense to weaken the prosecution's case (Irving 1983, 30).

Some of the guidelines by which the Nazi leadership was judged also brought uneasiness. Among them was the position to try men for crimes that were not part of the legal code when the actions were committed, the famous *nullum crimen lege* issue, and also the denial of "obedience to orders" as a defense. Third, no Allied atrocities were allowed to be used by the defendants to mitigate their own actions since, according to Lord Lawrence, British president of the court, the tribunal did not consider violations of human or international law or war crimes by other nations (Irving 1983, 34). Furthermore, a foggy impression of who would be charged prevailed until shortly before the opening date of the trials. Finally, 129 additional German officers were included in a subsequent indictment for the sole reason that they held high rank during the war. Top industrialists had been added to the list of accused as well, when it was made public on September 1, 1945.

Once the trial began, Jackson confided in his private notes, it became embarrassingly clear, though to a lesser degree, that the Allies themselves had committed some deeds for which the Germans now stood to lose their lives. For instance, some of Germany's enemies had killed masses of civilians in air raids, had occupied neutral countries, had mistreated POWs, and in the case of the Soviets under Stalin, had invaded Poland in 1939 and killed thousands of her officers at Katyn (Irving 1983, 51).

What finally came out as the indictment was understandably emotionally charged and contained numerous anti-German clauses, some of which today are considered void of historic authenticity (i.e., the attempt to blame the Germans for the murder of the Polish Officer Corps).

The charge against the employment of slave laborers was also embarrassing.

After all, the Soviets already had deported many Germans to Russia and were holding an estimated 2.5 million POWs under slave labor conditions. German soldiers in French control were likewise severely mistreated. The Allies themselves passed a law in February 1946 by which German males between the ages of fourteen and sixty-five and women between fifteen and fifty could be called up as forced laborers. Those who refused could be denied ration cards (Irving 1983, 57). However, this plan was not implemented.

The indictment brought mixed reactions from the defendants. Robert Ley left the proceedings through suicide. International Red Cross visits to the accused were denied, as was delivery of Red Cross Christmas packages. The court procedures themselves favored the prosecution, making the defense dependent on such excerpts as were available from the prosecution. Witnesses for the defense were often detained, whereas the defense attorneys received many amenities from their opposite number.

During the trials, the prosecution opened with a four-hour speech by Jackson, whereas the defendants were not allowed to make even an explanatory statement prior to declaring themselves guilty or not guilty. The Office of Strategic Services (OSS) film was devastating in its portrayal of evil done under the Hitler regime and fully justified the prosecution and the world's press in their call for revenge. General Jodl confided after viewing the film that the charge of general knowledge, by the defendants, of the atrocities in the concentration camps was false, certainly in his case. The film was heavily edited; removed were all scenes of the jubilant civilian populations greeting German troops upon their entering the Rhineland, Austria, and the Sudetenland (Irving 1983, 70).

The case of Schacht became tinted with appeals for his acquittal by the world of banking, and military charges against Dönitz had to be dropped. He was, however, convicted of not resisting Hitler's orders to execute members of Allied commandos. Hitler had based his decision on the contents of a captured British commando manual, which suggested unconventional warfare methods. Later, when Deputy Soviet Foreign Minister Andrei Vyshinsky appeared in Nuremberg, the implications of the latter's toast to the accused mortified even the most anti-German members of the Tribunal.

At the conclusion of the trial, Jackson felt justified in his efforts at fairness. Of all the death sentences, the one against Colonel General Jodl had been most contended and, in fact, in 1953 the general was posthumously cleared of the conviction by a German court. All those sentenced to die requested the firing squad. This was denied so that the rope, affixed by Master Sergeant John C. Woods of the U.S. Army's Third Execution Team, could do its work. It did so on October 16, 1946, but not before Göring had taken poison. The ashes of the executed were scattered into the Isar River.

They followed into death the Third Reich, which had gone fourteen months earlier. By this time, there were no werewolves, and no secret group of men to carry out a jailbreak of their former leaders. Nazi Germany had died. The German people were beaten—physically, spiritually, and morally. Other Nuremberg trials against organs and functionaries of the Third Reich continued until 1950 (Orthbandt 1968, 596).

When Admiral Dönitz was released from Spandau Prison after having served his ten-year sentence, American opinion about the Nuremberg trials had the benefit of hindsight and a decade of mutually supportive relations with Germany. However, in 1985, some forty years after the end of the war, Rudolf Hess, one of Hitler's early lieutenants, was still being held in Berlin's Spandau Prison by the wartime Allies.

Not all American officials at the time felt that the trials were proper in all respects. Senator Robert A. Taft was one politician who voiced his dissatisfaction (Kennedy 1956, 238). Although Senator Taft's sentiments have been echoed by some historians who now agree that the Nuremberg trials were only an imperfect attempt at meting out justice to those who had caused unprecedented suffering, it cannot be denied that the proceedings represented a positive step away from the summary execution of defeated leaders. Though unwelcome at first, the revelations of criminal misdeeds by Third Reich leaders gradually found acceptance among the German public and gave the subsequent denazification and reeducation efforts of the Allies a substantial chance at success.

THE MALMEDY TRIAL

One of the most controversial postwar trials resulted from events that surrounded the advance of the Sixth Panzer Army during Hitler's Ardennes offensive on the western front. On December 16, 1944, Colonel Jochen Peiper's armored battle group from the SS Division *Leibstandarte Adolf Hitler* (Hitler's Personal Guard Divison) was spearheading the drive for the Channel coast. During the initial assault, several American units were caught by surprise and suffered heavy casualties. At Malmedy, near Stavelot, the Panzers ran upon a U.S. mobile observation unit. Shelled by German tanks, the Americans jumped from their vehicles, their trucks running into each other or into the trees along the road. In the ensuing melee, according to a German source, some GIs returned fire; some tried to reach the nearby woods; others surrendered and were sent to the rear while Peiper's group pushed on.

The next Germans to meet the Americans, who in the meantime had been rallied by an officer, saw them as enemies and opened fire on them. Once the Panzers had closed in, the Americans surrendered. After that, a shot was fired by the German side, and the U.S. troops hit the ground. Another shot sent them scurrying. According to conflicting reports, depending on which side gives the account, a machine gun now opened fire to stop their escape. Within twelve minutes, sixty-seven Americans lay dead. Four others faked death and later escaped. From them the story of the Malmedy massacre came to the attention of the U.S. command. The German senior commander heard the news of the incident first from an Allied radio broadcast (Ziemssen 1981, 16).

This account is contradicted in its crucial points by several Allied authors who, from the trial transcripts, have identified the *SS* man who (allegedly under orders) opened fire on the American POWs. He was followed by other *SS* grenadiers using machine guns on the captured Americans, in an obvious effort to kill them all (Gallagher 1964, 110–113). This description agrees with the recollection of an American survivor, who felt that the GIs were doomed, apparently by the order given to the *SS* field commanders to suspend the rules of land warfare, normally adhered to in the fighting against Western allies, during the Ardennes offensive (Gallagher 1964, 117).

One thing is clear. Some of the members of Colonel Peiper's "blow-torcher" unit were in a foul mood. Not only were American POWs shot at Malmedy-Bagnez, but apparently also at Hoonsfeld, Bullingen, Stoumont, and other towns—a total of 308 soldiers, plus 111 Belgian civilians (Gallagher 1964, 109). Colonel Peiper was not present during the time the actual atrocities were being committed. He and his staff heard the news of the massacre over Radio Calais, the BBC propaganda station masquerading as a bona fide German field station. Being in overall command and realizing what this news portended, he accepted responsibility for his soldiers, one of whom had had seventeen members of his family circle killed by American bombardment earlier (Gallagher 1964, 107).

It was in the wake of the Malmedy incident at Chegnogne that on New Year's Day 1945 some sixty German POWs were shot in cold blood by their American guards. The guilty went unpunished. It was felt that the basis for their action was orders that no prisoners were to be taken (Gallagher 1964, 98).

The Malmedy incident was one of those terrible occurrences in which soldiers are killed after surrendering. An American survivor, James Mattera, one of the four mentioned earlier, stated that the *SS* troops apparently acted under orders to liquidate the prisoners (Mattera 1981, 32–39). No such specific order was officially given as far as the German commanders were concerned; however, it has been admitted that the taking of prisoners was not to impede the progress of Hitler's last gamble.

In the summer 1945, U.S. authorities rounded up over 1,000 former members of the First *SS* Panzer Division for a full investigation. Seventy-four of that number were indicted for murder, and a month later they were deprived of the protection afforded other POWs. They were treated as war criminals from then on. Following months of interrogations, they were brought to trial at the former concentration camp at Dachau.

During the preceding interrogations they had been subjected to threats, promises, mock trials, physical mistreatment, and trickery. From the beginning, Peiper was told that his life was forfeited and that he was America's number one enemy. He agreed to accept complete responsibility for the incident if his men would be freed. His interrogator, however, reportedly stated that even if Peiper committed suicide, his men would still be prosecuted (Ziemssen 1981, 21).

Colonel W. M. Everett, U.S. chief defense counsel, discovered that some confessions had been obtained under conditions that violated American law principles.

On July 17, 1946, the seventy-three accused were sentenced as follows:

Death	43
Life imprisonment	22
Imprisonment of 10–20 years	8

(*One prisoner escaped to East Germany where he died.

Nearly two years later, after appeals by both Colonel Everett and German counsels, General Lucius Clay, U.S. military governor of the American Zone, decided that of the forty-three death sentences, twelve would stand, four would be set aside, and twenty-seven would be reduced. Similar adjustments were made in the case of those sentenced to prison terms.

In May 1948, General Clay ordered the twelve death sentences to be executed. Army Secretary Stimson issued a stay of execution, and in September an American review judge, Mr. Simpson, recommended all death sentences be commuted. By now the Malmedy trial had become a thorn in the side of many. Clouded by improprieties, the issue was overshadowed by political polarization within the government. Although General Clay reaffirmed the death penalty for six defendants, General Handy in 1951 commuted all capital punishment. By now, some of the prisoners had been on death row for five years. By now, also, there was a new Germany. The Korean war was in full fury, and America's former enemy in Europe had become her most important ally there. Still the Malmedy case was not closed until April 1, 1952. On that date, the imprisonment sentences were finalized as follows:

Life	13
25 years	6
20 years	12
18 years	1
15 years	7
12 years	2
10 years	1

Thirty prisoners had been released, some for good behavior (Ziemssen 1981, 9).

The Malmedy trial is mentioned not to whitewash any German guilt for the killings, but to illustrate that the German side did not escape being called to account for its misdeeds. Colonel Peiper, after years in prison, was killed by assassins in 1979 in France, where he had been living under an assumed name after his release (Quarrie 1983, 106).

In connection with prisoners' losing their lives after capture or during escape attempts, it is worth noting that during General Patton's advance in Sicily in 1943, a U.S. army sergeant in charge of a group of German POWs near Butero

Airfield had them lined up by the side of the road and personally shot them with his submachine gun. The sergeant was tried and "Old Blood and Guts" had to explain to investigators from Washington that his rather forceful speech to his troops concerning the "Huns," prior to the campaign, did not go so far as to encourage the shooting of prisoners (Blumenson 1974, 431). This author's review of the speech confirms this assessment.

Nevertheless, Edward C. Williamson, a young officer in the Eighth Division, felt that Patton's speech to the men at Enniskillen Manor in Northern Ireland, and later in Africa, came close to advocating killing prisoners. In any case, the sergeant who had shot the prisoners used the speech in his defense. In another incident, forty-three captured German soldiers, five of whom dressed in semimilitary attire, were all shot without a trial (Blumenson 1974, 432). Though these types of incidents were admittedly rare on the western front, they did constitute atrocities, and in these cases, the victims were German troops.

THE GALLOWS OF LANDSBERG

Whereas the *SS* men indicted for the Malmedy tragedy were allowed to live, several hundred Germans, military and civilian, were tried and hanged by the Americans. The location for the execution was Landsberg Prison, where Hitler was jailed after his abortive coup against the Bavarian government in the early 1920s.

Landsberg had become U.S. war crimes prison number one. The condemned men had a sign hung in front of their doors reading "Death." Some waited up to thirty-three months for the hangman, who at first was a Bavarian. Later, he was replaced by an American, Sergeant Britt, whom the former had trained for the job. The next-of-kin of those to be executed were notified and allowed a one-hour visit to extend their support, comfort, and good-byes. The next morning, to the pealing of the little prison church bell, the death row candidates, dressed in their red jackets, would be allowed exactly ninety seconds to make their last statements. Virtually all maintained that they had acted under orders, just as the hangman was now obeying his orders in putting the rope around their necks.

By the summer 1948, a total of 152 had been executed. Later, conditions in the prison improved and after appeals and reviews, 203 of the remaining "red jackets" could change their coats to another color, their lives having been spared (Kiegeland 1979, 515). After Lucius Clay's return to the United States following his self-initiated retirement, and the arrival of John McCloy, U.S. high commissioner for Germany, the final seven at Landsberg died on June 7, 1951, six years after cessation of hostilities.

Altogether, in addition to the Malmedy proceedings, Americans presided over twelve major trials, not counting the famous Nuremberg war crimes trial. Accused were German doctors, lawyers, Field Marshal Milch of the *Luftwaffe*, the I. G. Farben chemical conglomerate, the Krupp concern, the entire staff of the

Wehrmacht's High Command, the infamous *Einsatzgruppen*, and those charged with crimes in relation to the administration of the concentration camps. In the latter trial alone, 426 death sentences were handed down, 199 received life sentences, and 791 got prison terms of various lengths (Kiegeland 1979, 515).

General Clay himself gave some indication as to the weight of the responsibility for confirming death sentences, including those resulting from the Malmedy trial. Out of 1,090 convictions on which he had to rule, 426 called for the death penalty. Of the latter, he eventually commuted 127, letting stand 299 executions, for which he took final responsibility as highest reviewing officer (Clay 1950, 252–255).

The British tried numerous Germans in their custody, sentencing 110 to death (Kiegeland 1979, 515). French courts had sentenced 2,853 persons to death, of whom 767 were executed. Over 8,000 Germans and their collaborators had been killed earlier by the French resistance.

These statistics, of course, do not include those cases prosecuted by German courts of the Federal Republic, a process that is still going on forty years after the war. In recent years, the statute of limitations was to make an end to these proceedings, but the timely showing of the "Holocaust" production on West German television caused the *Bundestag* to further exempt crimes committed during the Hitler years from any provisions of the statute. The West German government still employs a staff of thirty-five persons, among them public prosecutors, to collect, evaluate, and refer any cases that can be tried. The office files contain over 1 million entries. As of December 1983, 129 cases were still pending. One of these, involving the infamous Dr. Josef Mengele, may soon be closed as his remains were identifed in Embu, Brazil, in June 1985.

The 6,465 sentences handed down by West German courts involved 89,000 people. Of course, as the successor to a very harsh regime, the Federal Republic has no legal provision to impose the death penalty. Some of the accused have died in the meantime; others are too sick to be put in the dock. But the continuation of the task force can be seen as a very real effort by the present government to come to grips with Germany's painful past. The disavowal of the death penalty for past or present crimes has become an issue in recent years as German citizens and even U.S. servicemen have become victims of cold-blooded murder by sophisticated terrorists. Even if it were instituted, however, it appears virtually certain that remaining cases against Nazi criminals would not result in capital punishment.

14

SUMMARY AND FINAL THOUGHT

From the foregoing accounts, it is clear that no segment of the German people escaped the effects of the war. No doubt, members of the military services bore the brunt of the losses—in dead and wounded, and in suffering and death while prisoners of war. But the civilian population likewise sustained astonishing losses—from the air war, while feeling the onslaught of battle on land and on sea, and, finally, as expellees under very inhumane conditions.

Toward the end of the war, teenagers were drafted into combat units, such as in the case of the Hitler Youth and the anti-aircraft helpers. Girls aided on the home front and served in other auxiliaries. Both of these groups suffered casualties. The old, pressed into service in the ill-fated *Volkssturm*, rarely survived any serious encounter with battle-hardened troops. Germany's women bore a special cross—as anxious mothers, sisters, or wives, later in widowhood, and finally in the often-fatal embrace of enemy soldiers. In addition, some of the country's greatest leaders, in uniform and out, fell victim to a regime that tolerated no dissidence.

Material losses were staggering. Nearly 100 of Germany's major cities, long a significant part of Europe's centuries-old culture, had sunk into ashes. Many irreplaceable art treasures were lost to the world. People had lost their lives, their loved ones, and their livelihoods. Hitler's boastful, prophetic statement at the onset of the war that he needed only ten years of time and one would not recognize Germany again, had found a terrible fulfillment. After six years of war, Germany indeed lay "in extremis."

In conclusion, it might be helpful to compare the quantitative losses of Germany with those of the other combatants. Such comparison is made somewhat difficult by the lack of precise differentiations, in the commonly available American and British casualty figures, between losses sustained in Afro-European combat operations and in the Pacific campaigns. In addition, there are the differences in the numbers given for men killed in action, missing, and wounded—a problem certainly not surprising considering the monumentous events that engulfed the world and its record keepers during the war years.

According to sources used in this study, American casualties of dead, wounded, and missing totalled 1,218,000—essentially all military personnel. British losses, including colonials, amounted to 610,900, plus 146,780 civilian casualties due to aerial bombing, for a total of about 757,000. The USSR has listed its military losses at 7.5 million with another 12.5 million in civilian dead, for a total of 20 million. German losses are given as approximately 8,156,000, to which another 600,000 civilians must be added for a total of nearly 9 million ("World War II" 1975, 530).

Total world casualties are estimated to be about 55 million. Thus Germany's quantitative share of losses amounts to 17 percent of the world's total, or 12 percent of the Reich's pre-war population. This should in no way suggest that the suffering or death of even one innocent human being, no matter from what country, can ever be accepted. Neither is it intended to deny that Hitler and his executives bear a large responsibility for a giant share of the losses cited above. The statistics listed here are intended to point out that Germany paid with the blood of millions of its citizens for the military actions and racial and political policies of its rulers during the years from 1939 to 1945.

It is hoped that the evidence presented throughout this book will assist readers in countries formerly at war with Germany to realize that its initial victories were not without significant costs, and that its catastrophic suffering in defeat might be considered as at least a partial atonement for the losses Germany inflicted upon others. That the sacrifice of his own life would be counted as such was Dr. Carl Goerdeler's last wish as he was led to the gallows after his involvement in the unsuccessful plot against Hitler.

The realization of Germany's casualties, both in lives and in the attendant emotional suffering, should permit a greater degree of objectivity in the popular and historic treatment of the German nation during and subsequent to the war years, when so many of the world's people counted themselves among its enemies. Only then can there be substance to the sincere hope of all people, expressed by the biblical prophet, that swords will be beaten into plowshares and that men will learn war no more.

BIBLIOGRAPHY

Allied Forces. 1944–1945. Supreme Headquarters, G–1. *Daily report of enemy prisoners of war, 12 June 44–18 May 45*. Carlisle Barracks, Pa.: U.S. Army War College.

Anders, Wladyslav. 1953. *Hitler's defeat in Russia*. Chicago: Henry Regnery Co.

Andersen, Ludwig. 1965. *Mein Heimatland* [My homeland]. Mainz: B. Schott's Söhne.

App, Austin J. 1979. *The Sudeten-German tragedy*. Takoma Park, Md.: Boniface Press.

Armstrong, John A. 1964. *Soviet partisans in World War II*. Madison: The University of Wisconsin Press.

Balabkins, Nicholas. 1971. *West German reparations in Israel*. New Brunswick, N.J.: Rutgers University Press.

Baldwin, James. 1966. *Battles Lost and won*. New York: Harper & Row, Publishers.

Balzer, Karl, and Erich Kern. 1980. *Alliierte Verbrechen an Deutschen*. Preussisch-Oldendorf: Verlag K. W. Schütz.

Barker, Ralph. 1965. *The Thousand Plan*. London: Chatto and Windus.

Bauer, Yehuda. 1982. *A history of the Holocaust*. New York: Franklin Watts.

Baumbach, Werner. 1972. *The life and death of the Luftwaffe*. Translated by Frederick Holt. New York: Ballantine Books.

Beck, Earl R. October 1982. The Allied bombing of Germany, 1943–1945, and the German response: Dilemmas of judgment. *German Studies Review* 5, no. 3: 325–337.

Bekker, Cajus. 1968. *The Luftwaffe war diaries*. London: MacDonald and Company.

———. 1974. *Hitler's naval war*. Garden City, N.Y.: Doubleday and Company.

———. 1983. *Angriffshöhe 4000: Ein Kriegstagebuch der deutschen Luftwaffe* [Attack altitude 4000: A war diary of the German air force]. Munich: Wilhelm Heyne Verlag.

Benton, Wilbourne E., and Georg Grimm. 1961. *Nuremberg: German views of the war trials*. Dallas, Tex.: Southern Methodist University Press.

Bergander, Götz. 1985. *Dresden im Luftkrieg: Vorgeschichte—Zerstörung—Folgen* [Dresden in the air war: Prior events—destruction—consequences]. Munich: Wilhelm Heyne Verlag.

Berthold, Will. 1981. *Getreu bis in den Tod: Sieg und Untergang der Bismarck* [Faithful unto death: Victory and sinking of the *Bismarck*]. Munich: Wilhelm Heyne Verlag.

Bird, Eugene K. 1974. *Prisoner 7 Rudolf Hess: The thirty years in jail of Hitler's Deputy Führer*. New York: The Viking Press.

Blumenson, Martin. 1961. *Breakout and pursuit*. Washington, D.C.: Office of the Chief of Military History, Dept. of the Army.

————. 1974. *The Patton papers: 1940–1945*. Boston: Houghton Mifflin Company.

Böddeker, Günther. 1985. *Der Untergang des Dritten Reiches* [The demise of the Third Reich]. Munich: Herbig Verlagsbuchhandlung.

Bracher, Karl Dieter. 1970. *The German dictatorship. The origins, structure, and effects of national socialism*. Translated by Jean Steinberg. New York: Praeger Publishers.

————. 1984. *Das Gewissen steht auf. Lebensbilder aus dem deutschen Widerstand 1933–1945* [The conscience rises. Portraits of the German resistance 1933–1945]. Mainz: V. Hase and Koehler.

Brittain, Vera. 1946. Massacre bombing—the aftermath. *Christian Century* 62, no. 2: 880–881.

Browning, Christopher R. 1978. *The final solution and the German Foreign Office*. New York: Holmes and Meier Publishers.

Butler, Rupert. 1979. *The Black Angels: A history of the Waffen-SS*. New York: St. Martin's Press.

Caidin, Martin. 1960. *The night Hamburg died*. New York: Ballantine Books.

————. 1974. *The Tigers are burning*. New York: Hawthorn Books.

Campbell, James. 1974. *The bombing of Nuremberg*. New York: Doubleday and Company.

Carrell, Paul. 1964. *Hitler moves East*. Translated by Ewald Osers. Boston: Little, Brown and Company.

Chamberlin, William H. 1963. *The German phoenix*. New York: Duell, Sloan and Pearce.

Chaney, Otto Preston, Jr. 1971. *Zhukov*. Norman: University of Oklahoma Press.

Clay, Lucius D. 1950. *Decision in Germany*. Garden City, N.Y.: Doubleday and Co.

Climo, J. 1959. A study of casualties and damage to personnel and equipment caused by some air and artillery bombardments in European operations. (Unclassified.) Carlisle Barracks, Pa.: U.S. Army War College.

Cole, Hugh M. 1950. *The Lorraine campaign*. Washington, D.C.: Historical Division, U.S. Army.

————. 1965. *The Ardennes: Battle of the Bulge*. Washington, D.C.: Historical Division, Dept. of the Army.

Collier, P. F., ed. 1946. *Photographic history of World War II*. New York: P. F. Collier and Son.

Collier, Richard. 1966. *Eagle Day: The Battle of Britain August 6–September 13, 1940*. New York: E. P. Dutton & Co.

Congdon, Don, ed. 1963. *Combat: The war with Germany*. New York: Dell Publishing Co.

Conquest, R. 1960. *The Soviet deportation of Nationalities*. London: Macmillan & Co.

Control Council, Allied Military Government. February 25, 1947. *Abolition of Prussia*. Law No. 46. Official Gazette of the Control Council for Germany.

Cooper, Matthew. 1978. *The German Army 1933–1945: Its political and military failure*. New York: Stein and Day Publishers.

————. 1979. *The Nazi war against Soviet partisans, 1941–1944*. New York: Stein and Day Publishers.

————. 1981. *The German Air Force 1933–1945*. New York: Jane's Publishing.

Craig, William. 1974. *Enemy at the gates: The battle for Stalingrad*. New York: Ballantine Books.

Craven, Wesley Frank, and James Lea Cate, eds. 1951. *The Army Air Forces in World War II*. U.S. Air Force Historical Division, U.S. Air Force. Chicago: The University of Chicago Press.

Curtis, Monica, ed. 1965. *Norway and the war: September 1939–December 1940*. Documents on International Affairs. London: Oxford University Press. Johnson Reprint Corporation, New York.

Dabel, Gerhard. 1981. *KLV: Die erweiterte Kinder-Land-Verschickung* [KLV: The extended relocation of children into the countryside]. Freiburg, FRG: Verlag Karl Schillinger.

Dallin, Alexander. 1981. *German rule in Russia 1941–1945*. Boulder, Colo.: Westview Press.

Degrelle, Leon. Winter 1982. The Waffen-SS. *The Journal of Historical Review* 3; 441–468.

Demeter, Karl. 1965. *The German Officer-Corps in society and state*. Translated by Angus Malcolm. New York: Frederick A. Praeger, Publishers.

Der Spiegel. July 11, 1983. vol. 28, no. 32.

Der Spiegel. March 26, 1984. vol. 38, no. 13.

Deschner, Günther. 1968. *Der Zweite Weltkrieg* [The Second World War]. Gütersloh: Bertelsmann Lexicon Verlag.

Detwiler, Donald S., ed. 1979a. *Department of the Army Pamphlet No. 20–230* (1950). Historical study: Russian combat methods in World War II. Reproduced in *World War II German Military Studies*. 18, pt. 7. New York: Garland Publishing.

————. 1979b. *German Military Histiography Before 1945*. Maj. Percy E. Schramm, Notes on the Execution of War Diaries in the German Armed Forces. Reproduced in *World War II German Military Studies* 1, pt. 1. New York: Garland Publishing.

————. 1979c. *Oberkommando der Wehrmacht war diary* [German High Command war diary]. Compiled by Major Prof. Percy Schramm, Wehrmacht Historian Office. New York: Garland Publishing, 1, pt. 1.

Deutschland heute [Germany today]. 1958. Wiesbaden: Presse und Informationsamt der Bundesregierung.

de Zayas, Alfred M. 1979. *Die Wehrmacht-Untersuchungstelle: Unveröffentliche Akten über alliierte Völkerrechts-Verletzungen im Zweiten Weltkrieg* [The Wehrmacht Investigations Office: Unpublished documents of Allied human rights violations during the Second World War].

————. 1980. *Die Anglo-Amerikaner und die Vertreibung der Deutschen: Vorgeschichte, Verlauf, Folgen* [The Anglo-Americans and the expulsion of the Germans: Prior history, execution and consequences]. Munich: Deutscher Taschenbuch Verlag.

Dieckmann, Volker. December 2, 1983. Nazi crimes—the hunt continues. *Nürnberger Nachrichten*, reprinted in *The German Tribune*, January 8, 1984, p. 14.

Die Oase. June 1983. Zeitschrift des ''Verbandes Deutsches Afrika Korps'' [Journal of the German Afrika Korps association] 33, no. 6.

Djilas, Milovan. 1977. *Wartime*. New York: Harcourt, Brace, Jovanovich.

Dobson, Christopher, John Miller, and Ronald Payne. 1979. *The cruelest night: The untold story of one of the greatest maritime tragedies of World War II*. Boston: Little, Brown and Company.

Dollinger, Hans. 1982. *The decline and fall of Nazi Germany and Imperial Japan. A pictoral history of the final days of World War II.* Translated by Arnold Pomerans. New York: Bonanza Books.

Ehrenburg, Ilya. 1945. *The Russian reply to Lady Gibb.* London: Soviet War News.

Engelmann, Bert. 1984. *Germany without Jews.* Translated by D. J. Beer. New York: Bantam Books.

Engelmann, Joachim. 1979. *Zitadelle 1943: Die grösste Panzerschlacht im Osten* [Citadel 1943: The greatest tank battle in the East]. Frieberg, FRG: Podzun-Pallas Verlag.

Epstein, Julius. 1973. *Operation Keelhaul: The story of forced repatriation from 1944 to the present.* Old Greenwich, Conn.: Devin-Adair Co.

Euler, Helmut. 1984. *Als Deutschlands Dämme brachen: Die Wahrheit über die Bombardierung der Möhne-Eder-Sorpe Staudämme 1943* [When Germany's dams broke: The truth about the bombardment of the Möhne-Eder-Sorpe dams 1943]. Stuttgart: Motorbuch Verlag.

Federal Republic of Germany. 1953. *Statistical pocket-book on expellees in the Federal Republic of Germany and West Berlin.* Wiesbaden: Federal Statistical Office.

———. 1956. *Wirtschaft und Statistik* [Economy and statistics] 8, no. 6. Bonn.

———. 1960. *Deutsche Kriegsverluste* [German war losses]. Statistisches Jahrbuch für die Bundesrepublik Deutschland 1960. Wiesbaden: Federal Statistical Office.

———. 1971. *The treaty between the Federal Republic of Germany and the People's Republic of Poland.* Wiesbaden: Press and Information Office of the Federal Government.

———. 1974a. *The basic law of the Federal Republic of Germany,* May 23, 1949, as amended to August 31, 1974. Bonn: Press and Information Office of the Government of the Federal Republic of Germany.

———. 1974b. *Treaty on mutual relations between the Federal Republic of Germany and the Czechoslovak Socialist Republic of 11 December 1973.* Bonn: Press and Information Office of the Government of the Federal Republic of Germany.

———. 1977. CDU/CSU Group in the German Bundestag. *White paper on the human rights situation in Germany and of the Germans in eastern Europe.* Bonn.

———. 1980. *A mandate for democracy. Three decades of the Federal Republic of Germany.* Bonn: Federal Press and Information Office.

Fehling, Helmut. 1951. *One great prison: Documents concerning German and Japanese war prisoners in the Soviet Union.* With a foreword by Konrad Adenauer and Josef Cardinal Frings. Boston: The Beacon Press.

Feist, Uwe. 1973. *Fallschirmjäger in action.* Carrollton, Tex.: Squadron/Signal Publications.

Fest, Joachim C. 1974. *Hitler.* New York: Harcourt, Brace, Jovanovich.

Flower, Desmond, and James Reeves, eds. 1960. *The taste of courage: The war, 1939–1945.* New York: Harper and Brothers, Publishers.

Förster, Gerhard, and Richard Lakowski. 1985. *1945 Das Jahr der entgültigen Niederlage der faschistischen Wehrmacht: Dokumente* [1945 The year of the final defeat of the fascist Wehrmacht: Documents]. Leipzig, GDR: Militärverlag der Deutschen Demokratischen Republik.

Foy, David A. 1984. *For you the war is over. American prisoners of war in Nazi Germany.* New York: Stein and Day Publishers.

Franken, Bert. 1978. *Der Grosse Treck: Das Kriegsende in Ostdeutschland* [The big trek: The end of the war in East Germany]. Bayreuth: Hestia Verlag GmbH.

Frederiksen, Oliver J. 1953. *The American military occupation of Germany 1945–1953*. Headquarters, U.S. Army, Europe: Historical Division.

Gaertner, Georg, with Arnold Krammer. 1985. *Hitler's last soldier in America*. New York: Stein and Day Publishers.

Gallagher, Richard. 1964. *The Malmedy Massacre*. New York: Paperback Library.

Galland, Adolf. 1969. *The first and the last*. Translated by Mervyn Savill. New York: Ballantine Books.

Gansberg, Judith M. 1977. *Stalag: USA*. New York: Thomas Y. Cromwell Co.

Gatzke, Hans W. 1980. *Germany and the United States. A "special" relationship?* Cambridge, Mass.: Harvard University Press.

Gebhardt, Bruno. 1965. *Handbuch der deutschen Geschichte: Die Zeit der Weltkriege* [Handbook of German history: The time of the world wars]. Stuttgart: Union Verlag.

General losses, World War II. 1961. Chicago: Encyclopedia Britannica.

German casualties—World War I. 1939. Chicago: Compton's Pictured Encyclopedia.

The German Tribune. January 8, 1984, p. 14.

Glaser, Hans Georg. February 26, 1984. The thorny path toward reconciliation between Germany and Poland. *The German Tribune reprint*.

Gollancz, Victor. 1947. *In darkest Germany*. Hinsdale, Ill.: Henry Regnery Company.

Goolrick, William K., and Ogden Tanner. 1979. *The Battle of the Bulge*. Chicago: Time-Life Books.

Graber, G. S. 1978. *The history of the SS*. New York: The David McKay Company.

Great events of the 20th century. 1977. Pleasantville, N.Y.: The Reader's Digest Association.

Grenfell, Russell. 1954. *Unconditional hatred: German war guilt and the future of Europe*. New York: The Devin-Adair Company.

Groehler, Olaf. 1981. *Geschichte des Luftkriegs 1910 bis 1980* [History of the airwar 1910 to 1980]. Berlin: Militärverlag der Deutschen Demokratischen Republik.

Gröner, Erich. 1976. *Die Schiffe der deutschen Kriegsmarine und Luftwaffe 1939–45 und ihr Verblieb* [Ships of the German navy and air force 1939–45 and their fate]. Munich: J. F. Lehmanns Verlag.

Guderian, Heinz. 1957. *Panzer leader*. Translated by Constantine Fitzgibbon. New York: Ballantine Books.

Haffke, Jürgen, and Bernhard Koll. 1983. *Sinzig und seine Stadtteile—gestern und heute* [Sinzig and its areas—yesterday and today]. Sinzig: Stadt Sinzig.

Harris, Air Marshal, Sir Arthur. 1976. Motion picture. BBC-TV and Time/Life Films. New York: Time/Life Multi Media.

Harrison, Gordon A. 1951. *Cross channel attack*. Washington, D.C.: Office of the Chief of Military History, Dept. of the Army.

Hart, B. H. Liddell. 1953. *The Rommel Papers*. New York: Harcourt, Brace and Co.

Haupt, Werner. 1970. *Als die Rote Armee nach Deutschland kam: Die Kämpfe in Ostpreussen Schlesien und Pommern* [When the Red Army entered Germany: The battles in East Prussia, Silesia and Pomerania]. Friedberg: Podzun-Pallas Verlag.

Hechler, Ken. 1978. *The bridge at Remagen*. New York: Ballantine Books, a division of Random House.

Historical Division. 1944–1945. *Fifth Panzer Army surgeon: (1944–45)*. Headquarters, U.S. Army Europe, Foreign Military Studies Branch, APO 403. Carlisle Barracks, Pa.: U.S. Army War College.

————. 1945–1952. Headquarters, U.S. Army Europe, MS# B–715 OCMH. Manuscripts prepared by former German officers. Carlisle Barracks, Pa.: U.S. Army War College.

Hoffman, Peter. 1979. *The history of the German resistance 1933–1945*. Translated by Richard Barry. Cambridge, Mass.: The MIT Press.

Höhne, Heinz. 1979. *Canaris: Hitler's master spy*. Translated by J. Maxwell Brownjohn. Garden City, N.Y.: Doubleday & Company.

Hopkins, J.A.H., comp. 1944. *Diary of world events*. Baltimore, Md.: National Advertising Company.

Irving, David. 1977. *Hitler's war*. New York: The Viking Press.

————. 1981. *Der Untergang Dresdens* [The destruction of Dresden]. Munich: Wilhelm Heyne Verlag.

————. 1983. *Der Nürnberger Prozess: Die letzte Schlacht* [The Nuremberg trial: The last Battle]. Munich: Wilhelm Heyne Verlag.

Jackson, W.G.F. 1975. *The Battle for North Africa 1940–43*. New York: Mason/Charter.

Kaps, Johannes, ed. 1952/53. *Die Tragödie Schlesiens 1945/46 in Dokumenten . . .* [The Silesian tragedy 1945–46 in documents . . .]. Munich: Verlag "Christ Unterwegs."

Kehr, Helen, and Janet Langmaid. 1982. *The Nazi era 1919–1945*. London: Mansell Publishing.

Kemnitzer, Hans-Georg. 1964. *Nitschewo: Über Dornen Sibiriens zur Freiheit* [Nitschewo: Through Siberia's thorns to freedom]. Vlotho/Weser, FRG: Verlag für Volkstum und Zeitgeschichtsforschung.

Kennedy, John F. 1956. *Profiles in courage*. New York: Harper and Row.

Kern, Erich. 1964. *Dokumente alliierter Grausamkeiten 1933–1949* [Documents of Allied atrocities 1933–1949]. Preussisch-Oldendorf: Verlag K.W. Schütz KG.

Kesaris, Paul L., ed. 1980. *ULTRA and the history of the United States Strategic Air Force in Europe vs. the German Air Force*, by the U.S. Army Air Force. Classified Studies in twentieth-century diplomatic and military history. Frederick, Md.: University Publications of America.

Kiegeland, B., ed. 1979. *Weltgeschichte seit 1945* [History of the world since 1945]. Hamburg: Verlag fur Geschichtliche Dokumentation.

Kieser, Egbert. 1984. *Danziger Bucht 1945: Dokumentation einer Katastrophe* [Danzig Bay 1945: Documentation of a catastrophe]. Munich: Wilhelm Heyne Verlag.

Kissel, Hans. 1962. *Der Deutsche Volkssturm 1944/45*. Frankfurt/Main: Verlag E. S. Mittler und Sohn.

Kolyshkin, I. 1985. *Russian submarines in Arctic waters*. Translated by David Svirsky. New York: Bantam Books.

Konev, I. 1984. *Year of victory*. Translated by David Mishne. Moscow: Progress Publishers.

Krammer, Arnold. 1979. *Nazi prisoners of war in America*. New York: Stein and Day Publishers.

Krausnick, Helmut. 1985. *Hitler's Einsatzgruppen: Die Truppen des Weltanschauungskrieges 1938–1942* [Hitler's special mission units: Troops of the ideological war 1938–1942]. Frankfurt am Main: Fischer Taschenbuch Verlag.

Kuby, Erich. 1968. *The Russians and Berlin*. Translated by Arnold J. Pomerans. New York: Hill and Wang.

Kühn, Volkmar. 1985. *Deutsche Fallschirmjäger im Zweiten Weltkrieg* [German paratroopers during the Second World War]. Stuttgart: Motorbuch Verlag.

Kurowski, Franz. 1981. *Der Luftkrieg Über Deutschland*. Munich: Wilhelm Heyne Verlag.

Lang, Daniel. 1979. *Germans remember: A backward look*. New York: McGraw-Hill Book Company.

Langsam, Walter Consuelo. 1958. *Historic documents of World War II*. Princeton: D. Van Norstrand Co.

Last letters from Stalingrad. 1962. Translated by Franz Schneider and Charles Gullans. Introduction by S.L.A. Marshall. New York: William Morrow and Company.

Lewin, Ronald. 1977. *The life and death of the Afrika Korps*. New York: New York Times Book Co.

————. 1978. *Ultra goes to war*. New York: McGraw-Hill Book Company.

Liddell Hart, B.H. 1971. *History of the Second World War*. New York: G. P. Putnam's Sons.

Longmate, Norman. 1983. *The Bombers. The RAF offensive against Germany, 1939–1945*. London: Hutchinson and Co., Publishers.

Lucas, James. 1979. *War on the Eastern Front 1941–1945*. Briarcliff Manor, N.Y.: Stein and Day Publishers.

————. 1980. *Alpine Elite: German mountain troops of World War II*. New York: Jane's Publishing.

Ludwig, Max. 1965. *Aus dem Tagebuch des Hans O. Dokumente und Berichte über die Deportation und den Untergang der Heidelberger Juden* [From the diary of Hans O. Documents and reports on the deportation and demise of the Heidelberg Jews]. Heidelberg: Verlag Lambert Schneider.

Ludwigshafen am Rhein. Undated. *Air raids on Ludwigshafen am Rhein, 1940–1945*. City archives, Ludwigshafen am Rhein, FRG.

Mabire, Jean. 1977. *Berlin im Todeskampf 1945* [Berlin's death struggle 1945]. Translated by Dr. Erich Kopp. Preussisch-Oldendorf: Verlag K. W. Schütz KG.

MacDonald, Charles B. 1963. *The Siegfried Line campaign*. Washington, D.C.: Office of the Chief of Military History, Dept. of the Army.

————. 1973. *The last offensive*. Washington, D.C.: Office of the Chief of Military History, Dept. of the Army.

MacIsaac, David. 1976. *Strategic bombing in World War Two: The story of the United States strategic bombing survey*. New York: Garland Publishing Company.

McKee, Alexander. 1971. *The race for the Rhine bridges 1940, 1944, 1945*. New York: Stein and Day Publishers.

————. 1984. *Dresden 1945: The Devil's tinderbox*. New York: E. P. Dutton.

Macksey, K. J. 1968. *Afrika Korps*. New York: Ballantine Books.

Mann, Fritz. Undated. *Frühling am Rhein anno 1945. Das Drama deutscher Kriegsgefangener im Lager Remagen-Sinzig* [Spring on the Rhine anno 1945. The drama of German prisoners of war in the Remagen-Sinzig camp]. Frankfurt am Main: Verlag Bornheimer Brücke.

Marienfeld, W. 1981. *Verschleppt: Frauen und Mädchen von Ostpreussen nach Sibirien verschleppt* [Deported: women and girls deported from East Prussia to Siberia]. Leer, FRG: Verlag Gerhard Rautenberg.

Marshall, George C., H. H. Arnold, and Ernest J. King. 1947. *The War Reports*. Philadelphia, Pa.: J. B. Lippincott Company.

Maschke, Erich. 1983. *Zur Geschichte der deutschen Kriegsgefangenen des Zweiten Weltkriegs* [On the history of German prisoners of war during the Second World War]. Bielefeld: Gieseking Verlag.

Matloff, Maurice, ed. 1980. *World War II*. New York: David McKay Company.

160   BIBLIOGRAPHY

Mattera, James P. December 1981. Murder at Malmedy. *Army*, pp. 32–39.

Mayer, S. L., ed. 1976. *Signal: Hitler's wartime picture magazine*. Englewood Cliffs, N.J.: Prentice-Hall.

Meinicke, Friedrich. 1950. *The German catastrophe*. Translated by Sidney B. Fay. Cambridge, Mass.: Harvard University Press.

Messenger, Charles. 1984. *"Bomber" Harris and the strategic bombing offensive, 1939–1945*. New York: St. Martin's Press.

Middlebrook, Martin. 1974. *The Nuremberg raid*. New York: William Morrow and Company.

————. 1980. *The battle of Hamburg: Allied bomber forces against a German city in 1943*. New York: Charles Scribner's Sons.

————. 1983. *The Schweinfurt-Regensburg mission: American raids on 17 August 1943*. New York: Charles Scribner's Sons.

Mitcham, Samuel W., Jr. 1985. *Hitler's legions. The German army order of battle, World War II*. Briarcliff Manor, N. Y.: Stein and Day Publishers.

Mollo, Andrew. 1980. Dachau. The Webling Incident. *After the battle* No. 27, Battle of Britain Prints. Stratford, London.

Morrison, Wilbur H. 1982. *Fortress without a roof: The Allied bombing of the Third Reich*. New York: St. Martin's Press.

Moulton, J. L. 1966. *The Norwegian campaign of 1940*. London: Eyre and Spottiswoode.

Nawratil, Heinz. 1982. *Vertreibungs-Verbrechen an Deutschen* [Expulsion crimes against Germans]. Munich: Universitas Verlag.

Nichts vergessen. July 4, 1983. *Der Spiegel* 37, no. 27: 90–91.

Nicolaisen, Hans-Dietrich. 1985. *Die Flakhelfer: Luftwaffenhelfer und Marinehelfer im Zweiten Weltkrieg* [The anti-aircraft auxiliaries: Air Force and Navy auxiliaries during the Second World War]. Frankfurt/Main: Verlag Ullstein GmbH.

Noakes, Jeremy, and Geoffrey Priddham, eds. 1974. *Documents on Nazism, 1919–1945*. New York: The Viking Press.

Oelsner, Siegfried. 1981. *Sibirische Odyssee* [Siberian Odyssey]. Preussisch Oldendorf: Verlag K. W. Schütz KG.

Orthbandt, Eberhard. 1968. *Illustrierte Deutsche Geschichte* [Illustrated German history]. Munich: Südwest Verlag.

Parnell, Wilma. 1981. *The killing of Corporal Kunze*. Secaucus, N.J.: Lyle Stuart, Inc.

Paul, David W. 1983. *Czechoslovakia: Profile of a Socialist Republic at the crossroads of Europe*. Boulder, Colo.: Westview Press.

Paul, Wolfgang. 1981. *Der Heimat Krieg 1939–1945* [The war on the home front 1939–1945]. Munich: Wilhelm Heyne Verlag.

Peillard, Leonce. 1978. *Affäre Laconia*. Translated by Hans W. Braunert. Bergisch Gladbach, FRG: Gustav Lübbe Verlag.

————. 1983. *Geschichte des U-Boot Krieges 1939–1945* [History of the U-Boat war 1939–1945]. Munich: Wilhelm Heyne Verlag.

Phillips, Peter. 1969. *The tragedy of Nazi Germany*. New York: Praeger Publishers.

Pogue, Forrest C. 1973. *George C. Marshall: Organizer of victory*. New York: The Viking Press.

Polevoi, Boris, Konstantin Simonov, and Michael Trachmann. 1974. *Liberation*. Moscow: Progress Publishers.

Political Affairs Review. June 12, 1983. *The German Tribune*. New York.

Powers, Thomas. November 1984. Nuclear winter and nuclear strategy. *The Atlantic* 256, no. 5: 53.

Prcela, John, and Guldescu Stanko. 1970. *Operation Slaughterhouse: Eyewitness accounts of postwar massacres in Yugoslavia.* Philadelphia, Pa.: Dorrance and Co.

Price, Alfred. 1979. *Battle of Britain: The Hardest Day 18 August 1940.* New York: Charles Scribner's Sons.

Prittie, Terence. 1965. *Deutsche gegen Hitler* [Germans against Hitler]. Tübingen, FRG: Rainer Wunderlich Verlag.

————. 1974. *Willy Brandt: Portrait of a statesman.* New York: Schocken Books.

Prokhorov, A.M. 1980. The Great Patriotic War. *Great Soviet Encyclopedia*, vol. 4. New York: Macmillan Educational Company.

Quarrie, Bruce. 1983. *Hitler's samurai in action.* New York: Arco Publishing.

Reichsregierung. 1939. *Das Auswärtige Amt. Urkunden zur letzten Phase der deutsch-polnischen Krise* [Foreign Office. Documents of the last phase of the German-Polish crisis]. Berlin: Reichsdruckerei.

Rogers, Thomas F. February 6, 1984. Huebener against the Reich. *The Utah Statesman.* Logan, Utah.

Römer, Karl, ed. 1979. *Facts about Germany.* Gütersloh: Bertelsmann Lexicon-Verlag.

Ropp, Theodore. 1979. World War II. *World Book and Childcraft International*, vol. 21. Chicago: World Book Enclyclopedia.

Roskill, S. W. 1961. *The war at sea: 1939–1945.* London: Her Majesty's Stationery Office.

Ryan, Cornelius. 1959. *The longest day: June 6, 1944.* New York: Popular Library.

————. 1967. *The last battle.* New York: Pocket Books, Simon and Schuster.

Sag mir, wo die Gräber sind [Tell me where the graves are]. February 1983. *Kriegsgräberfürsorge—Stimme und Weg* [Care of wargraves—voice and path]. Kassel. Volksbund Deutsche Kriegsgräberfürsorge.

Scheiberg, Horst. 1979. *Bis Stalingrad 48 Kilometer* [Until Stalingrad 48 kilometers]. Friedberg, FRG: Podzun-Pallas Verlag.

Scheurig, Bodo. 1969. *Deutscher Widerstand 1938–1944* [German resistance 1938–1944]. Munich: Deutscher Taschenbuch Verlag.

Schicksal in Zahlen [Fate reflected in numbers]. 1979. Kassel: Volksbund Deutsche Kriegsgräberfürsorge.

Schmitt, Hans A. 1978. *U.S. occupation in Europe after World War II: Papers and reminiscences from the April 23–24, 1976 conference held at the George C. Marshall Research Foundation, Lexington, Virginia.* Lawrence: The Regents Press of Kansas.

Schneeberger, Josef. 1979. *Verständigung, Versöhnung, Frieden* [Understanding, reconciliation, peace]. Kassel: Volksbund Deutsche Kriegsgräberfürsorge.

Schoenberner, Gerhard. 1981. *Wir haben es gesehen: Augenzeugenberichte über die Judenverfolgung im Dritten Reich* [We saw it: Eyewitness accounts of the persecution of the Jews in the Third Reich]. Wiesbaden: Fourier Verlag.

Scholl, Inge. 1984. *Die Weisse Rose* [The White Rose]. Frankfurt am Main: Fischer Taschenbuch Verlag.

Schütz, W. W. 1943. *German home front.* London: Victor Gollancz.

Seidewitz, Max. 1945. *Civil life in wartime Germany—The story of the home front.* New York: The Viking Press.

Shulman, Milton. 1966. *Defeat in the West.* New York: E. P. Dutton and Co.

Sir Arthur Harris, Marshal of the Royal Air Force. 1976. Motion Picture. BBC-TV and Time-Life Films. New York: Time-Life Multi-Media.

Smith, Jean Edward, ed. 1974. *The papers of General Lucius D. Clay: Germany 1945–1949*. Bloomington: Indiana University Press.

Smyser, W. R. 1980. German-American Relations. The Washington Papers, vol. 8, no. 74. Beverly Hills, Cal.: SAGE Publications.

Snyder, Louis L., ed. 1958. *Documents of German history*. New Brunswick, N.J.: Rutgers University Press.

———. 1979. *Hitler's Third Reich: A documentary history*. Chicago: Nelson-Hall.

Solovyov, Boris. 1982. *The turning point of World War II*. Translated by Robert Conquest. New York: Farrar, Straus and Giroux.

Soltau, Hans. 1979. *Volksbund Deutsche Kriegsgräberfürsorge: Sein Werden und Wirken*. [National Union for the care of German war graves: Its inception and activities]. Kassel: Volksbund Deutsche Kriegsgräberfürsorge.

Solzhenitsyn, Alexander. 1977. *Prussian nights*. Translated by Robert Conquest. New York: Farrar, Straus and Giroux.

Speer, Albert. 1971. *Inside the Third Reich*. Translated by Richard and Clara Winston. New York: Avon Books, The Macmillan Company.

Steinert, Marlis. 1967. *Die 23 Tage der Regierung Dönitz* [The 23 days of the Dönitz government]. Düsseldorf: Econ-Verlag.

———. 1977. *Hitler's war and the Germans: Public mood and attitude during the Second World War*. Translated by Thomas E. J. de Witt. Athens: Ohio University Press.

Stier, Erich Hans. 1960. *Deutsche Geschichte* [German history]. Frankfurt am Main: Verlag Heinrich Scheffler.

Strawson, John. 1974. *The battle for Britain*. New York: Charles Scribner's Sons.

Streim, Alfred. 1982. *Sowjetische Gefangene in Hitler's Vernichtungskrieg* [Soviet prisoners of war in Hitler's war of annihilation]. Heidelberg: C. F. Müller Juristischer Verlag.

Sulzberger C. L. 1966. *The American heritage picture history of World War II*. New York: Simon and Schuster.

Sweetman, John. 1982. *Operation Chastise. The dams raid: Epic or myth*. London: Jane's Publishing Co.

Taylor, A.J.P. 1962. *The origins of the Second World War*. New York: Atheneum.

Thompson, H. K., Jr., and Henry Strutz, eds. 1983. *Dönitz at Nuremberg: A re-appraisal*. Torrance, Cal.: Institute for Historical Review.

Thorwald, Jürgen. 1979a. *Das Ende an der Elbe* [The end at the Elbe (river)]. Munich: Droemersche Verlagsanstalt Th. Knaur Nachf.

———. 1979b. *Es begann an der Weichsel* [It started at the Vistula (river)]. Munich: Droemersche Verlagsanstalt Th. Knaur Nachf.

Toland, John. 1981. *Adolf Hitler*. New York: Ballantine Books.

Trevor-Roper, Hugh R. 1964. *Blitzkrieg to defeat*. New York: Holt, Rinehart and Winston.

———, ed. 1979. *Final entries 1945: The diaries of Joseph Goebbels*. New York: Avon Books.

Tully, Andrew. 1963. *Berlin: Story of a battle*. New York: Simon and Schuster.

Turnwald, Wilhelm K. 1951. *Documents on the expulsion of the Sudeten Germans*. Translated by Greda Johannsen. Munich: University Press.

U.S. Annual report of the Immigration and Naturalization Service, FY 1950. Washington, D.C.: U.S. Government Printing Service.

U.S. *United States Strategic Bombing Survey.* September 30, 1945. Overall Report (European War). Washington, D.C.: Government Printing Office.

U.S. Bureau of the Census. 1953. The population of Czechoslovakia. International Population Statistics Reports Series P–90, No. 3.

U.S. Congressional Record. 1976. Washington, D.C.: Government Printing Office. *122.*

U.S. Department of Justice. June 1949. *Monthly Review* 6, no. 12: 168.

U.S. Department of State. June 1950. *Current problems in the occupation of Germany.* Office of Public Affairs.

U.S. Military Government, Germany. September 20 1945. *Denazification.* Monthly Report of Military Governor, U.S. Zone, vol. 2. Washington, D.C.: Government Printing Office, pp. 1–3.

————. September 20 1945. *Displaced persons, stateless persons and refugees.* Monthly Report of Military Governor, U.S. Zone, vol. 2. Washington, D.C.: Government Printing Office, p. 4.

U.S. National Archives. 1945. *Germany surrenders unconditionally.* Facsimilies of the documents. Washington, D.C.: Government Printing Office.

U.S. Office of Military Government for Germany. April 1, 1947. *German denazification law and all implementations American directives.* Special Branch Office of Military Government, Bavaria. Washington, D.C.: Government Printing Office.

————. September 22, 1947. Returning POWs. *Weekly Information Bulletin,* no. 111. Washington, D.C.: Government Printing Office, pp. 11–12.

————. May 31, 1949. *Summary of verdicts.* Military Government Information Bulletin. Washington, D.C.: Government Printing Office.

U.S. Office of the Chief Counsel for Prosecution of Axis Criminality. 1947. *Nazi conspiracy and aggression: Opinion and judgment.* Washington, D.C.: Government Printing Office.

Villard, Oswald Garrison. April 23, 1945. Must we kill neutrals? *Christian Century* 60, no. 1: 483–485.

Van Creveld, Martin. 1982. *Fighting Power. German and U.S. Army performance, 1939–1945.* Westport, Conn.: Greenwood Press.

Verfügungen/Anordnungen/Bekantgaben [Decrees, regulations, proclamations]. 1942, 1944. Vols. 3, 6. Munich: Zentralverlag der NSDAP., Frs. Eher Nachf. GmbH.

Völkischer Beobachter. 1940. Kriegsgefallene Anzeigen.

Volksbund Deutsche Kriegsgräberfürsorge e. V. 1979. *Verständigung, Versöhnung, Frieden.* Denkschrift über die deutschen Kriegsgräber in Ost-und Südost-Europa [Understanding, reconciliation, peace. White paper on German war graves in eastern and southeastern Europe]. Kassel: Volksbund Deutsche Kriegsgräberfürsorge.

von Kardoff, Ursula. 1966. *Diary of a nightmare: Berlin, 1943–1945.* Translated by Ewan Butler. New York: The John Day Company.

von Lehndorff, Count Hans. 1963. *East Prussian diary: A journal of faith.* London: Oswald Wolff Publishers.

von Manstein, Erich. 1958. *Lost victories.* Translated by Anthony G. Powell. Chicago: Henry Regnery Company.

von Salomon, Ernst. 1955. *Fragebogen* [The questionnaire]. Translated by Constantine FitzGibbon. Garden City, N.Y.: Doubleday and Company.

von Schlabrendorff, Fabian. 1965. *The secret war against Hitler.* New York: Pitman Publishing.

Webster's Geographical Dictionary. 1969. Springfield, Mass.: G. & C. Merriam Co.

————. 1972. Springfield, Mass.: G. & C. Merriam Co.

Weinberg, Gerhard L. May 1985. Hitler and England, 1933–1945: Pretense and Reality. *German Studies Review* 8, no. 2: 299–309.

Wellner, Cathryn J. 1982. *Witness to war: A thematic guide to young adult literature on World War II, 1965–1981.* Metuchen, N.J.: The Scarecrow Press.

Welter, Michael. December 10, 1983. The continuing burden of the *Rucksack* German. *Saarbrücker Zeitung.* Reprinted in *The German Tribune,* January 1, 1984.

Werner, Herbert A. 1982. *Die eisernen Särge* [The iron coffins]. Munich: Wilhelm Heyne Verlag.

Werth, Alexander. 1964. *Russia at War. 1941–1945.* New York: E. P. Dutton and Co.

West Germany emphasizes space effort. June 2, 1975. *Aviation Week & Space Technology* 102, no. 22: 223.

Whiting, Charles. 1971. *Massacre at Malmedy. The story of Jochen Peiper's battle group Ardennes, December 1944.* New York: Stein and Day Publishers.

————. 1972. *Hitler's Werewolves. The story of the Nazi resistance movement 1944–1945.* New York: Stein and Day Publishers.

————. 1973. *The end of the war in Europe: April 15–May 23, 1945.* New York: Stein and Day Publishers.

————. 1974. *Hunters from the sky. The German parachute corps 1940–1945.* New York: Stein and Day Publishers.

Wild, Alfons. 1931. *Hitler und das Christentum* [Hitler and Christianity]. Augsburg; Verlag Hass und Grabherr.

Wilder-Smith, Beate. 1982. *The day Nazi Germany died.* San Diego, Cal.: Master Books.

Winterbotham, F. W. 1984. *The Ultra secret.* New York: Dell Publishing Co.

World War Two. 1975. *The World Almanac and Book of Facts.* New York: Newspaper Enterprise Association.

Wulf, Josef. 1960. *Heinrich Himmler.* Berlin-Grunewald: Arani Verlags GmbH.

Wytwycky, Bohdahn. 1980. *The other Holocaust: many circles of hell: a brief account of 9–10 million persons who died with the 6 million Jews under Nazi racism.* Washington, D.C.: The Novak Report on the New Ethnicity.

Zeitgeschichte: *Kriegsverbrecher* [War criminals]. 1970. *Der Spiegel* 24, no. 31: 45, 48, 50.

Ziefle, Helmut W. 1981. *One woman against the Reich.* Minneapolis, Minn.: Bethany House Publishers.

Ziemke, Earl F. 1968. *Stalingrad to Berlin: The German defeat in the East.* Washington, D.C.: Office of the Chief of Military History, Dept. of the Army.

————. 1980. *The Soviet juggernaut.* Chicago: Time-Life Books.

Ziemssen, Dietrich. 1981. *The Malmedy trial.* Torrance, Cal.: Institute for Historical Review.

Zimmermann, Erich. 1969. *Germans against Hitler July 20, 1944.* Wiesbaden: Press and Information Office of the Federal Government of Germany.

Zweiter Weltkrieg—Kriegsgefangene [Second World War—prisoners of war]. 1969. *Der Spiegel* 23, no. 16; 68–92.

INDEX

About the Author

MARTIN K. SORGE, Maj. ret., was born and raised in Germany. He came to the United States in 1955 and served in the U.S. Air Force for twenty years. He holds a Master's degree from Utah State University. He has been awarded three Freedom Foundation awards from Valley Forge, Pennsylvania. Currently Major Sorge teaches talented and gifted children in grades 3-8.